MW00335918

# CAUSAL POWERS AND THE INTENTIONALITY CONTINUUM

Why does anything happen? What is the best account of natural necessity? In this book, William A. Bauer presents and defends a comprehensive account of the internal structure of causal powers that incorporates physical intentionality and information. Bauer explores new lines of thought concerning the theory of pure powers (powerful properties devoid of any qualitative nature), the place of mind in the physical world, and the role of information in explaining fundamental processes. He raises probing questions about physical modality and fundamental properties, and explores the possibility that physical reality and the mind are unified through intentionality. His book will be valuable for researchers and students working in metaphysics, philosophy of science, and philosophy of mind.

WILLIAM A. BAUER is Associate Teaching Professor in the Department of Philosophy and Religious Studies at North Carolina State University. He has published articles in journals including *Acta Analytica*, *Erkenntnis*, and *Science and Engineering Ethics*.

# CAUSAL POWERS AND THE INTENTIONALITY CONTINUUM

## WILLIAM A. BAUER

*North Carolina State University*

CAMBRIDGE
UNIVERSITY PRESS

# CAMBRIDGE
## UNIVERSITY PRESS

University Printing House, Cambridge CB2 8BS, United Kingdom

One Liberty Plaza, 20th Floor, New York, NY 10006, USA

477 Williamstown Road, Port Melbourne, VIC 3207, Australia

314–321, 3rd Floor, Plot 3, Splendor Forum, Jasola District Centre, New Delhi – 110025, India

103 Penang Road, #05–06/07, Visioncrest Commercial, Singapore 238467

Cambridge University Press is part of the University of Cambridge.

It furthers the University's mission by disseminating knowledge in the pursuit of
education, learning, and research at the highest international levels of excellence.

www.cambridge.org
Information on this title: www.cambridge.org/9781009214889
DOI: 10.1017/9781009214858

First published 2023

*A catalogue record for this publication is available from the British Library.*

*Library of Congress Cataloging-in-Publication Data*
NAMES: Bauer, William A., 1974– author.
TITLE: Causal powers and the intentionality continuum / William A. Bauer,
North Carolina State University.
DESCRIPTION: New York : Cambridge University Press, 2022. | Includes
bibliographical references and index.
IDENTIFIERS: LCCN 2022022793 | ISBN 9781009214889 (hardback) |
ISBN 9781009214858 (ebook)
SUBJECTS: LCSH: Causation. | Intentionality (Philosophy) |
BISAC: PHILOSOPHY / General
CLASSIFICATION: LCC BD541 .B38 2022 | DDC 122–dc23/eng/20220815
LC record available at https://lccn.loc.gov/2022022793

ISBN 978-1-009-21488-9 Hardback

In the series of things, those that follow are always aptly fitted to those that have gone before; for this series is not like a mere enumeration of disjointed things, which has only a necessary sequence, but it is a rational connection: and as all existing things are arranged together harmoniously, so the things that come into existence exhibit no mere succession but a certain wonderful relationship.

Marcus Aurelius, *Meditations* IV, 45

# Contents

# Figures

# *Preface*

Two electrons repel each other, thus displaying their charge. A particle responds to a gravitational field. Why do these entities behave as they do? Across space and time, why do any events happen? Science answers questions about *what happens* and *how it happens*. The metaphysics of science, however, answers questions about *why it happens*. That is what this book is about. Specifically, it argues that things happen because causal powers are at work. Causal powers – including fundamental powers such as charge and mass as well as nonfundamental powers like flammability – are modal properties that carry information for various manifestations. The causal powers of particles and other objects explain why things happen.

Take a step back. Should natural properties be understood as powers, qualities, or as simultaneously powerful and qualitative? The roots of this question spread throughout the history of philosophy, and in recent decades it and related questions have become central to the metaphysics of science. I defend the powers view of properties, specifically that properties are pure powers devoid of any qualitative nature.

If causal powers have no qualitative nature, then what are they like? Accounts of powers' nature and identity often focus on their relationship to other powers. Such networking accounts of powers focus on powers from the outside. Although they are not wrong, they are incomplete because they leave the inside nature of powers – the nodes in the network – underexplored and mysterious. After arguing for an ontology of pure powers, I argue that two metaphysical theses conjointly yield an informative and plausible nodal account of powers. The first is the Physical Intentionality Thesis (that powers are intentional, or have directedness, just as mental states are intentional) and the second is the Informational Thesis (that powers carry information for their potential manifestations). Together these theses undergird my account of powers from the inside, the **3d** account: powers (**d**ispositions) possess physical intentionality (**d**irectedness) and carry information (**d**ata) for various manifestations.

The 3d account has a number of significant implications, one of which is that nature possesses an intentionality continuum. Given that everything is physical and physical intentionality is real, intentionality runs throughout nature, from the smallest particles up through complex organisms with conscious minds. But fundamental intentionality, found in the causal powers of the smallest particles, is not conscious intentionality. This is not panpsychism, but a kind of panintentionality, where everything with causal powers possesses an important precursor to full, conscious mind.

# Acknowledgments

I received valuable assistance from many people along this intellectual journey.

John Carroll and Eric Carter provided detailed, constructive feedback on Chapter 1. Moreover, they discussed many topics in this book with me over the years. I thank them for their philosophical acumen and exceptional collegiality.

Either in the form of discussions, correspondence, or comments, the following individuals were very helpful in thinking about various aspects of this work: Lauren Ashwell, Joseph Baltimore, Isaac Bauer, Alexander Bird, Gary Comstock, Ronald Endicott, Toby Handfield, John Heil, Marc Lange, David Limbaugh, Gary Merrill, Michael Pendlebury, Stathis Psillos, Stephen Puryear, Benjamin Rancourt, Kris Rhodes, Jeffrey Snapper, Orlin Vakarelov, Neil Williams, and Jessica Wilson.

I would like to recognize audience members who attended my virtual presentation titled "Powers from the Inside," which was part of the Mereology of Potentiality online seminar series, on February 24, 2021. The discussion with the organizers – Christopher Austin, Anna Marmodoro, and Andrea Roselli – and all the participants was rewarding and helped me refine many aspects of my account of powers.

Early drafts of various chapters, or parts of these, were presented at multiple conferences, including the Alabama Philosophical Society (meetings in Pensacola, Florida on October 2, 2015; October 11, 2014; and October 6, 2012), the Central States Philosophical Association (Detroit, Michigan, September 24, 2010), the Indiana Philosophical Association (University of Indianapolis, November 17, 2012), a Joint Meeting of the North Carolina Philosophical Society and the South Carolina Society for Philosophy (Elon University, February 25, 2012), the Kansas Philosophical Society (Kansas State University, February 28, 2009), the Metaphysics of Science Conference (University of Melbourne, July 5, 2009), the North Carolina Philosophical Society (University of North Carolina Wilmington,

February 25, 2017), the Sixth Workshop on the Philosophy of Information (Duke University, May 16, 2014), the Society for Exact Philosophy (meetings at University of Miami on May 8, 2016; University of Montreal on May 25, 2013; University of Manitoba on May 27, 2011; and University of Alberta on May 7, 2009), the Society for the Metaphysics of Science (University of Geneva, September 16, 2016), and the South Carolina Society for Philosophy (Spartanburg, South Carolina, March 27, 2015). I thank the organizers of all these conferences for the opportunity to present my work. I also presented work in progress at two philosophy colloquia at North Carolina State University (March 20, 2012 and March 17, 2011). Audience members at all these events gave constructive comments for which I am grateful.

My editor at Cambridge University Press, Hilary Gaskin, provided helpful and timely guidance while conducting a highly efficient review process. I thank her and other Cambridge staff, including Abi Sears and Thomas Haynes, who helped bring this book to publication. Sarah Wales-McGrath did a wonderful job copy-editing the book. Thirumangai Thamizhmani of Lumina Datamatics Limited oversaw the book's production process with great attentiveness.

I am extremely grateful to the two anonymous reviewers assigned by Cambridge for rigorous feedback that helped me improve the structure and content of this book in many ways. It is undoubtedly better because of their expertise and goodwill.

I wish to acknowledge publishers of articles of mine that I incorporated into the present work. Although a large majority of the material in this book is new, Chapter 2 contains selections (modified both for clarity and consistency with surrounding text) from my article published in *Disputatio* (although *Disputatio*, owned and formerly published by the Philosophy Centre of the University of Lisbon but now published by De Gruyter/Sciendo, is an open access journal and authors maintain copyright, I requested and received permission from the editors to reuse content from my article 'Dispositional Essentialism and the Nature of Powerful Properties,' William A. Bauer, 2013, *Disputatio* 5[35]: 1–19), Chapters 5 and 8 contain selections (modified both for clarity and consistency with surrounding text) from an article I published in *Acta Analytica* (reprinted by permission from Springer Nature Customer Service Centre GmbH: Springer, *Acta Analytica*, 'Physical Intentionality, Extrinsicness, and the Direction of Causation,' William A. Bauer, Springer Nature Switzerland AG, 2016; permission obtained through the Copyright Clearance Center), and Chapters 6–8 contain selections (modified both for clarity and consistency with surrounding text) from an article published in *Sophia* (although authors retain rights to reuse published material according to the Copyright Transfer Statement, I requested and received permission from *Springer Nature* Customer Service Centre GmbH: Springer, *Sophia*, 'Powers and the Pantheistic Problem of Unity,' William A. Bauer, *Springer Nature*, Switzerland AG, 2018; permission obtained through the Copyright Clearance Center). I thank all the aforementioned publishers for granting me permission to reuse published material, as well as anonymous reviewers from the aforementioned journals for helpful comments. I also want to acknowledge that my *Sophia* article was completed with the support of a Summer Stipend from the Pantheism and Panentheism Project, led by Andrei Buckareff and Yujin Nagasawa and funded by the John Templeton Foundation.

Some of the ideas herein trace back to my doctoral dissertation, *The Ontology of Pure Dispositions*, completed in 2010. Chapters 2 and 7 include selections from that work. I thank the University of Nebraska–Lincoln and the Department of Philosophy there for providing an academic home where some key ideas in this book were born, and I thank Jennifer McKitrick for valuable feedback and guidance during my doctoral studies. However, this book as a whole was conceived and completed as a member of the Department of Philosophy and Religious Studies at North Carolina State University. I warmly thank my colleagues and the University for providing a stimulating and supportive environment for scholarship.

To Marcy and Isaac: thank you for reminding me of what is most important. You inspire me and have great power in my life.

To anyone that I unintentionally left out but should acknowledge, thank you.

It should go without saying that, despite the help I have received, all mistakes are mine.

# *Abbreviations*

PIT     The Physical Intentionality Thesis
IT       The Informational Thesis

# Introduction
## The Metaphysics of Powers and the 3d Account

### 0.1  A World of Causal Powers

Look around. The world is constantly unfolding. Objects move and interact, and their properties change.

Science aims to answer questions about what occurs and how it occurs. We have highly developed physical sciences – physics, chemistry, biology, geology, astronomy. These sciences uncover the nature of objects and their properties as well as how these are related to the unfolding of events in the world. The properties we find in the world include mass, charge, spin, shape, hardness, elasticity, flammability, and many others. These properties, according to the scientific image of the world, make a genuine difference to what occurs. A particle is affected by gravity because it has mass; oil ignites because it is flammable.

We investigate the role of these and other properties in natural events and processes as we attempt to accurately identify and mathematically formulate the laws behind them. But philosophical questions lurk close by these scientific efforts – abstract questions about the ultimate nature of these properties – answers to which can help reveal not just *what* is happening or *how*, but *why*. What are these physical properties like? What are they like beyond their appearances and beyond their mathematical structuring?

Is ours a world of pure qualities – that is, categorical properties? Qualities are, at a first glance, static features of objects that are fully manifest at all times. On this view, properties only play the causal roles they do owing either to the governance of the laws of nature (on a realist, universals-based approach to laws) or they exhibit regularities and patterns over time that we identify as laws of nature (on a Neo-Humean, systems-based approach to laws). If the qualities view of properties is correct, mass is involved in massive displays (e.g., resisting motion or continuing in motion) solely because there are laws of nature – laws of motion and gravity – that determine what happens.

Or is ours a world of powers – that is, dispositional properties? If properties are powers, the mass of an object is involved in massive displays because that is what mass does: it is the nature of mass. If so, then we should view mass as inherently powerful – as a causal power or a disposition to behave in certain ways under certain conditions in response to certain stimuli. These stimuli are the powers of other objects; therefore, the unfolding of the world is due to a vast array of powers interacting with each other. On this view, the laws of nature – while perhaps true statements about what could or would happen – are metaphysically secondary to the primacy of the powers. Causal powers themselves make the world go – the lawful, modal force of things is owed to their powers.

The debate between powers theorists and their rivals is not new. For instance, Aristotle (1941a: *Metaphysics* 1046a28-1052a12) and Locke (2004: Book II, Chapter VIII), in different ways, were committed to the reality of powers.[1] Aristotle's views on potentiality and actuality, as well as other topics, informs Neo-Aristotelianism (Groff and Greco 2013), represented by philosophers such as Ellis (2001, 2012), Molnar (2003), and Heil (2003, 2012), amongst others.[2] Hume (2002, 2003) denies the reality of powers and necessary connections between events. For Hume, any event could follow from any other event, so there are no powers directed at certain types of outcome. This line of thinking informs Neo-Humeanism, most prominently represented by Lewis (1986a, 1986b) but also other twentieth and twenty-first-century philosophers.[3]

This book is structured around two basic questions. First: Why powers? Second: What are powers like? These questions raise more specific questions. On the first question: why accept a powers view of properties over views based on pure qualities? Intricately related to this are further questions: Why accept a powers-based view of physical modality over accounts based on qualities in conjunction with laws of nature, such as Neo-Humeanism (David Lewis' view) or the universals account of laws (David Armstrong's view)? Moreover, why posit *pure* powers over powerful qualities (powers conceived as simultaneously qualitative)? On the second question: What

---

[1] Locke, however, wants to fit powers into a mechanical philosophy (contra Aristotelianism) and thereby seems to treat them relationally (Ott 2009: 12).

[2] However, we should be careful to not equate Aristotelianism and powers theory (Meincke 2020: 4). Despite common emphasis on potentiality and activity, powers theorists need not, for example, accept Aristotle's substance ontology.

[3] In this book, I will not conduct historical analysis reaching back into modern philosophy and early twentieth century philosophy. I will, however, refer to historical precedents to contextualize contemporary issues where appropriate. For some historical discussions of the debate, see, for example, Joy (2013) on Hume's theory of powers as well as Anjum and Mumford (2018: 24–46) on precursors to what they call the "dispositional modality" (a notion I will critique in Chapter 6).

are powers like? We can approach this question from an outside point of view, so to speak, by investigating the relationships that powers have to each other. But what explains why powers have the relationships to each other that they have? What are powers like *from the inside*? Why do they do what they do and what would they be like absent other powers?

Two terminological notes are important before proceeding. First, I use the terms "causal power," "power," "disposition," "capacity," and similar terms interchangeably – though not everyone does[4] – unless a distinction makes a real difference to a specific issue. I prefer "causal power" and its cognates because it accurately connotes causal productivity; however, for efficiency I will mostly just use "power."[5,6] Second, qualities are often called categorical properties by philosophers, but "quality" is fairly common too. I will use the term "quality" unless "categorical property" makes discussing an author's view easier.

In the rest of this Introduction, I explain my approach to metaphysics and how it overlaps with science (Section 2), further explain the differences between powers and qualities (Section 3), explain my stance on properties and substances (Section 4), show how we can "know" powers (Section 5), and distinguish different powers "isms" (Section 6). I then make a distinction between networking and nodal accounts of powers (Section 7) before briefly outlining my proposed view, the 3d account, which is a nodal account of powers (Section 8). The concluding section provides a roadmap for the rest of the book.

## 0.2   Metaphysics and Science

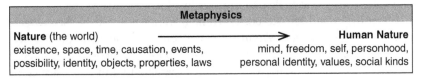

Figure 0.1   The primary concerns of metaphysics (our understanding of Nature influences our understanding of Human Nature)

---

[4] For example, see Bird (2013) and Fara (2005).

[5] Ellis (2010b: 98–99) distinguishes between "power" and "causal power." Powers are a larger class of properties that include causal powers; the latter's manifestations necessarily involve energy transmission, while the former's manifestations do not (2010b: 87); for instance, mass is a power but not a causal power because its manifestations do not involve energy transmission. This is an idiosyncratic, and in my view dubious, distinction that does not affect my argumentation.

[6] Mumford and Anjum (2011: 3) maintain that all properties in the world are *composed of* powers, which are primitive, as Shoemaker (1980) argues. On this view, powers are parts of properties, a kind of protoproperty. On my view, there is no need to distinguish powers and properties. Rather, powers are a kind of property – and the only real kind.

Metaphysics aims to understand the most abstract, fundamental features of reality, including *nature* and *human nature*. The understanding of fundamental aspects of nature (the world in itself) informs our understanding of human nature since humans are necessarily part of nature. Humans live in time and space, have identities, possess properties, are subject to laws of nature, and so on. The idea that our understanding of *nature* influences our understanding of *human nature* is captured by the right arrow in Figure 0.1.[7]

My primary concern in this book is with the metaphysics of nature, in particular powers: what they are like and why we should accept them in the groundwork of reality. The metaphysical debate over properties, laws, and related phenomena is highly relevant to our understanding of the nature of the world. Science has a lot to say about these matters, of course. So, an important question arises: What is the relationship between science – rightfully seen as the producer of definite knowledge about the world – and philosophy?

In my view, philosophy and science form a continuum of investigative inquiry, both in methodology and content. There is no sharp cut-off point. There are strong family resemblances to be found in the kinds of questions that philosophers and scientists ask in their different disciplines. Despite occupying different areas of thought along the continuum, some areas of research (e.g., how to interpret quantum mechanics) require both philosophy and science in order to formulate plausible, complete answers to our deepest questions. But the boundaries of philosophy (especially metaphysics) extend beyond science. If science identifies, explains, and applies the laws of nature (or forces of nature more generally) in order to understand and predict reality, then metaphysics asks: Why are the laws true? What grounds reality's modal features? What is the underlying, fundamental reality that makes all this possible (or necessary)?

Metaphysics and science possess some commonalities: they share cognitive tools, emphasizing to varying degrees deductive logic, conceptual analysis, and thought experiments; they both search for and incorporate evidence produced by either empirical or thought experiments; and they have common concern with discovering truths about the world and our place in it. Moreover, to answer some metaphysical questions requires interpretation of scientific theories and ideas. Quantum mechanics, the nature of space and time, and the mind–body problem all involve scientific and philosophical aspects. However, in some important areas metaphysics necessarily goes

---

[7] Others might wish to include different issues than those listed in Figure 0.1 or to organize the issues differently. For example, Esfeld and Deckert (2018: 1) propose a narrower list of key metaphysical issues – the nature of matter, space, and time – and how these, following certain laws, explain phenomena.

beyond science, such as what laws of nature are, whether reality is fundamentally unified, and whether properties (if properties are real at all) are powers or qualities.[8] In short, there are meaningful questions about reality that science alone cannot adequately answer (Trigg 2015) and some metaphysical claims are arguably even essential to the advancement of science (Maxwell 2020).[9]

In the areas identified above and more, we often must speculate about the nature of things. Such speculation is justified, so long as the contents of our speculations are logically consistent with what we think we know from science and we can show that such speculations offer some explanatory payoff. Despite its value and importance, we should not expect certainties in metaphysics (Lowe 1998: 27). Although much of my work here should be regarded as speculative metaphysics, I do think that it contributes to part of a complete, scientifically informed metaphysics. Science is generally comfortable with positing causal powers (Cartwright 2017; Ellis 2002: 74–75; Mumford 2006: 476), powers arguably plan an important role in interpreting some of our most successful scientific theories such as quantum mechanics (Dorato 2007) and genetics (Mumford and Anjum 2011: 214–235), and powers arguably form part of a proper understanding of human nature and society (Ellis 2002: 145–166; 2013). In this book, the most speculative parts concern themes in Part II, particularly the Physical Intentionality Thesis and the Informational Thesis concerning powers. I see these as quintessentially answers to "why" questions – Why do causal power behave the way they do? Why are they inherently modal?

The metaphysical question concerning whether properties are powers or qualities (or both) at its root concerns the correct interpretation of fundamental reality and what lies beyond (or beneath) the appearances of things. The "appearances," as I am using the term, include not just the everyday events involving ordinary objects, but the results of scientific experiments as well. Experimental science has proven marvelous at revealing underlying structures and mechanisms, from quantum reality to genetics to geological processes. If these are not *mere* appearances, they are *deep* appearances, things as revealed through observation-enhancing tools and techniques as well as sophisticated scientific theorizing. Yet deeper, more abstract questions remain concerning the underlying ontology of the world.

---

[8] Concerning what laws of nature are, see, for example, Armstrong (1983); concerning whether reality is fundamentally unified, see, for example, Maxwell (2020); concerning the reality of properties, see, for example, Armstrong (1989) and Campbell (1990); and concerning whether properties are qualities or powers, see, for example, Armstrong (2010) and Mumford (1998).

[9] Maxwell (2020) sees significant implications of the metaphysics of science for how we do science and therefore for practical questions about our basic institutions.

Ontology is the study of what exists. The outcome of doing ontology well is a warranted list of the kinds of things that exist: properties, objects, laws, forces, events, persons, minds, and so on. Philosophers, particularly metaphysicians, argue about what this list should include and what these things are like. Metaphysics includes not only ontology but the study of the relationship between all types of entities in an ontology, as well as other questions about reality such as identity, essence, time, freedom, and teleology.

This project falls squarely within the purview of the metaphysics of science. I take the metaphysics of science to include the investigation of metaphysical and ontological assumptions – concerning laws of nature, kinds, causal powers, causation – that help make science possible (Mumford and Tugby 2013: 14).[10] The metaphysics of science assumes that both metaphysics and science are serious, rigorous disciplines that try to understand reality from different, but complementary points of view.

I assume a generally scientific realist approach in the philosophy of science, as do most working in the metaphysics of science (Bird, et al. 2012; Schrenk 2017: 298). We have good reason to believe that the entities (objects, properties, forces) posited by our best science are real. This does not mean that science reveals or can understand everything we want to know about these entities. Their ultimate natures might not be fully subject to scientific discernment, based on either observation or inference from observation, because there are background philosophical ideas and commitments that prove more abstract than those that science is able to investigate without the aid of philosophical analysis and insight.

Many metaphysicians and philosophers of science seem to view science as providing a kind of model for metaphysics, where science is the driver of knowledge and metaphysics plays an important but secondary role.[11] Although I agree that metaphysics can and does play a helper role for science, for example in elucidating conceptual implications and assumptions of quantum mechanics and evolutionary theory, I think it can do more. It can break new ground that opens up space for science to operate within. Maudlin (2007: 1) argues that scientific practice should guide choices in building a fundamental ontology; however, I do not think scientific practice should set boundaries for ontology. If we took all the properties of particles posited in fundamental physics into our ontology, we would have mass, charge, spin, and so on. But meaningful questions remain: What *are*

---

[10] Mumford and Tugby also include the study of the relationships between various sciences, which I am not opposed to although it seems more like pure philosophy of science.

[11] For examples of this approach to the relationships between science metaphysics, see Bird (2007a: 8), Callender (2011: 48), and Maudlin (2007: 1). See Schrenk (2017: 296–297) for further discussion.

properties? Are they qualities? Are they powers? Are they both? What is their connection to the laws of nature?

By carefully, if speculatively, stretching our understanding of how everything hangs together beyond what science alone shows us, we can put ourselves in position to explore new possibilities that can enhance and deepen our scientific picture of the world. Philosophy can explain things – though, to be sure, with less certainty – that science alone cannot explain.

I agree to an extent with Reichenbach (1951: vii) that there is "a scientific approach to philosophy." Many philosophers today would affirm this – particularly metaphysicians of science and experimental philosophers. It is a good thing that philosophy takes science into account and tries, to some extent, to model its methods. However, contrary to Reichenbach (1951: vii), philosophy has *not* fully "proceeded from speculation to science." Speculation is crucial, though it must be carefully done in a way that it could reasonably fit into a naturalistic picture of the world. Speculation can be part of a legitimate scientific approach to metaphysics. In my estimation, philosophy – especially, but not only, metaphysics – and science need each other: the former to supply the background conception of reality, identify methodological assumptions, and study normative frameworks, and the latter to fill out the empirical details and develop mathematical equations to analyze and predict phenomena.[12]

Descartes (1985: 186), in *Principles of Philosophy*, suggested that "philosophy is like a tree. The roots are metaphysics, the trunk is physics, and the branches emerging from the trunk are all the other sciences."[13] I largely agree. This metaphor makes clear that the boundaries between metaphysics and science are vague; all subjects of study are connected likes branches of one tree, rooted in philosophy.

If the roots are metaphysics, these roots have causal powers.

## 0.3   Powers, Qualities, and Powerful Qualities

This section characterizes powers, qualities, and powerful qualities. Whether properties are powers or qualities is a metaphysical question. The question is not asking about all the specific types of properties (colors, shapes, etc.), but about how to categorize properties themselves: are they essentially powerful, or qualitative? Powers are properties that have potential for various manifestations. For example, the property of elasticity has the potential to stretch in various ways. To view properties as powers is to view them operationally, in terms of what they can *do*. By

---

[12]  See Bauer (2015) for an overview of why science needs philosophy. See also Laplane et al. (2019).
[13]  See Ariew (2014: 106–107) for discussion of the tree metaphor's Scholastic roots.

contrast, to view properties as qualities is to view them as just being a certain way. For example, the property of circularity just is being circular. To view properties as qualities is to view them nonmodally, in terms of what they are manifestly or categorically. As we will see in Chapter 1, Humeans and Neo-Humeans strongly resist the claim that properties are inherently modal and productive (Schrenk 2017: 71). This commitment to modally inert properties is what Wilson (2010) has called "Hume's Dictum" and helps specify what I mean here by "quality."

To put it too briefly: A quality is what it is; a power is what it can do.

It might be that all properties are powers or that all properties are qualities. Those are monistic views. Alternatively, the world might contain some combination of the two; this is a mixed or dualistic view. A fourth option is that property instances are amalgams of quality and power – on this view, properties are powerful qualities. This is also known as the identity thesis, akin to the identity thesis in philosophy of mind; to distinguish these, I shall call the view that powers and qualities are identical the Identity View. Powerful qualities are not simply powers or pure powers but simultaneously both qualitative and powerful.

Whereas a pure power lacks any trace of quality, and a pure quality lacks any trace of power, a powerful quality features both at once. Powerful qualities have the "just-there-ness" (Armstrong 2004: 141) of pure qualities combined with inherent powerfulness. The difference between powerful qualities, pure powers, and pure qualities can be visualized as follows.

Pure power   Powerful quality   Pure quality

Figure 0.2    Three conceptions of properties

In Figure 0.2, the boundary between each type of property is discrete, not continuous. Each type is represented as homogeneous, as expected for pure powers and pure qualities, but powerful qualities are also represented as homogeneous since the power and quality are one and the same. The gray area is *not* meant to indicate that powerful qualities have a mix of power and quality or possess distinct bits of quality and power. What is meant is that it is a single property: a quality that *is* powerful. (This is, at least, the identity interpretation of powerful qualities; some suggest that powerful qualities have a powerful part and a qualitative part, a view that I will address in Chapters 1 and 2.)

A further characterization of powers will prove helpful. Pure powers theorists as well as powerful qualities theorists often either explicitly or implicitly provide identity conditions for powers based on the idea of a *causal profile* (a term from Hawthorne 2001). The causal profile of a power is the total set of conditions and possible stimuli that prompt the power's activation, along with the total set of possible manifestations it can undergo when activated. Essentially, a causal profile describes the power's role in system of properties (other powers) with which it can interact.

Here I am just setting up an initial framework. In Chapter 1, I will show how these different conceptions of properties – qualities on one hand and powers (either pure powers or powerful qualities) on the other hand – figure into different conceptions of physical modality. Physical modality is concerned with possibilities consistent with the laws of nature; different senses of modality will be explained in Chapter 1. I will argue for what I call the Powers Model (subsuming either the Pure Powers Model or the Powerful Qualities Model). In Chapter 2, the differences between powers and powerful qualities, including whether powerful qualities could have two "parts," will be discussed further and the notion of a causal profile will be revisited. There I will argue against the Powerful Qualities Model, thus advocating for the Pure Powers Model.

It is quite possible that any one of the conceptions of properties in Figure 0.2 is logically compatible with the way the world appears or presents itself to us. It seems that the appearances would remain the same under these different ontologies. Furthermore, these conceptions might very well be compatible with our best science. For instance, perhaps both powers theorists and non-powers theorists can in principle explain gravity, electromagnetism, and evolution.[14] What occurs – and the mechanisms and forces at play in the unfolding of the world – remain the same in terms of their mathematical representation. But the metaphysics is different – and the underlying, fundamental ontology that grounds these metaphysical views is different. However, the logical compatibility of a metaphysic with science is one thing. The explanatory power and depth of a metaphysic is another thing. Here, I think, powers are favored. Furthermore, as I will argue in Chapter 1, nonpowers theorists might not be able to get away with avoiding powers in explaining physical modality.

## 0.4   Properties and Substances

How do my views on powers fit with closely related metaphysical issues regarding the reality of properties and substances?

This book assumes both the reality of properties and that there is a real ontological distinction between "sparse" (or natural) and "abundant" (or

---

[14] There are some details where one or the other view might fit better with certain scientific theories, particularly in physics – see, for example, Balashov (2002) and Livanios (2017b).

nonnatural) properties (Lewis 1986b: 59–61). Nominalists hold that properties are unreal, that they are just concepts or terms that we apply to the world. We talk about properties as if they are real, but in doing so we are only learning about our conceptualization of how objects are propertied. Realists, however, hold that properties are real entities existing independently of our conceptualization. Among the realists, there is a storied disagreement. Some realists claim that properties are universals, according to which each property is an abstract entity that might have multiple instances, yet all these instances are numerically identical; each universal, such as red or mass, can be spread out over many instances. The universals are either transcendent or immanent. Plato's theory of Forms is a theory of transcendent universals. Aristotle, by contrast, holds a theory of immanent universals, according to which universals are not independent of their instances. One can, however, be a realist about properties without accepting universals. Trope theory holds that property instances are particularized, independent entities, not strictly numerically identical to any other instance (Campbell 1990; Williams 1953). Trope theory accounts for the particularity and universality of properties in one ontologically lean package.

Although I assume properties (including powers) are real, I take no definite stance here on whether they are universals or tropes. I intend that all my main claims about powers comport with different realist interpretations of the reality of properties. However, all things considered, I think that the trope theory is most likely to be correct. It is the simplest and most metaphysically unifying view of properties. As such, powers as I conceive them are particularized properties, bounded by spacetime, and not numerically identical to any other instance but exactly similar in some cases.[15,16]

Are there, metaphysically, substances that properties are pinned to, so to speak, or is reality substance-less? Are what we perceive as substances simply bundles of properties? Substances can be admitted into one's ontology whether properties are powers, qualities, of powerful qualities. Some theorists, like Heil (2012), argue that substances fit best with a powerful qualities view and consequently accept a substance-property ontology. Having substances nicely accounts for the apparent permanence of things in the world, even as it changes, propelled by powerful qualities. However, positing substances is not the most economical view. Trope theory, which I tentatively affirm, eschews substances. The substance-like particularity of things in the world is generated by collections (or bundles) of tropes.

[15] So, on my view, properties are not universals in either a Platonic or Aristotelian sense. If I were forced to commit to a universals approach to powers, I would take up the Aristotelian perspective and maintain that they are repeatable properties whose reality is entirely instantiated in space and time.

[16] Amongst powers theorists, some accept that powers are tropes and others accept that powers are universals. For example, Molnar (2003) is a trope theorist while Ellis (2001) accepts a universals approach.

Tropes are abstract particulars that constitute the basis for reality and, if they are powers, inherently drive changes within the cosmos.

## 0.5 Knowing Powers

Powers are hidden from direct empirical observation. They are theoretical posits. As such, those with strong empiricist or logical positivist leanings, such as the Vienna Circle and its sympathizers, have been reluctant to accept powers.

So how do we infer that some property is a power? Or, at least, what characteristics raise suspicions that some property is a power? I contend that we can in many cases justifiably infer the existence of powers through their common marks. McKitrick (2003a: 157, 2018: 2) identifies five marks of powers.[17] In Figure 0.3, I formulate these marks and include one additional mark found in Heil (2003: 198, 2012: 75) and Martin (2008: 3).[18]

| Mark | Explanation and example |
|---|---|
| Mark 1: Characteristic manifestations | Powers have characteristic manifestations when triggered (e.g., the fragility of a vase can manifest in breaking, cracking, etc.). |
| Mark 2: Circumstances of manifestation | Powers have circumstances of manifestation (e.g., a vase needs to be in a certain temperature range: if too hot it will be melty and thus not fragile). |
| Mark 3: Can remain unmanifested indefinitely | Powers need not ever manifest (e.g., a vase is fragile throughout its existence but never breaks or cracks). |
| Mark 4: Association with counterfactuals | Powers are closely associated with, or support, true counterfactual conditional statements (e.g., 'if the glass were struck by a hammer, then it would break').[19] |
| Mark 5: Relevance of overtly powerful locutions | Once identified, overtly powerful locutions apply to powers (e.g., fragility is "the power to break when struck"). |
| Mark 6: Partners in manifestation | A power typically requires one or more powerful partners in order to manifest; the partners are jointly responsible for the manifestation (e.g., hardness and fragility work together to manifest the vase's breaking). |

Figure 0.3   Marks of powers

[17] McKitrick (2018: 4–5) advocates a deep and broad dispositional pluralism according to which dispositions (powers) can be extrinsic or intrinsic, fundamental or nonfundamental, natural or unnatural, causally relevant or irrelevant, and so on. Nonetheless, McKitrick thinks that all powers share the marks she identifies.

[18] Martin (2008: 87) advocates for the idea of "reciprocal disposition partners" according to which two (or more) powers causally interact to produce "mutual manifestations." In other words, powers are "inherently directed towards shared results" (Baltimore 2020: 691). The manifestation of an instance of fragility, for example, is equally the manifestation of a hammer striking a glass and the glass responding to the strike, thus shattering.

[19] This does not imply that the conditional analysis of powers, which analyzes powers in terms of counterfactual statements, is true.

The observable evidence for powers – their supposed effects – is likely to be consistent with a Neo-Humean, qualities-based view of properties. But this does not obviate the relevance and importance of the marks of powers. Any inference that a property is a power based on observable events (manifestation events) and processes (continuous manifestations), linguistic data, and other clues (those indicated by the marks), is going to be an inference to the best explanation, not a deductive inference. So, these marks are not put forward as jointly necessary and sufficient conditions for being a power (although each mark itself might be necessary). But together they help us infer that we are dealing with powers. At least, they serve to introduce some of the most important features of powers.

Mark 6 is somewhat controversial. In order to manifest, it seems that a power needs a powerful partner, that is, a manifestation partner. The trigger or stimulus of a power is, in fact, another power. The hardness of a hammer is a manifestation partner for the fragility of a vase. Hardness is the power to break something fragile, and fragility is the power to break when struck by something hard (or when subject to intense freezing, high-pitched sounds, etc.). This seems intuitive enough if one is already committed to a power-based ontology. However, it might not be a universal thesis, for there might be special cases of self-manifesting powers. Jaworski (2016: 58–59) challenges a common example that radioactive decay is self-manifesting (Harré and Madden 1975) by conjecturing that an environment free of inhibiting factors can itself be interpreted as a powerful partner; the example he gives is that the environment surrounding an atomic or molecular nucleus must be free of inhibiting factors. One might say that this is a circumstance of manifestation, not a power, therefore not a powerful partner. However, environments have properties, which can include the property of not having properties (powers), therefore doubt remains about the possibility of self-manifesting powers. Thus, Mark 6 remains plausibly intact.

Besides the marks of powers, how else might we know powers? Vetter (2015: 12) argues that with "a sufficiently rich view of perception" it is possible that we perceive objects to have powers: for example, "I can see that the glass is fragile, just as I can see that it is a champagne glass." (Inference to the best explanation certainly plays a role as well, as Vetter notes.) It is often assumed that powers are hidden from empirical observation, and I generally agree with that claim. However, if "perception" somehow goes deeper, it could be another way we know powers, although I do not expect that this point would apply to fundamental powers. Fundamental powers are theoretical posits to explain the behavior of microscopic particles. Here, inference and indirect observation are required to "know" them.

## o.6   Powers "isms"

A number of powers or dispositional "isms" have arisen: dispositional essentialism, dispositional monism, and pandispositionalism.

Dispositional essentialism is a brand of scientific essentialism. While scientific essentialism holds that objects possess some essential features or properties, dispositional essentialists specifically maintain that at least some fundamental properties are essentially dispositional or powerful. Prominent proponents include Ellis and Lierse (1994), Ellis (2001, 2010a, 2010b, 2012), and Molnar (2003). Ellis and Molnar hold that some fundamental properties, for instance locations, are qualities. So, they accept a mixed view allowing both powers and qualities. Dispositional monism (Bird 2007a) is a subtype of dispositional essentialism and maintains that *all* fundamental properties are essentially powerful. Pandispositionalism (Bostock 2008; Mumford 2004; Mumford and Anjum 2011) takes dispositional monism a step further, maintaining that all properties (fundamental or not) are essentially powerful.

In contrast to these dispositional or powers-based views, pure qualities theorists deny views that centralize powers. They hold that properties are essentially qualitative in character. According to Ellis (2002: 71), this view "is the established metaphysic of our culture." This was true at the time of the remark and likely remains so, although powers theorists are gaining ground.

There are two major forms of the qualities view that I will discuss in Chapter 1, but for now it is useful to contrast the form based on David Hume's philosophy with the powers view to get a better grasp of what the various powers "isms" have in common against the qualities view of properties. Humeans (both old and new) regard powers "as a kind of pre-scientific animism" – the world for them is "not potent" but "inert" (Groff 2013: 4). Neo-Humeans maintain that there are no real, inherent powers. Although we can talk as if objects have powers based on the perceived flow of events, this does not represent an ontological commitment to powers. By contrast, powers theorists hold that matter is essentially active (not passive) because objects have irreducible causal powers, that there are necessary causal connections between events (which causal powers underpin), and – if they allow them in their ontology – that laws of nature describe how natural kinds must behave (Ellis 2002: 59–60; Groff 2013: 7–9).

The view of this book is firmly situated in the family of powers views. All three powers "isms" require the reality of at least some pure powers, powers devoid of any qualitative character. I am very confidently committed to dispositional monism and, with slightly less confidence, to pandispositionalism. But the major claims of this book could in principle be accepted by pure powers theorists of all stripes (pandispositionalists, dispositional monists, and dispositional essentialists) insofar as those claims are applied only to pure powers.

## 0.7   Networking versus Nodal Accounts of Powers

Assume that we accept that there are systems of powers, that is, systems of properties that consist entirely of powers. What kinds of accounts of the nature of powers in that system are available? By "account" I do not mean a reductive or conceptual analysis, but a general characterization that illuminates the nature of powers. An account should be explanatory, informative, and, ideally, raise new questions.

There are two types of accounts of powers – or, at least, approaches to developing more specific, detailed accounts: *networking accounts* and *nodal accounts*.[20] Networking accounts present an outside point of view of powers, so to speak. By contrast, nodal accounts focus on the what the nodes of the network are like, from their own point of view and not the system's point of view. Contrasting these approaches can help better situate my view of powers.

Networking accounts understand powers only in terms of their relation to other powers, by claiming that powers (i) are essentially related to possible stimuli and manifestations where (ii) these stimuli and manifestations are also powers and (iii) these connections or relations define what it means to be a power (i.e., they determine a power's nature).[21] A networking account is implied by the various conditional analyses of

---

[20] The term "nodal" should not be confused with "modal" – although in the case of power networks the nodal units are, of course, inherently modal.

[21] I am not claiming that anyone holds exactly the networking account of powers – though some dispositional essentialists come close enough to it. Instead, my intent is to illustrate a way of conceiving the nature of powers in order to contrast with and better explain my own view (a nodal account). Moreover, I am not trying to outright falsify the networking account but to show that it is inadequate because an account of powers needs to go beyond the network. From the outside, there is the network – we can "see" that powers relate to each other – but what about the situation from each power's point of view?

powers, according to which powers are analyzable through counterfactual statements (such that an object, $x$, possesses a power to manifest if and only if, if $x$ were subject to the appropriate stimulus, then such-and-such manifestation would occur).[22] Powers theorists who accept some version of the conditional analysis do not need to claim anything about powers' internal nature other than that powers are essentially powerful such that it is in their nature to manifest in appropriate circumstances. So, they should be satisfied to accept a networking account of powers. But this leaves many questions about what powers are like from the inside. What does their *directedness* toward manifestations consist of? *How* do powers connect with other powers in their networks? A networking account leaves the "inside" of powers a mystery – or implies they do not really have an inside nature and that their relational nature is exhaustive.[23]

What explains why powers do what they do and why they have the relations to each other that they have? To see powers from the inside is to look beyond the activity of powers and beyond their relations to each other. It is to imagine a lone power – a power token in a one-property world – and ask what it is like. Such one-power universes are clearly possible. Consider two thought experiments. In the first, subtract the entire network of powers around one select power, which remains capable of activity despite having no partners. What is this power like? Why can it do what it is capable of doing? In the second thought experiment, consider a bare world absent any properties and install a single, lone power. Again, it remains capable of activity. What is this power like?

To take this question seriously is to take the directedness of powers seriously and ask what makes them directed toward their merely potential, thus perhaps always nonexistent, manifestations. It is to dig into their hidden nature. To see powers from the inside is to provide a nodal account. My 3d account is such an account.

## 0.8   The 3d Account of Powers

I contend that the following interrelated theses conjointly yield an informative and plausible account of powers from the inside.

---

[22] Conditional analyses will be further discussed in Section 6.5.

[23] The idea of a power's "internality" or "inside" is metaphorical, for properties do not literally have insides and outsides. "Intrinsic" (versus "extrinsic") might be the better term, yet the intrinsic/extrinsic distinction itself is contentious. And, to say a property is intrinsic or extrinsic does not tell you everything about that property's genuine, inherent nature independent of other instantiated properties – which is my main interest here.

**The Physical Intentionality Thesis** (PIT): Powers and thoughts share the marks of intentionality.

**The Informational Thesis** (IT): Powers carry information for their potential manifestations.

The core commitment of PIT is that powers are directed toward manifestations that might not occur (e.g., an electron is directed toward accelerating but it need not ever do so), akin to how desires are directed toward objects that might go unfulfilled (e.g., one's desire for chocolate might remain unrealized). The core commitment of IT is that powers carry counterfactual information for the various manifestations that they might undergo.

PIT has explicit and extensive precedence in the debate concerning powers, with some metaphysicians defending it and others criticizing it. Something like IT has also been discussed in previous accounts of powers.[24] However, my development and defense of these theses is original in several regards. First, in defending PIT, I argue that directedness – arguably *the* central feature of intentionality – is best interpreted as representational in nature. As such, powers represent their possible manifestations. This stands in contrast to the nonrepresentational interpretations of directedness advanced by influential PIT advocates such as Molnar (2003). Second, beyond the original five marks of intentionality (Martin and Pfeifer 1986), I extensively discuss five additional marks of intentionality, setting my analysis apart from many opponents and proponents of PIT. Third, with regards to IT, I take seriously the idea that powers carry informational contents and show that this has important implications for the power/quality distinction and other key debates in the metaphysics of powers. Fourth, my combination of both physical intentionality and information sets my account apart from others, and, I hope, illuminates powers from the inside better than other accounts to date.

Given both PIT and IT, my account of **d**ispositions (i.e., powers) combines **d**irectedness (i.e., intentionality) and **d**ata (i.e., information), therefore I call it the **3d** account of powers. The term "directedness" here is meant to suggest all of the marks of physical intentionality more generally (though, strictly speaking, I take directedness to be *the* essential mark of intentionality – if only one were allowed), and the term "data" refers to information more generally.[25]

---

[24] I will give a robust account of supporters and critics of PIT in Chapters 3–5 and a robust account of previous support for something akin to IT in Chapter 6.

[25] In some contexts, we might want to characterize information as *meaningful data* or something similar; more on this in Chapter 6.

## 0.9   Roadmap

Part I of this book argues that we should conceive of properties as pure powers. Chapter 1 argues for the Powers Model of physical modality (this is the powers-based view of modality that includes two main subvarieties, the Pure Powers Model and the Powerful Qualities Model). I argue for the Powers Model by showing that the two principal rival accounts, the Universals Model and the Neo-Humean Model (which are based on qualities combined with laws of nature) implicitly employ powers.[26] Having established the plausibility of the Powers Model, Chapter 2 explores the differences between powerful qualities and pure powers, and argues that interpreting powers as pure is the better way to go, hence the Pure Powers Model should be adopted over the Powerful Qualities Model. I interpret the Pure Powers Model strongly to imply pandispositionalism, although most of my theses and arguments are compatible with weaker interpretations (dispositional monism and dispositional essentialism) provided appropriate adjustments in the domain of relevant properties (more on this in Section 1.4). Moreover, Chapter 2 attempts to solve the problem of being: how pure powers exist through periods of nonmanifestation. This is a Level 1 objection to powers because it concerns the inherent nature and existence of powers. By contrast, Level 2 objections concern systems of two or more pure powers.[27] This book focuses primarily on Level 1 problems: the being of powers and what they are like.

Part II presents a theory of powers from the inside in the form of the 3d account introduced above. Chapter 3 introduces two arguments for the Physical Intentionality Thesis (PIT): the Argument from the Marks of Intentionality and the Argument from the Unity of Nature. In Chapters 3, 4, and 5, I primarily develop the first argument; in Chapter 8, I revisit and develop the second argument. Chapter 6 defends the Informational Thesis (IT), which complements PIT while extending our understanding of powers from the inside. With these supporting theses and arguments in place, the 3d account – especially how PIT and IT are interrelated – will

---

[26] There are implications of powers theory for philosophical issues beyond physical modality, including areas closely related to physical modality such as causation (Mumford and Anjum 2011) and philosophy of physics (Balashov 2002; Bauer 2011; Dorato and Esfeld 2010), but also more distant issues such as free will (Mumford and Anjum 2015), ethics (Anjum et al. 2013; Doyle 2018), and the nature of social powers and society (Ellis 2013; Groff 2013). However, my focus in this book concerns fundamental questions about the nature of powers and physical modality, although I will have some comments about larger issues in Chapter 8.

[27] These levels of objections are not rigid, but it is a dialectically useful distinction.

be explained in Section 6.6.[28] Chapter 7 focuses more on Level 2 concerns and accomplishes two tasks. First, it explores how powers might be systematized. Second, it discusses the appearance of qualities: given a system of powers, how can we account for the appearance of qualities in our common, everyday experience? It is argued that qualities are mere appearances generated by the activity of powers. The possibility of emergent qualities is discussed. Chapter 8 (the concluding chapter) argues for the Intentionality Continuum Thesis, that there is a continuum of intentionality throughout nature. Physical intentionality diminishes the mystery of psychological (i.e., mental) intentionality. Physical intentionality, as I see it, is a phenomenon continuous with psychological intentionality. The resulting view provides a foundation for conceptually unifying our understanding of basic physical systems, increasingly complex physical systems to include living systems, and psychological systems. Since powers are everywhere, intentionality is everywhere. This implies a mild form of panpsychism, namely panintentionality.[29]

---

[28] The 3d account is compatible with any theory regarding the *extent* of pure powers (mixed views allowing both powers and qualities, dispositional monism, or pandispositionalism), insofar as pure powers themselves in those theories are concerned.

[29] Pfeifer (2016), whose view I will discuss in Chapter 8, formulates panintentionality as a brand of panprotopsychism, according to which some precursor states for full mind are everywhere.

## PART I

# *Why Powers?*

# CHAPTER I

# The Need for Powers
## Three Models of Physical Modality

## 1.1   Three Models of Physical Modality

What accounts for the fact that some physical events occur while others do not? This is a question of physical modality, that is, natural necessity and possibility. Physical modality is typically conceived as narrower or more restricted than logical or metaphysical necessity and possibility.[1] Physical modality generally concerns what Carroll (1994: 7) calls the "*nomic concepts*" (italics original) such as chance, causation, and dispositions. As I see things, a conception of physical modality should at least account for possibilities consistent with our best understanding of the actual laws of nature (using the term "laws of nature" loosely so as not to assume any particular account of what laws are). In sum, it covers scientific possibilities – which constitute only some metaphysical possibilities, unless physical or natural possibility exhausts metaphysical possibility.[2]

Three models in contemporary analytic metaphysics have dominated the investigation of physical modality: the Neo-Humean Model, the Universals

---

[1] No stance is taken here on whether logical and metaphysical modalities are coextensive, only that physical modality is narrower than both of those.

[2] A sampling of how other philosophers conceive physical modality: Lange (2009: 45) holds that although the laws are naturally "necessary," they could be different and could allow exceptions, unlike metaphysical, logical, or conceptual necessity; Borghini and Williams (2008: 21–22, n. 2) envision a kind of modal necessity weaker than logical or metaphysical necessity; Barker (2013: 605) envisions physical modality as including "physical necessitation and possibility, causation, disposition, and chance"; Fine (2005: 235) argues that physical (or natural) and metaphysical modalities (as well as normative modality) are each fundamental, independent notions (thus, he accepts modal pluralism); Müller (2010: 118) disagrees, claiming that physical modality is not fundamental and that the best modal notion for philosophy of science is what he calls real or historical possibility, emphasizing the connection between modal and tense operators, which Müller traces to Prior (1957).

Model,[3] and the Powers Model.[4] Each of these views aims to explain, in ontologically conspicuous ways, the unfolding of possibilities in space and time. In this chapter, I first argue (in Sections 1.2 and 1.3) that the Neo-Humean and Universals Models, while explicitly denying a place for powers in their fundamental ontologies, nonetheless involve powers. I show how these models subtly assume or can plausibly be interpreted as positing powers. As a result, I contend that the Powers Model is the way to go in explaining physical modality; however, there are different ways of conceiving powers that I outline in Section 1.4 and explore more deeply in Chapter 2.

In my critique of the Neo-Humean and Universals Models, I proceed by reversing a strategy designed by Barker (2013), who argues that (what I call) the Universals and Powers Models collapse into the Neo-Humean Model; thus, the so-called metaphysics of powers is illusory. By contrast, I contend that the Universals and Neo-Humean Models implicitly assume powers (Barker thinks the same of the Universals Model, but not the Neo-Humean Model).[5] Therefore, the Powers Model (not Neo-Humeanism) should be the default position. But my critique of the Neo-Humean and Universals Models is limited. A comprehensive evaluation of these views would be a lengthy endeavor and trace over ground covered many times by others. My more modest goal is to investigate the issue of physical modality by showing how the Universals and Neo-Humean Models require powers.

---

[3] The most influential Neo-Humean Model is Humean Supervenience (Lewis 1986a); the Universals Model is defended most prominently by Dretske (1977), Tooley (1977), and Armstrong (1978, 1983); and the Powers Model has prominent defenders in Heil (2003, 2012), Molnar (2003), Martin (2008), Bird (2007a), Mumford and Anjum (2011), and Williams (2019). All three models of physical modality discussed here are realist about properties and laws (although some Powers Model theorists eliminate laws; e.g., Mumford [2004] is antirealist about laws). The first two models are closely linked to laws of nature: the Universals Model holds that laws are contingent necessitation relations between universals (more on this in Section 1.3), while Neo-Humean Model proponents accept the Best System Account of laws or the Regularity Theory.

[4] Besides their great influence on contemporary metaphysics, I focus on these three accounts of physical modality since they centrally involve the question of the nature of properties (powers or qualities?) and their relation to laws of nature. However, there are also antirealist views of laws (Mumford 2004; Van Fraassen 1989) and antireductionist views of laws (Carroll 1994, 2008; Maudlin 2007), which clearly have ramifications for physical modality. For instance, if laws are not real, the question of where physical modality comes from arises (Mumford's answer, and one with which I agree: the properties – powers – themselves); and if laws are primitive, irreducible entities, then physical modal necessities are presumably primitive and irreducible facts about the world's ordering.

[5] What Barker (2013) calls "degrees" (first, second, and third) of physical modality I call *models*. Are the three views better termed theories, not models? If my argument is sound, then the three models discussed here all share the same underlying theory: that powers drive modality. Hence, the three views are, effectively, three models of the powers theory of modality.

In the concluding part of this chapter, after describing variations of the Powers Model, I return to the main question posed in the introductory chapter: What is the nature of powers from the inside?[6] Stricter attention to the internal reality of powers, the focus of Part II, is necessary for a better understanding of the Powers Model and its metaphysical commitments.

## 1.2   The Neo-Humean Model Needs Powers

The Neo-Humean Model is antirealist about powers. Neo-Humeans accept quidditism about properties – that properties are fundamental qualities possessing a perfectly nonmodal this-ness. I will focus my discussion on Humean Supervenience (Lewis 1986a: ix–x, 1986b: 14) since this is the most influential Neo-Humean Model, although much of my critique will apply to any account of physical modality couched in terms of nonpowerful qualities behaving in accord with external lawful regularities. On Humean Supervenience, the supervenience base consists entirely of local, intrinsic, nonmodal categorical properties (qualities or quiddities) spread out over spacetime with no necessary connections between them, that is, these properties have no essential causal powers (Jaworski 2016: 82).[7] At best, powers are derivative – certainly not found in the supervenience base of perfectly natural properties.[8] The appearance of dispositional action and physical modality in general is explained in terms of qualities acting in accord with the contingent laws of nature, that is, fitting into patterns or regularities (see Figure 1.1).[9] There are no primitive causal connections between events, just a series of particular facts. The qualities in the supervenience base, unchanging in themselves, will be involved in different kinds of power displays (manifestations), depending on global, nomological conditions.

---

[6] For discussion of the term "inside," see footnote 23 in the Introduction.

[7] Lewis (2008: 209) claims that "Quidditism is to properties as haecceitism is to individuals." The point being that each property (quiddity), like individuals (particulars) according to haecceitism, has "nothing but a (naked) primitive identity" to distinguish it from other properties (Schrenk 2017: 73). For further discussion of quidditism about properties, see Barker (2013: 611).

[8] Lewis (1997) is committed to a reductive account of powers and provides a revised counterfactual analysis that blocks some potential counterexamples. Although powers on his view are derivative and grounded entirely on intrinsic qualities, Lewis could arguably be considered a kind of "moderate realist" about powers (Azzano 2019). See McKitrick (2021: 279–285) for further discussion of Lewis' ontological commitments with respect to dispositions.

[9] Lewis (1986a: xiv, 1994: 478) makes the Best Systems Account of laws central to his Neo-Humean account. On this account, laws are a select set of regularities that fit into the best system of axioms, with "best" defined by reference to simplicity and strength.

| NEO-HUMEAN MODEL |
|---|
| the facts of physical modality<br>*are determined by*<br>regularities grounded in the total spatiotemporal distribution of qualities (i.e., categorical properties) |

Figure 1.1    Neo-Humean Model of physical modality

Further clarifying the commitments of Humean Supervenience, Vetter (2015: 7) explains that it excludes "modality – the whole modal package – from the supervenience base. The Humean world is, at root, thoroughly nonmodal." This is what mainline Neo-Humeans are explicitly committed to. However, I will argue below that Humean Supervenience has a hidden feature that, when brought to light, implies powers. Before getting to that, I will consider some other possible criticisms.[10]

### Criticisms of Neo-Humeanism

Several strategies are available to criticize Neo-Humeanism. First, one could try to show that the view is incoherent; however, I do not think this is viable. It is a well-developed, complete metaphysic refined through the work of several philosophers tracing back to Hume, with several advantages and disadvantages that must be weighed against other views of physical modality. This suggests a second strategy: Comparatively analyze Neo-Humeanism against the other models based on the merits/demerits of each. For example, one might argue that Neo-Humeanism does not explain some feature of reality as it appears to us or does not explain our epistemic practices regarding those appearances.

Cartwright (2017: 17), for instance, argues that we need to posit powers in scientific theories: On her view, the inclusion of causal powers in our ontological picture gives us greater predictive power; yet powers are not reducible to Humean qualities. Our best scientific theories, in other words, should quantify over causal powers. In any purported chain of inference

---

[10] Vetter (2015: 8) suggests that Humean Supervenience goes against its principal proponent's stated aim "to resist philosophical arguments that there are more things in heaven and earth than physics has dreamt of" (Lewis 1994: 474) because physics says nothing "about any 'underlying' qualities or quiddities" (as well as, we might add, an infinity of genuinely real possible worlds). Without Humean Supervenience, says Vetter (2015: 9), the motivation for possible worlds realism also takes a hit. By contrast, because the Pure Powers Model eschews underlying qualities, it might more closely align with science's functionalist and operationalist tendencies; however, see Williams (2011) for a critique of the argument from science for pure powers.

for empirical predictions, "Powers [...] have to be there in the facts that we input at the very start or our derivations will not lead us to true results" (2017: 19). The problem with this argument is that there will probably always be a way for the Neo-Humean to add in one more fact or contingent relation between the facts to show that their view has equal predictive and explanatory power, that is, epistemic ability to explain the modal features of reality. Although this might increase the complexity of their position, so long as Neo-Humeans can accommodate all the essential behavior of what others will argue emanates from causal powers, the Neo-Humean Model will have equal epistemic force. However, it must be noted that an ontology of real causal powers can ground physical modality, since powers metaphysically explain modal features: Indeed, powers are inherently modal properties, whereas the qualities on Humean views are not.

In general, I worry that all three models of physical modality are internally consistent, can be made compatible (given plausible modifications) with the empirical data, and have equal predictive power.[11] That is to say, this is a genuine metaphysical debate concerning the way the world is beyond the empirical appearances. The criteria to employ in navigating such a debate include simplicity or parsimony, elegance, and logical fit with other accepted theories. But what if one could show that Neo-Humeanism (or another target view) has a metaphysical feature previously unrecognized by its proponents, which completely transforms the kind of view it is? I wish to contend – primarily based on the work of Cross (2012) and Strawson (2008) – that Neo-Humeanism cannot escape the ontology of powers: Powers and their modality are subtly inherent in the Neo-Humean Model, particularly Humean Supervenience.

### How Neo-Humeanism Implies Powers

Cross (2012) argues that Lewis' Humean Supervenience – although it explicitly eschews powers and necessary connections between spatiotemporal events – requires powers. Lewis adheres to the view that properties "endow *different* powers in *different* circumstances" (Cross 2012: 136). But Cross contends that these circumstances – global, nomological

---

[11] So, I do not hold, as Harré and Madden (1975: 1) do, that "There can be no doubt that the Humean conception of Causality and its linear descendant, the Regularity Theory, must be wrong." I take them to imply that Neo-Humean views are also undoubtedly false. Although I agree in general with them that there are real causal powers, and that there are good reasons to accept causal powers and deny Humeanism, my level of confidence in (or against) metaphysical theories stops short of certainty. Perhaps they were exaggerating when they opined "no doubt."

circumstances – effectively function as activation conditions for the (supposedly qualitative) properties endowing the objects that bear those properties with powers. As such, these supposed qualities are actually powers. Therefore, Lewis implicitly posits powers in his fundamental ontology.

The central insight in this argument is that the Humean laws of nature – global states or conditions – can be interpreted as conditions of manifestation for the point-like (and supposedly qualitative) properties in the Humean supervenience base. The global conditions, in a sense, "trigger" or "stimulate" these properties to reveal different potentialities. This is analogous to how the immersion of NaCl in water causes its dissolution and the striking of a match causes flame. On a (much) larger scale, "the laws of nature reveal the causal powers inherent in so-called categorical properties [qualities]" (Cross 2012: 142).[12] It is important, however, to note that the global conditions that reveal different potentialities of properties are not exactly triggering events or stimuli in the typical sense as, for example, in the striking of match. Nonetheless, natural properties are differently disposed in different worlds and the only difference in these worlds is the sequencing of events or regularities – that is, the global conditions.

In support of this claim, powers can have what is known as *alien sensitivity*: "radically nonactual" activation or triggering conditions that could subject them to manifestations that they would not ever undergo in the actual world (Cross 2012: 136). It is possible for our world to contain properties with effects capable of manifesting "only in the company of an alien" property (2012: 135). For example, there could be two particles that never, in fact, meet, but if they did, they would produce a new kind of particle with alien properties and powers (Martin 1993: 180, 1997: 224–226). We can also imagine exotic triggering conditions like a deity's predilections toward ensuring a vase breaks if even a lone dust particle touches it.[13]

Recognizing that some properties only reveal their powers under alien circumstances (triggers that are not part of the actual world but, if they were, could cause an actual-world property to manifest) brings us to the

---

[12] However, there is a disanalogous component: salt and water are powerful partners for specific token effects, whereas laws and properties are not powerful partners for specific token effects, but for the actualization of different powers than the property in question would otherwise have. Yet, there is a strong similarity with powers that remain actively manifesting when certain environmental conditions are satisfied. For example, arguably the mass of fundamental particles is generated by immersion in the Higgs field: as such, mass is a causal power that a particle obtains in virtue of total environmental conditions (Bauer 2011).

[13] The triggering property could be an "alien" property, and the manifested property – a new power – could also be an "alien" property, wholly foreign to this world, with no chance of manifesting because its partner is an alien property.

point of recognizing that the properties in Lewis' supervenience base are tantamount to powers. On Lewis' view, there certainly are "possible conditions such that" some property "F endows some power to objects in those conditions" (Cross 2012: 140). More specifically, there are global conditions – that is, some parts of the pluriverse – that trigger the Humean base properties to gain some powers different than they actually have.[14] Different laws activate different powers. While Lewis might not exactly hold this nomic theory of powers, Lewis' view is close enough to it and, besides, the point is that "there *are* possible conditions in which F disposes things to become Gs" (2012: 136). It is for these reasons that Cross (2012: 140) claims that "categorical properties [qualities], far from the inert, modally innocent creatures they purport to be, are in some sense *modal monads*, representing the full range of possible conditions (but unlike monads, causally interacting as well)." These modal monads are virtually indistinguishable from powers, directed toward various outcomes conditional upon appropriate global conditions.

This is a surprising interpretation of Humean Supervenience and not how Lewis himself sees things. *But it is surprisingly close.* Cross envisions a counterpart Lewis – "Dlewis." Lewis and Dlewis agree on nearly every count – the existence of discrete, spatiotemporally separate, concrete possible worlds; counterpart theory; and properties as sets of possibilia. However, they disagree on one point: Dlewis thinks fundamental properties (those in the supervenience base) are powers, not qualities. He accepts what Lewis denies: that the global states are conditions that "endow the powers [in the base] to bring about" effects or manifestations (Cross 2012: 144). Both Dlewis' and Lewis' metaphysics are coherent, and the view of properties is only "nominally different" (2012: 145). There are no differences in the behavioral modality of properties – it is just a different *interpretation* of Lewis' own fundamental metaphysical premises.[15]

---

[14] The manifestation here is not like a glass breaking, but the glass gaining the ability to break; the potential for gaining a power is itself a power. In other words, the type of manifestation Cross seems to have in mind is the *gaining* of a power: $x$ manifests its ability to gain a power, a power which can then be triggered by global conditions.

[15] If Humean Supervenience is a contingent thesis (Lewis 1986a: x–xi), then it is true only in a limited range of possible worlds including the actual world: worlds "Within the inner sphere of possibility" and without "alien" properties (1986a: x). (Comparing this remark about "alien" properties to the discussion of alien sensitivity in an earlier paragraph – while keeping in mind that Cross' argument invokes alien sensitivity – it is worth noting that despite the limited range of worlds of which Humean Supervenience is true, Lewis does allow alien triggers, such as sorcerers [Lewis 1997: 147–148].) Thus, Cross' Dlewis argument applies only to worlds in which Humean Supervenience holds. Still, this should be a large range of worlds with plenty of opportunities for the fundamental

To resist, Lewis would have to agree with Dlewis on every point while refusing to label as a *power* that which behaves like a power (Cross 2012: 145). In this way, given the total package of Lewis' metaphysics and the observation that the properties in the base behave as powers, Lewis not only could, but reasonably *should*, accept Dlewis' view. Lewis and Dlewis do not have different ontologies but different interpretations of one and the same ontology.[16] Lewis might well have said, "there is just one little disposition and then another" (2012: 141) in place of "just one little thing and then another" (Lewis 1986a: ix), where things are "local qualities" (1986a: x).

In further support of the Dlewisian interpretation, consider that in Lewis' pixel or computer screen metaphor (Lewis 1986a: 14), pixels are akin to qualities, independent of each other and capable of instantiating a vast range of colors (nearly 16.8 million, of which humans can only detect 10 million), such that any distribution of colors across the screen can be completely rearranged with different programming.[17] On Dlewis' interpretation, each pixel can be interpreted as modally rich: Each is packed with potential for a variety of outcomes, contingent on global conditions. Changing global conditions is akin to reprogramming the pixels.

Strawson (2008: 277) also develops a powers-oriented interpretation of Neo-Humeanism. His interpretation is, in some ways, a more general critique of Neo-Humeanism than Cross' targeting of Lewis' brand of Neo-Humeanism. Strawson argues that the powers of any object, *x*, include its

---

properties to have their world-relative powers activated (i.e., to become specific powers) owing to global conditions at that world. I further note that if Humean Supervenience really is a contingent thesis, then it would seem that in some worlds there are inherent, irreducible powers (i.e., dispositional essentialism appears to be true in those worlds). So, setting Dlewis aside, Lewis himself must be open to the possibility of irreducible powers. So, for example, in some worlds charge is a quality with contingent powers, but in other worlds, charge is an irreducible power. This makes it curious as to how, if one has empiricist leanings, we could know which kind of world we are in: a powers- or qualities-based world.

[16] In further support of the Dlewis interpretation, assume that properties are sets of individuals (Lewis 1986b: 50). So, a property is a set of objects not just in the actual world but across some range of possible worlds; for example, electric charge is the set of all electrons carrying charge, whether in this world or others. But what charge *does* – its causal role – differs across worlds owing to different regularities in the patterns of events. So, as a property (i.e., a set of individuals), charge (or any other natural property) has the power to manifest differently in worlds with different laws. It might be that each *instance* (borne by each particular) does not have the power to be a different power (though it does have the power to obtain the actual causal role in each world that it in fact has), for then it would be a different instance in a different world. However, properties – taken as sets of individuals, as Lewis does – do seem to have the power that Cross ascribes to them: to have different powers in their different instances across worlds. That is, Dlewis is correct.

[17] Lewis specifically tells the analogy in terms of a "dot-matrix picture" with "dots" and "non-dots," but Schrenk (2017: 76) helpfully frames the example in terms of computer screens and pixels.

powers to behave differently under different laws. Even if we suppose that laws can come apart from the (categorical) nature of matter – as the Neo-Humean maintains[18] – Strawson (2008: 277) thinks we cannot justifiably claim that $x$'s "fundamental dispositions [powers] will change on change of nomic environment" as Neo-Humeans maintain. This is because the fundamental powers of $x$ include the power to behave in different ways in different nomic environments or contexts (i.e., worlds with different orderings of events, per the regularity theory of laws). In nomic environment 1, $x$ has the power to behave in way M1; in nomic environment 2, $x$ has the power to behave in way M2; and so on. That is, objects have powers to gain (have activated) new sets of powers under different laws.[19] This is basically the Dlewisian view discussed above.[20] The intrinsic qualities of the Humean mosaic are, in short, "meta-powers" (powers to gain powers) because the specific causal roles that they have in different worlds are determinable by global conditions.[21] By contrast, nonmeta-powers – of the kind on the Powers Model to be discussed in Section 1.4 – just are the powers that they are (see Figure 1.2).

We can illuminate the idea that Neo-Humeanism implies that qualities are meta-powers (and therefore powers) by focusing on the quality/power distinction. Suppose we differentiate qualities and powers in terms of manifestations. Then powers are not always manifesting; they can remain latent. However, qualities *are* always manifesting; specifically, they are manifesting their meta-power to have certain world-specific, nomologically contingent powers.[22] Qualities are manifest under all conditions in

---

[18]  Strawson (2008: 277) rejects what he calls the "'separatist' habit of thought," which, as I understand it, is how he thinks the Humean approaches metaphysics, and according to which laws should be conceived as linguistic, human creations. By contrast, laws are to be understood "as non-linguistic objective principles" and cannot be independent of the categorical (=dispositional) nature of matter (Strawson 2008: 277).

[19]  This supports Strawson's overall argument that qualities and powers are inseparable, and in fact identical to each other. However, in accepting the claim that objects have powers to behave in different ways under different laws, I argue that the identity theory is not forced on us; for we can deny the identity claim by contending that powers are devoid of quality (more on pure powers in Section 1.4).

[20]  The power does not lie with the laws, for according to Humean Supervenience the laws are simply regularities; therefore, the power should be found in the only "real" things on this view: the properties of spacetime points.

[21]  Broad (1925: 432–433) distinguishes first-, second-, and higher-order powers, where the latter are powers to gain or lose lower-order powers; see McKitrick (2018: 9) for discussion. On the interpretation I am putting forward, Neo-Humean qualities have higher-order powers to gain new powers in different nomic situations (worlds).

[22]  Hüttemann (2009: 225) holds that while instances of dispositions are "*manifest under specific conditions only,*" categorical properties are "*manifest under all conditions*"; thus, "categorical properties are limiting cases of dispositional properties" – as such the distinction between property and

that their meta-power is always activated relative to some world; although they might not always be doing what they are activated for in a world *w*, they are always activated to have specific powers in *w*.

|  | Qualities | Powers |
|---|---|---|
| **Property F has a meta-power to *gain* power to φ** | Necessarily have power to gain world-specific, law-dependent powers to φ | No meta-powers; have law-independent modal natures |
| **Property F has power to φ** | Contingently have power to φ | Necessarily have power to φ |

Figure 1.2    Powers and meta-powers of qualities versus powers (φ is a manifestation type)

Livanios (2017b: 34) observes that Strawson ascribes to "properties either a transworld *functional* essence or the same *total* essence, *part of* which is instantiated in each possible world." This, he contends, is unorthodox because usually powers theorists maintain that a power presents its whole essence (not necessarily all of its actual *manifestations*, of course) in the world in which it exists or is instantiated. However, I do not think the unusualness of this claim presents a significant worry. This is because, on Strawson's interpretation of Neo-Humeanism, each power's total essence (its total causal profile) remains fully present in each nomic context; but the specific laws (and nonlaws) in each nomic context effectively *mask* part of each power's essence. As such, a power will only be capable of manifesting a subset of its full range of power upon a shift in nomic context. It is important to not overlook that this point assumes that the presence of nomic contexts is indeed relevant to modality, something powers theorists typically reject. But if powers theorists were to accept such nomic contexts, adopting a Neo-Humean view of laws while maintaining a powers view of properties, then, surely, they would correspondingly adjust the essence of powers so that each power's total essence would include its essence in different possible worlds/nomic contexts. They would accept a meta-view of powers. That is, they would accept that, from the point of view of particular nomic contexts, each power's potency (essence) is only partially in play, whereas normally they hold that all of a power's potency (essence) is in play in the world in which it exists. Nonetheless, on both views, each power has or embodies its full essence – the power it inherently has despite the nomic context masking some of that power.

manifestation "doesn't do any work." However, I disagree that it does no work; for the limiting case – *necessary* manifestations that signify categoricalness – is distinct from the *contingent* manifestations of dispositions.

Given that the supervenience base qualities are conceived only as conferring powers to objects in virtue of the laws of nature, they are in a sense mere intermediaries or "transit centers" for powers and their displays. But in having this primitive role, I claim – invoking Cross' and Strawson's arguments – that they do have powers: they must have the power to take on different causal roles, to be adaptable to different nomic environments. In other words, if quiddities can swap causal roles (Bird 2007a: 73–76) in different nomic environments, they must be capable of world-specific modal reprogramming; if they were truly *completely inert*, they could not and would not serve any modal role.

### Responses to the Powers Interpretation of Neo-Humeanism

One objection is that in extracting powers from the innards of the Neo-Humean Model, we are adopting the mystery of powers – supposed by some as occult, unobservable entities – in place of the more empirically oriented, mystery-less mosaic of particular facts. However, there is also great metaphysical mystery in the Neo-Humean Model. This is because it allows that "anything can be the cause of anything" – in one world hammer strikes *break* vases, while in another world they *liquefy* them – therefore, the Neo-Humean Model "involves an occult, even mystical, conception of the world's unfolding" (Campbell 1990: 116). This runs contrary, notes Campbell, to a scientific conception of the world in which scientists often frame happenings in terms of forces, powers, and the like to emphasize causal relations and interconnectedness. The point is not that the Powers Model presents no mystery (i.e., no unexplained features). No serious, complete conception of reality is free of that accusation. Rather, the Neo-Humean Model is no less mysterious, thus not on more secure grounds, than the Powers Model. This sense of mystery is exacerbated by the fact that qualities are supposed to be quiddities with an inherently unspecifiable this-ness that does not "prescribe anything" (Schrenk 2017: 73).

Another objection is that the powers-oriented Dlewisian interpretation of Neo-Humeanism appears to be less parsimonious than the qualities-oriented Lewisian interpretation. This is because, beyond qualities, the Humean mosaic of properties is supposed to contain only spatiotemporal relations. Everything that exists – including all ordinary "objects" within our experience – is supposed to be reducibly explainable in terms of the mosaics' qualities and their spatiotemporal relations (Lewis 1986a: ix–x).[23]

---

[23] See Nolan (2014: 34–38) for an illuminating discussion.

However, if the properties that make up the fabric of the Humean mosaic are powers, not qualities, then on networking accounts of powers the mosaic would need to also include stimulus and manifestation relations (e.g., as part of the identity conditions of a power). If these relations are added to the supervenience base, then things look less parsimonious than with the qualities-only view.

One way to respond is to argue that stimulus and manifestation relations are not fundamental: they arise from the mosaic of powers and their spatiotemporal relations. It seems that potential manifestations (i.e., potentialities for effects, including the stimulation of other powers) are inherently part of the identity and essence of powers – supposing, as seems reasonable, every power is a potentiality (Vetter 2015: 19). Therefore, the potency of powers is irreducible and part of what it means to be a power. Therefore, importantly, it is not the manifestations that need to be added to the fundamental picture of reality – only the *potential* for such. What I ultimately suggest is that each power inherently contains information about its directedness toward and possible interactions with other powers, and thus about its potential manifestations. Actual manifestations might be relational, produced by the relationality between two or more powers; but the information that drives powers toward these manifestations is not. (These claims will be developed in Part II.) This information is the source of the specific directedness that each power has toward its possible manifestations, and this is neither more mysterious nor less parsimonious than the hidden, haecceity-like essence that qualities have. The inherent nature of each power explains why powers do what they do.

The argument of this section strongly suggests but does not prove that Neo-Humeanism – in particular, Lewis' Humean Supervenience thesis – implies that properties are powers, contrary to the wishes of its adherents. This favors the Powers Model. However, could there be something short of powers but non-Neo-Humean in character that explains physical modality, perhaps a primitive necessary connection between properties? Enter the Universals Model.

## 1.3    The Universals Model Needs Powers

Some theories of laws of nature are best characterized as descriptive – in particular the regularity theory of laws that is part of the Neo-Humean package – whereas others are prescriptive such as necessitarian theories of laws (Dumsday 2019: 3). On the Universals Model, a necessitarian theory, prescriptive power comes from universals governing the order of events.

The Universals Model says that a law of nature is a necessitation rela-tion, N, that holds between two universals, F and G, understood as cat-egorical properties or nonpowerful qualities: N[F,G].[24] N is a nonlogical, contingent necessitation relation (Armstrong 1983: 71–102), thus repre-senting physical modality, not metaphysical or logical modality. For any particular *a* that is F, *a* will be G, provided that N[F,G] holds. N[F,G] undergirds all kinds of laws of nature; for instance, F could be an electron $e_1$'s negative charge, and G the repulsion of $e_1$ when approaching a second electron $e_2$.

However, it is important to note that just because some particular pos-sesses F does not mean that the law N[F,G] holds. The entailment goes from the general *law* to the instantiated *state of affairs*, not from the instan-tiation of F and G to the law N[F,G]. This is reflected in the metaphorical idea that laws of nature "*govern* particular states of affairs" (Armstrong 1983: 98).[25] Owing to the law represented by N[F,G], the Universals Model is an account of physical modality (see Figure 1.3).

---

**UNIVERSALS MODEL**

the facts of physical modality
are *determined by*
lawful connection between qualities (i.e., categorical properties) conceived as universals

---

Figure 1.3   Universals Model of physical modality

Borghini and Williams (2008: 35) ask, "What is the modal power inside a natural law?"[26] This is a revealing question for any account of laws of nature, especially the Universals Model. For this model posits laws as real, mind-independent entities that govern relations between objects, thus explaining physical modality. The model makes a law an *entity* (in the

---

[24] I focus on the view as formulated by Armstrong (1978, 1983), who calls it the Universals theory. A statement of the general idea can be found in Armstrong (1983: 83). Armstrong (1993: 422) has clari-fied that on his account N is a causal relation. Dretske (1977) presents a similar account, although his argument is conditional: *if* there are laws, they are relations between universals (1977: 267). Tooley (1977) also presents a universals-based account of modality, but for him universals are tran-scendent, unlike for Armstrong, who maintains that universals are immanent.

[25] The claim that laws govern holds significant sway in our thinking about the nature of reality (Roberts 2008: 1–5). However, it is metaphorical owing to the "imperfect analogy between social law and law of nature" (Armstrong 1983: 106). Yet it captures the idea that laws stand independently from their instantiations. By contrast, Armstrong notes, the regularity theory of laws (taken in sec-tion 1.2 as part of the Neo-Humean Model) cannot make sense of either the governing metaphor or of laws being independent of their instantiations.

[26] By "natural law" they mean "law of nature" (laws as in science, not in Thomism).

broadest sense of the term "entity," an existent of some sort) that affects the world. The lawfulness is found in N. But what does N do? On one hand, if N is utterly passive, incapable of producing change, then F would not be G due to N itself. On the other hand, if N is supposed to do something, then it *is* productive, implying modal force or power.

In this light, Barker (2013: 621) contends that the Universals Model (the second degree) seems to require a power-like necessary connection between properties, or it collapses into brute-modalism (the first degree, i.e., Neo-Humeanism). He continues:

> If there is to be a second degree at all, then second-order facts like N[F,G] have to *constrain* or *govern* first-order facts of natural property instantiation. But [...] that requires that N[F,G] necessitates lower order facts *by virtue of the inherent nature* of N. But this means N has to be powerful in a way analogous to the third-degreer's powerful natural properties.[27] (Barker 2013: 621)

The necessity between F and G cannot be a brute relation (2013: 617). If it were brute, it would be a brute fact about possible worlds – where "all Fs are Gs" is simply correlated with N[F,G] – and N[F,G] would not be the source of the necessity. In that case, we would be back to the Neo-Humean Model discussed in Section 1.2 (Lewis, not Dlewis). However, on the Universals Model, the necessity between F and G is due to an inherent necessity relation, N. Instead of being simply a brute fact, there is assumed to be an explanatory basis for "all Fs and Gs" as specified by N[F,G] where necessity "just *flows* from the nature of N. It is a kind of second-order power" (2013: 618).[28] N is a power-like source of the necessity that transpires between F and G.

Perhaps the power that N implies is a power of the *system* of law-abiding properties as a whole (e.g., of the universe or nature as a whole). Still, this is a power. Power must be present somehow to effectuate the connection between F and G. According to the Powers Model, F and G would themselves be powers. But on the Universals Model, the power is removed one step from F and G and given the designator N. Present and real is the power of N, so much that F necessitates G.

In *A Treatise of Human Nature*, Hume (2002: Sect. XIV) lumps together various nomic concepts: "EFFICACY, AGENCY, POWER,

---

[27] The third degree is what I call the Powers Model.

[28] A similar conclusion must be drawn, I suggest, from antireductionist views of laws (such as Carroll 1994, 2008): that the fundamental, irreducible laws are powers of nature to enforce physical ordering and necessity between events in the universe.

FORCE, ENERGY, NECESSITY, CONNEXION, and PRODUCTIVE QUALITY, are all nearly synonymous; and therefore it is an absurdity to employ any of them in defining the rest." If Hume is correct, consider what this means for Armstrong's analysis of laws and properties. Given that Armstrong touts a *necessary connection between universals* under the governance of law, this could reasonably be interpreted as akin to a *power's necessary manifestation under appropriate conditions*. In other words, the Universals Model and the Powers Model, on the face of it, have a lot more in common with each other than they do with the Neo-Humean Model. This implies that it is not a metaphysically big step from the Universals Model to the Powers Model.[29]

In sum, maintaining that N is inherently powerful – or sufficiently power-like to believe that N is powerful – seems like the only viable position for a Universals Model proponent to take. Therefore, according to Barker (2013), since the Powers Model collapses into brute-modalism (i.e., Neo-Humeanism), the Universals Model also does because it too invokes powers. By contrast, I have argued that the Neo-Humean Model requires powers, so no such collapse into brute-modalism can in fact occur – any collapse of the Powers Model would be a collapse into some *alternative* powers model. Therefore, the question becomes: which of the three different, ultimately powers-based, models is best? I think the Powers Model (and specifically the Pure Powers Model) is preferable because it is more economical: It need not refer to governing laws or possible worlds in explaining physical modality, and it keeps modal action simpler than the other models by placing modality squarely inside properties.

Like the Neo-Humean Model, the Universals Model provides a coherent account of properties, laws, and physical modality. Although both models claim to be nonrealist about powers, if the arguments of Sections 1.2 and 1.3 are on the right track, then both models implicitly posit powers. I do not take the arguments in Sections 1.2 and 1.3 to be completely decisive. However, they raise significant suspicion that powers are subtly (or not so subtly) involved in these two models. Therefore, let us look at the Powers Model.

---

[29] Bird (2005) also argues that the Universals Model (any in the Dretske-Tooley-Armstrong family of views) implies powers. If N is to explain why there is a necessary relation between distinct properties F and G, there is nothing to prevent one from simply positing that F has a necessary connection to G (a power and its manifestation), thus assigning modal force to F, thus making it a powerful property. And McKitrick (2021: 288) reiterates something similar to Bird (2005) and Barker (2013): locating a necessitating universal inside some particular to explain its activity is arguably no different than saying that the particular has the power to do the action.

## 1.4  The Powers Model

The Neo-Humean and Universals Models try to expunge irreducible powers from their ontologies. However, positing powers is unavoidable. To the extent that these supposedly nonpowers models are successful, it is because they implicitly posit powers. A weaker conclusion would be that those models only contain hints of powers (e.g., N displays some but not all of the characteristics of power-hood). Although I favor the stronger conclusion – that the other models are implicitly committed to a robust conception of powers – the weaker conclusion nonetheless gives sufficient reason to take seriously the hypothesis that real powers play an essential role in physical modality.

In light of the finding that the nonpowers models actually need powers, I adopt the Powers Model of physical modality. But beyond the *need* for irreducible causal powers, the Powers Model also appears to be more economical and elegant than the Universals Model and the Neo-Humean Model. This is because the modality needed to drive events is built right into powers and thus there is no metaphysical requirement for laws of nature, although it remains plausible that laws of nature are epistemically useful in scientific practice.[30] Moreover, a metaphysics of science based on powers has the potential to inform a number of key issues in philosophy besides modality, including causation, agency, free will, epistemology, and normative theory.[31] Although these ramifications are not my main concern, noticing them bolsters motivation for investigating powers from the inside.[32]

---

[30] The Powers Model, however, is consistent with the metaphysical reality of laws (Bird 2007a; Dumsday 2019).

[31] See Meincke (2020) for an overview concerning how powers relate to other philosophical issues.

[32] Powers according to the Powers Model are what Azzano (2019) calls *robust powers*: irreducibly powerful properties. There are also, Azzano suggests, *weak powers* and *moderate powers*. Weak powers are "obtained" simply through disquoting a statement about some particular *x* being disposed: for example, if "the glass is fragile" or "the glass has the power to break" is true, then the glass has the power to break. However, weak powers assume no ontological posit to explain or ground the truth of the dispositional statement. Logical empiricists would tend to be mere weak powers realists for wanting to avoid any commitment to any kind of hidden metaphysical reality. Moderate powers – as found in the Universals Model and Neo-Humean Model – are properties that are "at least partially responsible [...] for dispositional truths" (Azzano 2019: 342). These are real properties that feature in nomic-causal explanations of events. But, sans laws of nature, they would lose their power. Thus, Armstrong and Lewis are moderate powers realists. One might reasonably contend that Armstrong – or Dretske or Tooley for that matter – are strongly moderate powers realists, whereas Neo-Humeans like Lewis are weakly moderate powers realists. Regardless, if the arguments I have presented above are on the right track, it is likely that proponents of moderate powers are actually committed to *robust* powers. Note that the third degree of realism specified by Azzano – robust powers – aligns with the third degree of modality as specified by Barker (2013).

### Questions about the Powers Model

What do we accept in admitting irreducible powers into our ontology? Whereas qualities are perpetually manifest, powers reside in a state of real potential: they are real properties but their effects might not ever manifest. When triggered in the appropriate circumstances – with no interferences, finks, masks, and so on – powers will manifest: electrons will repel each other, fuel will explode, a fragile glass will break, a chocolate lover will eat chocolate.

The Powers Model can explain the same modal facts as the Universals and Neo-Humean Models but can do so more simply and elegantly by making properties inherently modal. The Powers Model combines the truthmaker for modality (a property) and the modal force (a power) – a powerful property just *is* the source of physical modality *and* that which is involved in modal relations. Thus, the Powers Model can eschew laws, unlike the other models, although it need not do so.[33] I am inclined to dismiss laws of nature as real, mind-independent things. Given a fully developed theory of powers, according to which powers are the modal force in the universe, we have enough to account for the cosmos' dynamic nature. However, law statements – as equations or summaries of what could happen – remain useful to scientific practice and everyday reasoning.

Despite advantages in elegance and simplicity, a problem haunts the Powers Model. What are powers like from the inside? If they are modal entities, as presumed, then exactly what about them explains their modality?[34] Is there anything further that we can discern about their internality

---

[33] Although powers theorists tend to eschew laws, holding that powers are the drivers of activity in the universe, recently some powers theorists have been advancing alternative accounts. These accounts attempt to show how the Powers Model is compatible with a robust, realist sense of laws (Dumsday 2019; Tugby 2016), contrary to eliminativist accounts (Mumford 2004) or weakly realist, supervenience accounts of laws (Bird 2007a) advanced by other powers theorists. For example, Dumsday (2019: 9–22) presents what I interpret as a middle ground between the Universals Model and the Powers Model of modality. He argues for a dispositionalist theory of governing laws according to which instantiated powers (conceived as universals) and uninstantiated universals – as specified in *ceteris paribus* clauses, which are necessary to the identity conditions of powers, according to Dumsday – conjointly underpin physical modality. These uninstantiated universals fit the bill for lawhood because "with them we have abstracta determining that certain events can or cannot take place under particular circumstances" (2019: 14). My suspicion is that these uninstantiated universals are still properties doing "powers work" along with the instantiated powers, so it is not fundamentally different from the Powers Model.

[34] It should not go unnoticed that the internal nature of quiddities (categorical properties or pure qualities) also remains something of a mystery. They have something of an ineffable "this-ness" apart from their merely contingent causal roles and relations to other properties.

other than that they are modally charged? Much of the discussion of powers has focused on their relationality in the form of networking accounts, as discussed in Section 0.7. But I contend that the nature of a power – what it is to be a power – is *not* fully revealed by examining its causal role in a system of powers. Their networked nature is important, and much of what I want to argue overlaps with this idea, but I think we can discern more about a power's internality.

What we would like to discern is a power's point of view, so to speak. Although the true internal nature of any entity – other than, perhaps, some aspects of our own minds – might forever be occluded from us, this should not stop us from offering careful interpretations of entities in the world that include hypotheses about their internal natures. Speaking of powers (and properties in general) from the "inside" is somewhat metaphorical. The term "inside" implies a boundary or spatial containment that could be misleading. What we are after is to understand their nature, to get a picture of their internal setup – the way powers are "through and through" beyond their relations to each other and things in the world.

### Varieties of the Powers Model

There are two primary ways to build the Powers Model: powers as *pure*, or powers as simultaneously *qualitative*. Pure powers have no qualitative nature, whereas powerful qualities are simultaneously powerful and qualitative (see Figure 1.4).

| POWERS MODEL | |
|:---:|:---:|
| the facts of physical modality<br>*are determined by*<br>the potentiality of powers (i.e., powerful properties) | |
| **Pure Powers Model** | **Powerful Qualities Model** |
| properties are entirely powerful and have no qualitative nature whatsoever | properties are simultaneously (P) powerful and (Q) qualitative |
| Scope of Pure Powers Model<br><br>pandispositionalism<br>dispositional monism<br>dispositional essentialism | Compound View (P + Q)<br>P and Q are "parts" or aspects of a property<br><br>Identity View (P = Q)<br>P is numerically identical to Q |

Figure 1.4   Variations of the Powers Model of physical modality

The Pure Powers Model claims that properties – at least some, but perhaps all – are entirely and essentially powerful.[35] This does not mean that they are mere potentials; pure powers are real, actual properties capable of manifesting when triggered in relevant conditions. A pure power's identity conditions consist of its causal profile – its range of possible causal effects within a variety of circumstances. By contrast, the Powerful Qualities Model combines quality and power into a single property.[36] Importantly, there are two ways to build the Powerful Qualities Model, as Figure 1.4 indicates: the Identity View and the Compound View. The Identity View says that properties are identical to both power and quality, that is, P = Q. Some might wish to characterize this view as a triple identity between *property*, *power*, and *quality* (Heil 2003: 111; Livanios 2017b: 31). However, since each of the latter two (power, quality) just are *property* types, the triple identity seems redundant. By contrast, according to the Compound View, powerful qualities are compounded of power and quality, that is, P + Q, such that P and Q are each "parts" of a whole property.[37] I will focus my assessment (in Chapter 2) on the Identity View mostly because the Compound View implies that one property is two properties, so it is *prima facie* incoherent.

What I call the scope of the Pure Powers Model, in the lower left box of Figure 1.4, concerns whether the model is interpreted to apply to all properties or just some subset of properties. The main options are pandispositionalism (all properties are pure powers), dispositional monism (all

[35] Advocates of pure powers, to varying extents, include Bird (2007a), Ellis (2001, 2002), Molnar (2003), Mumford and Anjum (2011), Anjum and Mumford (2018), and Shoemaker (1980), among others. Some (e.g., Bird) are dispositional monists, some (e.g., Mumford, Anjum) are pandispositionalists, and some (e.g., Ellis, Molnar) accept a mixed view (according to which some fundamental properties are powers and some, such as locations, are qualities). On the mixed view, Ellis (2010b: 105), for instance, maintains that fundamental categorical properties can play causal roles but only accidentally, not essentially.

[36] Advocates of powerful qualities – the Identity View, in particular – include Heil (2003, 2010, 2012), Ingthorsson (2013), Jacobs (2011), Jaworski (2016: 53–79), and Martin (2008), among others.

[37] Barker (2013: 622–623) classifies the pure powers and powerful qualities views as the two principal ways to interpret the Powers Model. However, he thinks that the identity version (P = Q) of powerful qualities is incoherent (2013: 649). That remains to be seen – powerful qualities are discussed in more detail in Chapter 2 – but for Barker (2013: 623) the real competition is between pure powers and the compound version (P + Q) of powerful qualities, according to which qualities "*generate* or *produce* modality." He identifies three ways to construct pure powers (2013: 623): (i) relational constitution (the identity of powers – which are bundles of relations – is fixed by higher-order relations), (ii) graphs (powers are "nodes in a graph, whose *arc* is a modal relation"), and (iii) functional roles (powers are essentially functional properties). Barker criticizes the P + Q version of powerful qualities (2013: 644–648) as well as the three understandings of pure powers (2013: 623–644). If my arguments in sections 1.2 and 1.3 are on the right track, then we must admit powers into our ontology as an explanation of physical modality.

fundamental properties are pure powers), and dispositional essentialism (some fundamental properties are pure powers). If one adopted dispositional monism, for instance, one would accept the Pure Powers Model for all fundamental properties but then accept that all nonfundamental properties are qualities or perhaps powerful qualities. If one accepted dispositional essentialism, one could take locations and spatiotemporal relations, for example, as qualities or powerful qualities, while asserting that all other fundamental properties are pure powers (thus accepting a limited scope of the Pure Powers Model). So, in general, one might maintain that pure powers, powerful qualities, and pure qualities are not mutually exclusive, thus that the correct view is a mixed view: taking any two or three of these models as true for different subsets of properties.[38]

I accept the Pure Powers Model conceived strictly to exclude the other models, that is, conceived as pandispositionalism. If others do not want to accept pure powers to the maximum extent, they could still accept my major claims as applied to the pure powers that *are* posited in their ontologies. So, one could accept my major claims without committing exclusively to the Pure Powers Model.

Before further distinguishing these models of powers as well as critiquing the Identity View in Chapter 2, I want to introduce another aspect of the debate over physical modality and powers. Beyond the standard dual modality of necessity and possibility, Mumford and Anjum (2011) and Anjum and Mumford (2018) argue for a third, unique modality: the dispositional (or powerful) modality. Anjum and Mumford (2018) advocate the powers view of reality, arguing that it provides the foundation for properly understanding several metaphysical issues, such as the nature of

---

[38] To explain further, the various Powers Models presented here could be combined in various ways. For instance, one could hold that all fundamental powers are pure powers (the Pure Powers Model applies comprehensively), or that some fundamental powers are pure powers while some are powerful qualities (Pure Powers Model + the Powerful Qualities Model), or that some fundamental properties are pure powers while some are pure qualities as on standard "mixed views" of properties. Similar kinds of mixed views could be claimed for nonfundamental powers as well. In summary, one could have an *exclusive* or a *nonexclusive* interpretation of any of the Powers Models (or, for that matter, models that posit pure qualities). However, the simplest and most unified interpretation would exclude the other models, and that is how I proceed in this book in defending the Pure Powers Model. This Pure Powers Model, interpreted in an exclusive manner, is synonymous with pandispositionalism. However, all my central claims about the nature of powers (Chapters 2–6) are about their internal nature and thus do not require accepting pure powers to the exclusion of other models. Any theorist who accepts a mixed view could accept my claims about the nature of pure powers while holding that other types of property instances have their own nature. I will further discuss mixed views in Chapter 7 and explore how a pure powers theorist might accommodate the appearance of qualities at higher levels of reality.

causation. But they think that the standard approach to thinking about modality in terms of either necessity or possibility is insufficient to capture the true nature of powers: powers *tend* toward their manifestations, without necessitating them while yet being more than merely possible. The dispositional modality is something "less" than necessity (be it metaphysical or physical necessity) and something "more" than mere possibility. And a power's tending toward its outcome cannot be reduced to probability; for Anjum and Mumford, tendencies (dispositional modalities) underlie probabilities.

In this chapter, I did not concern myself with the dispositional modality. As compelling as the idea might be to some, it is (at least) not yet widely accepted and needs further evaluation. In this initial dialectical context, it would beg the question against the first two models (the Neo-Humean and Universals Models) to assume that a dispositional modality must be taken on board. Moreover, the main theses about powers in this book can be maintained whether there is a genuine dispositional modality or not. Indeed, I think that one can be a realist about powers without accepting a unique dispositional modality if, for example, physical modality is explained by an informational structure within powers concerning only possibility and necessity – a point I will argue for in Chapter 6.

CHAPTER 2

# *The Reality of Pure Powers*

## 2.1   Pure Powers versus Powerful Qualities

Powers imbue the world with real possibilities and make things happen. Which version of the Powers Model, all things considered, is best? My answer is the Pure Powers Model, interpreted broadly to be pandispositionalism.[1] In this chapter, I further explore differences between pure powers and powerful qualities, argue for the Pure Powers Model, and discuss the problem of being for pure powers. Much work remains to be done in the debate over pure powers versus powerful qualities, and my investigation here is not definitive. My intent here is as exploratory as it is argumentative.

Examining the distinction between the powerful qualities and pure powers is important for two reasons. First, since I am defending pure powers, I need to reasonably demonstrate that they differ from powerful qualities. Second, one might wonder if powerful qualities illuminate powers from the inside. If powerful qualities are identical to pure powers, the question is moot since adding qualitativity adds nothing new to pure powers. But if there is a distinction between powerful qualities and pure powers, as I maintain, then one reason to prefer the Powerful Qualities Model is that it illuminates better what powers are like from the inside (i.e., that their qualitativity is explanatorily relevant to powers' internal nature). However, I do not think qualitativity helps much because qualities themselves are rather mysterious and thus uninformative regarding the inside of powers. Even if we suppose that powerful qualities help, I think there are independent reasons to be discussed in Sections 2.3 and 2.4 to dismiss this model of powers (nonetheless, my 3d account could, with appropriate modifications, reasonably be adopted by advocates of powerful qualities).

---

[1] Pure powers need defense if one is to accept even just one pure power in their ontology.

After tentatively rejecting the powerful qualities interpretation of powers, I will defend the reality of pure powers in the rest of this chapter (Sections 2.5–2.8).

### *Similarities between Pure Powers and Powerful Qualities*

Is there a real difference that sets powerful qualities apart from pure powers? It has been argued that there is no ontological distinction between powerful qualities (the Identity View) and pure powers. Taylor (2018) argues that despite a number of ways that advocates of each view try to distinguish pure powers and powerful qualities, the opponent in each case seems to include something that negates the supposed difference implied by the competing view, thus supporting the thesis that pure powers are the same as powerful qualities.

Powerful qualities theorists sometimes point to examples like shape and color as "paradigmatic qualities" (Heil 2012: 57), hence suggesting a need for powerful *qualities*, not just powers. But pure powers theorists accept the existence of these properties as well. So, pointing out the reality of shapes such as sphericity or colors such as redness cannot dictate a real difference between the views (Taylor 2018: 1426). Pure powers theorists simply interpret sphericity, for instance, as the power to roll down an incline, and redness as the power to cause red experiences in perceivers.

Speaking of qualitative experiences, some philosophers (Heil 2003: 76; Martin 1997: 222–224) claim a necessary overlap between qualities and phenomenal, or experiential, qualia (Taylor 2018: 1426–1428). Jacobs (2011) promotes this line of argument. He first distinguishes mental from physical qualia; the former are phenomenological properties, but the latter belong to physical objects.[2] Wanting to avoid implications of panpsychism, Jacobs (2011: 91) holds that qualia are not necessarily phenomenal since physical qualia are not phenomenal properties. Instead, he says, "To be qualitative [i.e., a physical qualia] is to be identical with a thick quiddity (a quality or a quale)," which differ from each other by their intrinsic

---

[2] It is not clear why physical qualities (powerful or not) should be likened to mental properties, but one motivation seems to be that, as powerful qualities theorists sometimes contend, pure powers theorists cannot account for mental, subjective states. Jacobs (2011: 87) says that if all properties are pure powers, "*everything* is zombie-like" with no "qualitative nature" whatsoever. However, pure powers theorists can account for mental qualia: Qualia are manifestations of mental powers (see, e.g., Gozzano 2020). Mental qualia might, in turn, be powers capable of causally influencing actions by the agent, or they might be epiphenomenal.

nature, not just numerically (2011: 90).[3] To encounter a thick quiddity is "emphatically not to have encountered them all" (2011: 91).[4] So, the suggestion is that the "thickness" that Jacobs ascribes to powerful qualities sets them apart from pure powers.

In response to this reasoning, pure powers have the same features that Jacobs ascribes to qualities (Taylor 2018: 1427): They differ from each other not just numerically, they have distinct natures, "and to encounter one is not to encounter them all." Pure power tokens are distinct existences with their own natures, Taylor suggests, which makes them no different than powerful qualities. I am somewhat skeptical of this response. This is because two token pure powers, though numerically distinct, might share the same causal profile and thus be intrinsically indistinct, thus not have their "own nature" as Jacobs claims for powerful qualities. However, to support Taylor's response, we could argue that two otherwise identical token powers (e.g., two instances of charge) are distinct in terms of their contingent causal history and future because of their unique spatiotemporal trajectories through the world. Two instances of charge might share all the same potential causal effects, yet they are their own charges with their own causal histories; electron 1 (carrying charge $c_1$) can (contingently) do things that electron 2 (carrying charge $c_2$) cannot because of its unique spatiotemporal path: It is on a different causal path from electron 2.[5] Each pure power token has its own identity, owing to its unique causal history (and future) or that of the object that instantiates it. Therefore, to see one instance of a property is not to see all of that property's instances in their causal-historical totality.

Besides the example-based argument and the comparison to qualia, there is a third possible way to distinguish powers and powerful qualities (Taylor 2018: 1425–1426): One might argue that powerful qualities, because of their qualitativity, are "real" or "actual" features of objects whereas powers are not.[6] The problem with this claim is that pure powers

[3] To avoid confusion with phenomenological properties, in my view it would be best to avoid talk of qualia or a quale in this context.

[4] Here, Jacobs is quoting Armstrong (1997: 168), who rejects thick quiddities although he accepts qualities, thus implying a distinction between quiddities (numerically distinct bare qualities analogous to numerically distinct bare particulars, as Jacobs appears to be assuming) and a standard conception of qualities (nonpowerful properties that are fully, always manifest). (Thanks to an anonymous reviewer for suggesting further clarification here.)

[5] I am inclined to accept this way of distinguishing otherwise identical instances of pure powers, thus challenging the claim that powers theorists cannot distinguish identical tokens of powers (Hawthorne 2001).

[6] See, for example, Heil (2012: 59) and Strawson (2008: 278).

theorists also hold that powers are real or actual features of objects.[7] No one holds, or should hold, that powers are real only when manifesting. During periods of nonmanifestation, there is a real potential – a power – to manifest. Thus, the claim that the "reality" or "actuality" of powerful qualities sets them apart from pure powers is insufficient to distinguish them. Relatedly, however, there remains a problem of explaining the being or reality of powers during latent periods. I will address this in Section 2.6.

### Are There Differences between Pure Powers and Powerful Qualities?

If the above discussion is correct, then pure powers and powerful qualities share much in common, not just their commitment to properties being inherently powerful. This is good news for pure powers theorists, because it shows that they can account for many of the phenomena that powerful qualities are claimed to account for: the supposed examples of "qualities" (colors, shapes) and the "real" features of things. However, there are reasons to continue treating pure powers and powerful qualities as distinct.

First, if Taylor (2018) is right, then arguments against powerful qualities – specifically those that focus on their qualitative nature – would also be arguments against pure powers. But such arguments,[8] including those I advance below, do not *prima facie* threaten pure powers. Thus, there must be some difference between the two views. Furthermore, pure powers and powerful qualities theorists certainly take their views of powers to differ. Metaphysicians of science by and large continue to distinguish between powerful qualities and pure powers. The various arguments for and against these views, despite Taylor's efforts, deserve further consideration before final judgment is made concerning their similitude. Finally, powerful qualities and pure powers are at least conceptually distinct, as Taylor recognizes, if not also ontologically distinct.

Before exploring further reasons why powerful qualities differ in nature from pure powers, and arguing against the former, I want to better clarify the difference between the two versions of the Powerful Qualities Model, that is, the Identity View and the Compound View.

The Identity View originates in the work of C. B. Martin. In one of his clearest statements of the view, Martin (2008: 51) contends that

---

[7] See, for example, Bostock (2008: 145), Molnar (2003: 99), Mumford (2006: 485), and Mumford and Anjum (2011: 4–5).
[8] See, for example, Livanios (2017b: 31–54).

properties "are at once dispositional and qualitative." Others, notably John Heil, have taken up Martin's advocacy of the Identity View. As Heil (2003: 111) maintains, "every property of a concrete spatiotemporal object is simultaneously qualitative and dispositional." As such, properties are powerful qualities, specifically in the identity sense (Heil 2010, 2012: 80–81). Martin and Heil (1999: 47) jointly claim that "A property just *is* a certain dispositionality that just *is* a certain qualitativity." So, on the Identity View, for any given property its powerful nature = its qualitative nature.

The Compound View, by contrast, denies the identity claim but maintains that properties simultaneously have both a powerful and a qualitative part. Taylor (2018: 1438–1439) urges reexamination of the Compound View and suggests that the view could define qualities negatively, as those parts of properties that do not contribute to the powers of objects exemplifying them. I do not see how this will do, however, since if some part of an actual property is ontologically real (how could it not be?) then it must have some positive features. I suggest that on the Compound View the powerful and qualitative parts or aspects should be conceived as distinct but inseparable, equally fundamental collaborators in the property's total nature (Williams 2019: 46, 113).[9] One problem with such a view, however, is that it is not clear what role the qualitative aspect plays in qualitative change when the power manifests (Marmodoro 2020). Powers presumably make "qualitative" changes to reality when they manifest, but if the power does all the work, what is the point of the qualitative part? (That is, what is the point other than providing a stable base for the power when it is not manifesting, a topic I will address later in this chapter.) It is not my aim here, however, to delve into a lengthy exploration of the theory behind the Compound View.

In my evaluation of the Powerful Qualities Model, I focus on the Identity View. The dialectical reason is that the Identity View is more commonly defended than the Compound View. The metaphysical reason is that the Compound View seems to violate the unity of a property token – that a single property is a unified existent. Theories attributing two sides or two natures to a property token seem unnecessarily complex and raise many onerous questions. Although the Compound View

---

[9] Borghini (2009: 209) also mentions the possibility of a compound view, which "makes the categorical and the dispositional two aspects of properties" such that they are not mutually exclusive but not identical either.

avoids some potential counterintuitive implications of the Identity View,[10] it introduces a host of new questions that are difficult to answer: How do the two parts collaborate to serve their dual role in a unified way? When the power manifests, does the quality change in any way or does it just get dragged along? When the quality does something – whatever that might be – is it acting as a power? If so, should we not simply consider the whole property powerful?

The Identity View theoretically issues the same advantages – those of power and quality – as the Compound View, without the worry about cramming two parts, natures, or sides into the space of one unified property. Therefore, I will focus my discussion on the Identity View. Going forward, when I use the term "powerful qualities" I mean the Identity View not the Compound View, unless otherwise specified. Sometimes I will use the term "Identity View" or related expressions such as "identity theory" or "identity theory of properties," and I will speak of "identity theorists."

Figure 2.1 displays a summary of the similarities and differences between pure powers and the Identity View of powerful qualities discussed above. In Sections 2.2–2.4, I explore the nature of powerful qualities and present some considerations against the Identity View, thus setting the stage to further explore and defend pure powers.

| Pure powers vs. powerful qualities | |
|---|---|
| **Purported similarities** | **Purported differences** |
| -They are actual, real properties. <br> -Each instance has a unique, distinct existence. <br> -They can equally account for shapes and colors. | -Powerful qualities (on the Identity View) have a dual (or, at least, a different) "nature" compared to pure powers. |

Figure 2.1  Pure powers and powerful qualities: purported similarities and differences

## 2.2  The "Nature" of Powerful Qualities

On the Identity View, what does it mean for a property to be both a quality and a power? On one hand, if we suppose that the quality is entirely powerful, then the quality simply adds power to the property beyond the pure

[10] Armstrong (2005: 315) finds the Identity View of properties "totally incredible" and a category mistake. Channelling Lewis Carroll, Armstrong vividly captures the counterintuitive nature of the Identity View when he states, "They are just different, that's all. An identity here seems like identifying a raven with a writing desk." However, in my discussion I give the identity theorist the benefit of the doubt.

power itself (and Taylor's conclusion that there is no difference between pure powers and powerful qualities would be correct). On the other hand, if my assessment in Section 2.1 is correct, there are differences between pure powers and powerful qualities. Supposing that the quality adds something beyond power – that it is fully integrated with the power to the point of identity and not merely compounded with power where quality and power are "side by side" – then whatever the quality is, its integration with the power does not add any causal or modal oomph (otherwise, powerful qualities would collapse into pure powers). The quality must add something to the power – or change its nature somehow – if there is to be a difference between these two conceptions. Let me explain why in further detail.

Assume the indiscernibility of identical objects, $x$ and $y$. If $x = y$, then $x$ and $y$ share all the same properties. Now suppose that all the properties that $x$ and $y$ share are powers and these powers completely and exclusively determine all possible events involving $x$ and $y$. So, it should make no causal or modal difference whether the powers are powerful qualities or pure powers. Call this No Causal Role Difference. There is no difference in their powers, so $x$ and $y$ will do all the same things in all the same circumstances. Yet, comparing pure powers to powerful qualities, the following observation – Qualitative Difference – also seems true: Supposing $x$ has pure powers and $y$ has powerful qualities, although No Causal Role Difference is true, $x$ and $y$ cannot be identical. For the *quality* of $y$ makes it metaphysically (if not epistemically) distinguishable from $x$. Object $y$ has, perhaps, a hidden essence inextricably mixed in with the power. This clarifies that, because the Powerful Qualities Model saturates every causal power with a qualitative nature, the identity conditions of a powerful quality should consist of something more than just a causal profile. If this were not the case, then we would simply be dealing with pure powers. If they are different, as I have suggested, what is the nature of the quality in a powerful quality?

The term "nature" is sometimes used in discussing properties without explicitly characterizing it (Jacobs 2011: 87; Martin and Heil 1999: 47). For starters, the "nature" of a property is not a further entity, but the way the property *is* (as a property is a way an object is). A property's nature yields identity conditions making it metaphysically distinct from other property instances. It not only differentiates powerful qualities and pure powers, but the qualitative from the powerful within powerful qualities. So, we should be able to conceptually distinguish these two natures.[11]

---

[11] Heil (2003: 173) holds that although properties are metaphysically inseparable from the objects that possess them, we can still consider objects and properties separately. Similarly, although the two natures of powerful qualities might be inseparable, we can still consider them separately.

On the Identity View, power and quality are not two parts collaborating in property-hood as on the Compound View.[12] Yet, properties posited by Identity View proponents are not simply (pure) powers. They are powerful qualities and as such they are – as I will call it – ontologically *denser* than pure powers. Their increased density is suggested, though not entailed, by their increased conceptual complexity. Supposing that there should be something ontologically to answer to this conceptual complexity, I suggest it is their increased ontological density. This is what we attend to in distinguishing pure powers from powerful qualities. We can begin to illuminate what this denser nature is by saying what it is not.

It is *not* a substance or something that instantiates properties. Qualities are properties. Properties do not instantiate properties unless the instantiated thing is a second-order property. But a second-order property cannot be identical to the first-order property, and on the Identity View the power must be identical to the quality. Furthermore, if the general concern is to include substance in one's total ontology to meet some metaphysical demand, a pure powers theorist can posit substances and powers as necessary co-existents just as well as a powerful qualities theorist can.[13]

It is *not* the source of qualitative experience or some sort of experiential component. Qualities, it is often thought, provide for "Technicolour vistas" and "experienced boomings and buzzings" (Heil 2012: 63). But why cannot pure powers provide such effects? Given that identity theorists accept powers – powerful qualities *are* powers – they recognize that powers provide the modal dynamics for events. If the supposed effects were merely experiential and defined exclusively in terms of nonpowerful qualities, then we would be accepting that some instances of qualities are powerless. But that is not the case. My contention – fully addressed in Chapter 7 – is that the continual manifestation of some set of two or more powers creates the illusion of what others posit as real qualities: They are quasi-qualities.

It is *neither* actuality *nor* actualization that quality adds to a powerful quality. Powers are actual properties with potentials for action and have as much "being" as qualities do.[14] What about actualization? Jaworski (2016:

---

[12] However, Giannotti (2021) gives an interesting interpretation of the Identity View that claims that properties have two aspects. If these aspects are no real addition of being to the property (i.e., they are given a lightweight interpretation), and provided that my further argumentation against the Identity View in this chapter is correct, then the dual-aspect interpretation issues no advantage over pure powers.

[13] For example, Heil (2012: 12–32) includes substances alongside powerful qualities.

[14] Strawson (2008: 278) argues otherwise.

56–57) substitutes "actualization" for "quality" in characterizing powerful qualities, thus revising the Identity View. He does so in order to avoid implications that qualities are only presented in experience (i.e., qualia), since some properties (such as those of subatomic particles) are clearly real but do not present themselves to us qualitatively in experience.[15] Approaching the issue with more of a linguistic bent than I would prefer, Jaworski (2016: 56) claims that one of the roles of nonpowerful property descriptions is to express the "statuses of properties as stable manifestations or actualizations." However, I suggest that the actualization of a supposed powerful quality just is a manifestation or realization of its power. The concept of a power entails the concept of a (potential or real) actualization; indeed, this is what it means to be a power. Therefore, it is not clear that "actualization" adds anything to a power that would suffice to count it as a "powerful quality."

Since I maintain that powerful qualities have increased density (being or something akin), I contend that it must be that identity theorists conceive of powers themselves differently than pure powers theorists conceive of powers. Both views are theories of powers, but the identity theorist envisions the nature of powers differently. The Identity View is simply a different way of envisioning powers themselves. It is a vision of powers as qualities, where the power itself is somehow different without adding any new further modal capacity beyond that found in pure powers; qualities cannot be postulated to add more *power* if we are to genuinely maintain the identity of powers and qualities. In sum, powerful qualities are modally indistinguishable from pure powers but have a denser nature.[16]

---

[15] For instance, Molnar (2003: 178) argues that properties of subatomic particles do not present themselves as qualities in our experience, but only as powers.

[16] Can we gain a further foothold on how powerful qualities differ from pure powers? Possibly. Coates (2021), making a distinction between "intrinsic nature" and "intrinsic property," theorizes that powerful qualities have an intrinsic, fixed nature independent of any other properties, whereas pure powers have a relational nature defined in terms of their relation to other properties (powerful partners) such that their nature is not independently fixed (both pure powers and powerful qualities are, however, intrinsic properties). Therefore, although we cannot distinguish powerful qualities from pure powers along intrinsic/extrinsic *property* lines, we can distinguish them along intrinsic/extrinsic *nature* lines. While pure powers are intrinsic properties (if the objects exemplifying them do so independently of other objects or properties – it remains possible that some pure powers are extrinsic properties, as I will argue in Chapter 5), their nature is relational. However, the property/nature distinction does not obviate all worries about powerful qualities. If powers remain identical to qualities, then it seems that powerful qualities would inherit the extrinsic (relational) nature of pure powers, thus collapsing the distinction. Furthermore, what is the nature of powers' relationality? In a sense, their relationality is illusory. They are really quasi-relational because they are only

I claimed that having a simultaneous qualitative nature makes powers ontologically denser. But this does not mean it provides any extra causal power (how could it?), any substance, or an experiential (phenomenal) component. Exactly what this density consists in remains an open question that deserves further attention by those interested in carving out a definitive distinction between pure powers and powerful qualities. At this point, I do maintain that that there is a genuine distinction between pure powers and powerful qualities, but the full nature of the distinction remains indeterminate. Although doubts remain about the distinction, there is enough argumentation in support of it to keep it as a working assumption. So, here I will assume that the Identity View attributes an increased ontological density to powerful qualities, thus affirming that there is a real difference between pure powers and powerful qualities.[17]

## 2.3 Considering Simplicity and Explanatory Relevance

Only one main concept – *power* – needs inclusion in the Pure Powers Model, whereas the Powerful Qualities Model demands two – *power* and *quality*. Therefore, the Pure Powers Model is conceptually simpler. What about ontological simplicity? Pure powers are clearly ontologically simpler than the Compound View's version of powerful qualities because the pure powers theorist need not posit two "parts" to a property. If pure powers are ontologically simpler than the Identity View's version of powerful qualities, then the Pure Powers Model would have a clear advantage over the Powerful Qualities Model as a whole. I claim to have shown just that in Section 2.2 in arguing that the Identity View is ontologically more complex than the Pure Powers Model due to the denser nature attributed to powerful qualities. Therefore, since the simpler model should be preferred, assuming all other factors are equal, the Pure Powers Model is preferred.

If powerful qualities add some sort of explanatory benefit, this could tip the balance in their favor. However, such considerations make the Pure Powers Model more attractive than the Identity View (as well as

---

related to *possible* relata (possible manifestations and possible powerful partners) captured by the informational content they must carry in order to potentially act. Since powers are quasi-relational, they do not depend on actual relations to other powers. Rather, they *point toward* other powers – they possess directedness. The nonrelationality of powers is discussed further in Section 5.6.

17 For further discussion of ways to interpret the Identity View, see Livanios (2017b: 35–44). Although he does not conclude that the Identity View is incoherent, there is "a metaphysically obscure triple identity" between a power, a quality, and a fundamental property at the heart of the view (2017b: 36).

the Compound View). Consider what I call the causal effects test: If a supposed spatiotemporal entity (property, force, substance) has no possible causal effects, then it is unreal.[18] The qualitative nature of a powerful qualities – its nonpowerful, denser nature – has no causal effects other than those given by its powerful nature. Thus, the qualitative nature is unreal and should not be posited. One could rejoin that since the qualitative and powerful natures are identical, the quality does have causal effects. However, it does so only in virtue of its powerful nature. The qualitative nature does not add power, although it adds *something* to a property, as discussed in Section 2.2: It "qualifies" the power by making it denser.

Consider this dilemma: Either the qualitative nature that is identical to the powerful nature adds something to the property's causal profile, or it does not. If it does not, then it does not lead us past the Pure Powers Model, for it does not add anything beyond that given by the powerful nature. But if the qualitative nature adds something to the causal profile of a property – making the self-same property denser than a pure power – then it is mysterious what explanatory value it adds beyond the possible effects issued by the powerful nature. Therefore, the combined considerations of simplicity and explanatory value favor the Pure Powers Model.

Because a qualitative nature adds no power to a property, the Identity View offers no explanatory benefit over the Pure Powers Model regarding the metaphysics of modality, causality, or the laws of nature. All these phenomena are explainable by reference to powers sans qualitative nature, therefore the qualitative nature is unnecessary.[19]

---

[18] Oddie (1982) formalized the idea that entities we posit should play some causal role, an idea having roots in the Eleatic Stranger in Plato (1997: *Sophist* 247D-E). Following this idea, Armstrong (2010: 2) claims that "if an entity plays no causal role at all, then that is a good argument, though perhaps not a conclusive one, for not postulating that entity."

[19] One might argue that powerful qualities offer two explanatory advantages over pure powers: one is that given their denser nature, they are better suited as truth-makers for counterfactuals associated with powers, thus explaining the being of powers through latency periods. However, this implies that pure powers are not real or actual and so cannot serve as truth-makers for counterfactuals; but this is not the case. Pure powers are just as real and any lingering questions about their reality – especially during nonmanifesting periods – will be answered in Sections 2.5–2.9. One might also argue that powerful qualities successfully address the various regress objections that are used to critique pure powers; this is because the qualitative nature can theoretically put a stop to the regress. The concern here is that the pure powers theorist needs to refer to an infinitude of pure powers in defining the identity conditions of these powers (there are, however, various types of regress, as mentioned in footnote 31 of this chapter). However, the view I develop in Part II effectively addresses identity-related regresses by placing the identity conditions of powers inside their being in the form of an informational blueprint, not in a network of instantiated powers.

## 2.4   The Identity Conditions of Powers and Powerful Qualities

On the Identity View, since power = quality and the power's identity conditions are defined by causal profiles, powerful qualities must have a causal profile as part of their identity conditions. But if the identity conditions for the qualitative nature of a powerful quality are *not* based entirely on a causal profile, then the quality must have some further identity condition(s). However, it is not clear what this should be, for it is hard to see how it would not be characterized in terms of stimulus and manifestation conditions. So, it appears theoretically economical to maintain the identity conditions of powerful qualities in terms of a causal profile. Powerful qualities on the Identity View are, simply put, denser powers but with all the same potential (thus the same causal profiles) as pure powers. This approach honors what pure powers theorists and identity theorists alike contend is true of properties – that they are powerful – while honoring their distinctness.

Suppose that powerful qualities have something beyond increased density compared to pure powers, some quiddity beyond a causal profile that forms their identity conditions. This might be acceptable for pure qualities, but it should not be welcome for powerful qualities, for the following reasons. On this view of the nature of powerful qualities, for any two powerful qualities $PQ_1$ and $PQ_2$, each will have a quiddity and a causal profile as part of its identity conditions. Suppose $PQ_1$ and $PQ_2$ are instances of the same type of property. Further suppose that the causal profiles of $PQ_1$ and $PQ_2$ are swapped. Now, since the causal profiles are identical to the quiddities, the quiddities are swapped.[20] But the quiddities, in this case, make no difference to the identities of the properties. $PQ_1$ and $PQ_2$ retain all the same powers, so are ontologically indistinguishable from what they were prior to the swap. Therefore, short of assigning a quiddity to powerful qualities, I have argued only for their increased density relative to pure powers.

I have argued that pure powers and powerful qualities are distinct (Section 2.2) but pure powers are preferred based on considerations of simplicity and explanatory relevance (Section 2.3). Furthermore, in this section, I suggested that attempts to go beyond causal profiles in stating identity conditions for powerful qualities are ill-advised. In the remainder of this chapter, I turn attention from powerful qualities to pure powers.

---

[20] This scenario compares similarly to the objection that quiddities could swap causal roles, but intuitively there is no difference between the actual world and a world in which they are swapped (Bird 2007a: 73–76). See Jaworski (2016: 84) for further discussion.

## 2.5   Central Argument for Pure Powers

Here is my main argument for the Pure Powers Model. The major rivals to the Powers Model of physical modality – Neo-Humeanism and the Universals Model – are implicitly committed to powers (see Chapter 1). Therefore, a powers view of properties is inevitable. The Pure Powers Model is both distinct from, and either conceptually or ontologically simpler than, the Powerful Qualities Model (see Sections 2.3 and 2.4). I do not claim that the Powerful Qualities Model is incoherent or leads to absurdities; it is just less plausible than the Pure Powers Model. Therefore, the Pure Powers Model is the best available view regarding the nature of properties.[21]

However, pure powers face two levels of objections. Level 1 objections concern the inherent nature and existence of pure powers, including but not limited to how powers are directed toward manifestations; what it means for a power to be directed toward manifestations[22]; and how powers are grounded or continuously instantiated through periods of nonmanifestation. Level 1 objections reflect the concerns that nodal accounts of powers aim to address (see Section 0.7). Level 2 objections concern systems of two or more pure powers, including but not limited to how qualities, or at least the appearance of such, can result from a powers foundation (Heil 2003: 114–115 and 2012: 67–69); how to individuate two or more powers with identical causal profiles (Hawthorne 2001); and the "always re-packing" objection (Armstrong 1997: 80), that is, that nothing would ever get done in a world of powers because every power is merely for some manifestation

---

[21] There are a number of other arguments for the reality of pure powers. These are not necessarily arguments for pandispositionalism or dispositional monism, but at least for dispositional essentialism (e.g., Ellis, whom I cite several times in this footnote holds that some fundamental properties are essentially dispositional while others are definitely categorical). The argument from science claims that our most successful sciences, especially particle physics, posit irreducible powers (Cartwright 2017; Cartwright and Pemberton 2013; Ellis 2001: 114–115 and 2002: 74; Mumford 2006); see Williams (2011) for critical analysis of the argument from science. The argument from the nature of laws of nature (Ellis 2001: 115 and 2002: 75) claims that dispositional concepts are essential to our formulation of laws of nature (this is related to yet different from the argument from science). Generally, scientific theories and findings have played a role in the growing support for the powers view of properties (Balashov 2002; Meincke 2020; Mumford 2006), but there are purely metaphysical arguments too. The argument from basic powers (Ellis 2001: 115–116 and 2002: 76) focuses attention on the need – as we unearth more layers of reality – to posit more basic powers to explain the instantiation of higher-level powers. Given these arguments, some combination of the first two (the arguments from science and the nature of laws) seems most plausible to me. Again, these arguments do not necessarily support pandispositionalism (i.e., the Pure Powers Model interpreted broadly), only that at least some fundamental properties are powers. I do not intend to evaluate these arguments here.

[22] The first two level 1 objections listed are also problems for powerful qualities.

that is simply another power. Level 2 objections roughly reflect the concerns that arise on networking accounts of powers (see Section 0.7).

A big Level 2 worry is that any network of pure powers is completely relational, therefore implausible, because the identity conditions of pure powers must be understood solely in terms of their relation to other powers (Heil 2003: 97–107). The worry then concerns *what* enters the various relations that hold between the powers and how they maintain their being over time (Jacobs 2011: 85). This brings us back to the more fundamental worries, that is, Level 1. Mitigating Level 1 worries would help alleviate some Level 2 concerns because reference can then be made to the nature of the relata in a system of pure powers.[23]

Indeed, it seems that any network of pure powers must have relata: the individual quality-free pure powers themselves. If so, an entirely pure powers ontology need not commit to a purely relational world of the variety proposed by Holton (1999). Such an ontology can affirm that pure powers are nodes of being given identity conditions by their relatedness to other powers, yet which also have their own internal reality independent of other powers. That is, even though a pure power's identity conditions might be understood in relation to other powers, its being is independent of them. Powers have manifestation partners and are typically instantiated in collaborative systems, but they do not need these other powers to be powerful; they only need them to actually do their work. A lone power is still a power.

I contend that it is possible that there exists only a single instance of a pure power – a "lone power world" (as discussed in Section 0.7). One might suggest that this lone power must be directed at some manifestation, which is true, but since the manifestation is just another power, at least two powers are required. However, the manifestation need not occur for the power in question to be real. The manifestation is a potentiality, not an actuality. The Physical Intentionality Thesis, to be defended in Part II, will further support this claim. Even if the manifestation were actual, it is possible for there to be powers that are self-directed, so to speak: directed at persisting or maintaining their own reality. So, an instance of a single power does *not* necessitate the existence of other powers; thus, Level 1 concerns arise. What does it mean for a power to exist during

---

[23] I will not attempt to defend pure powers from all existing objections, for two reasons: It could overwhelm the larger goals of my project and significant discussion of these objections already exists in the metaphysics of science community. Rather, I focus on the problem of being, which is most relevant to my larger goals.

nonmanifestation periods such that counterfactuals associated with it are true? What, intrinsic to the power, admits of its being? Psillos (2006: 137) asks: If a pure power consists entirely of potential to manifest – and supposing that any power need *not* manifest – then what is it doing when it is not manifesting?[24]

If pure powers are to provide a stable basis for physical modality, the problem of their being needs resolution. Below I analyze the problem of being and suggest that pure powers are self-grounded. Note that I am using the terms "grounding," "being," and "continuous instantiation" equivalently as terms that get at the existence of unmanifested powers. After discussing the problem of being, I discuss a regress argument advanced by Psillos (2006) that challenges the self-grounding of pure powers. Lastly, I develop Point Theory as a way of explaining the self-grounding of pure powers.

## 2.6  The Problem of Being and Potential Solutions

Since pure powers are sometimes in states of nonmanifested potential, in what does their reality consist when not manifesting? That is the problem of being.

On any of the models that challenge the possibility of pure powers – the Powerful Qualities Model, the Universals Model, or the Neo-Humean Model – there is a qualitative property or property-complex (on the latter two views), or a simultaneously instantiated qualitative nature or property (on the Powerful Qualities Model) that accounts for the work of powers. On the non-Powers Models (Universals and Neo-Humean Model), powers are either absent or given a second-class, derivative ontological status. On the Identity View, power and quality have equal ontological priority (because they are identical), but the qualitative nature can be justifiably claimed to ground (if grounding can be reflexive) the being of the powerful nature. And because it is always manifest, the qualitative nature can seemingly stop various powers-related regresses.[25]

However, the grounding story must be different for pure powers. They have no qualitative nature. So, what grounds their instantiation through periods of nonmanifestation?[26] I will argue that at least some types of

---

[24] Mumford (2006: 481) calls this the "question of *Being*."

[25] See Psillos (2006: 151–152) for discussion of the claim that qualities can stop powers regresses.

[26] Ellis (2001: 114; 139–140, footnote 120), who posits some pure powers and some categorical properties in his mixed view of properties, maintains that the being or grounding of pure powers needs no explanation. However, attending to the problem of being can illuminate the internal nature of pure powers, my main goal.

pure powers are self-grounded and I will develop a theory of their self-grounding. However, there are ways of grounding pure powers in other properties or objects that would *not* necessarily violate their pureness because they need not involve qualities.[27] First, one could argue for a global grounding theory (Handfield 2008), that is, that the ontological ground of a pure power consists of every possible property, including extrinsic properties.[28] Second, one could take up a monistic grounding theory according to which pure powers are grounded by the cosmos or world as a whole – invoking monism of one or another variety (Horgan and Potrč 2008; Schaffer 2010b) as an ontological basis for pure powers' being. Finally, if one rejected a bundle theory of objects (contrary to my position) one could adopt a substance-based grounding theory and ground pure powers in objects conceived as ontological substances.

In contrast to these non-self-grounding options, the simpler approach (both conceptually and ontologically) is that pure powers are self-grounded. The second and third options require robust ontological commitments (monism; substantivalism) needing further defense. Concerning the first option – the global grounding theory – I grant that "abundant" powers can be extrinsically grounded (McKitrick 2003a). I also maintain that some pure powers, such as mass, are extrinsic (i.e., extrinsically grounded): The mass of fundamental particles is generated by their interaction with the Higgs field (Bauer 2011). However, I doubt that *all* pure powers are extrinsically grounded as global grounding theory implies. Instances of extrinsic pure powers such as mass ultimately require some sort of premass or proto-mass – a property of a particle that disposes the particle to gain mass via its interaction with the Higgs field – which arguably must be self-grounded (2011: 89).[29]

---

[27] For evaluation of these alternative options for the grounding of pure powers, see Bauer (2012: 145–154).

[28] Supposing pandispositionalism is correct, then on the global grounding hypothesis every pure power would be grounded in every other pure power. This sounds a lot like powers holism of the variety advocated by Williams (2010) and Mumford (2004), which I will discuss in Chapters 6 and 7. However, I do not interpret this as a grounding thesis. Powers holism explains how powers are individuated and what their identity condition are relative to other powers, but it does not necessarily explain their continuous instantiation. It remains possible that a token power could be implemented all alone; it would be self-grounded and have directedness toward its possible manifestations all by itself. In sum, assuming powers holism is correct (as I do in Part II), as I interpret powers holism it is not a theory of the *grounding* of powers but of their *identity* or *individuation*. Therefore, it is not the same as the global grounding theory.

[29] One might suppose that extrinsic factors only partially ground an extrinsic power, so something about the power itself is at also at work. If each extrinsic power must contribute something to its own grounding, in addition to the extrinsic factor's contribution, it must be partially self-grounded

Moreover, in support of the need for the self-grounding of at least some pure powers, as discussed in Section 0.7 and Section 2.5, it is possible to have "lone power worlds" – for instance, worlds with only one power token and no other property tokens. Since such a power should be grounded and assuming there is nothing else to ground it, it must be self-grounded.[30] However, a special sort of regress challenges this idea. If sound, this regress argument would prevent the self-grounding of pure powers, because an endless series of properties would be required to ground a single instance of a pure power.

## 2.7　Psillos' Pure Powers Regress

### *The Pure Powers Regress Argument*

What do pure powers do when they are latent, that is, unmanifested or not manifesting? Pure powers, especially those at the fundamental level, have no independent causal bases (either in qualities or further powers) to anchor them during latent periods. Psillos (2006) argues that this leads to a vicious regress, given two assumptions (both of which I accept).[31]

The first assumption is that powers are directed toward their manifestations (Molnar 2003).[32] The second assumption is that properties are defined in terms of the contributions they make to the causal powers of their possessors (Shoemaker 1980); they make such contributions to their possessors because these properties simply are powers. Given these assumptions, it

---

and for that reason we need a theory of self-grounding. However, this is mistaken. The extrinsic power (e.g., mass) *wholly comes into being* from some extrinsic factor (e.g., the Higgs field) plus some intrinsic factor (proto-mass, or the capacity to gain mass) of a particle that is *not* the power (mass) itself.

[30] Is the term "self-grounding" – used, for example, by Mumford (2006: 486) – appropriate here? I take this term, when applied to a pure power, to imply that the property is ungrounded in any other distinct properties or objects, beyond the pure power itself. "Self-grounded" is a more positive way of saying that a pure power is ungrounded by any properties distinct from the power in question. However, this is significant in my view because "self-grounded" compared to "ungrounded" connotes the idea that a pure power is responsible for its own being. Characterizing pure powers as ungrounded has some unwanted connotations, such as implying that they should be grounded but are not. Self-grounding is a positive, minimalist conception of grounding.

[31] Although there are many varieties of powers regress argument – see Bird (2007a: 132–146 and 2007b) and Ingthorsson (2015) for discussion – I focus on Psillos' regress because it reveals important lessons about the directedness of powers, which is crucial to the Physical Intentionality Thesis that I argue for in Chapters 3–5.

[32] Psillos (2006: 138–139) assumes that Molnar (2003: 60–81) is right in attributing directedness to powers, which I will defend in Chapter 4 and is essential to the Physical Intentionality Thesis.

appears that "directedness is a power of powers: it is the power they have to manifest themselves" when they are unmanifested (Psillos 2006: 139).

The pure powers theorist can contend that when latent, any pure power, F, remains directed, or maintains directedness, toward its manifestation, M. That is what F *does* while latent. However, Psillos (2006: 139–140) argues that this entails that F has a power, Q, that is, the directedness of F toward F's manifestation, and thus (according to Psillos), the power of F to manifest itself. Q manifests when F manifests. Yet, since Q is a power, Q is directed toward manifesting but does not actually manifest when F is not manifesting. Thus, Q requires a power, R, the directedness of Q toward Q's manifestation, and so on … ad infinitum (see Figure 2.2). This is the Powers Regress.[33]

```
F-----------------------------> M1 (F's possible manifestation)
    directedness, Q (of F toward M1)

Q-----------------------------> M2 (Q's possible manifestation)
    directedness, R (of Q toward M2)

R-----------------------------> M3 (R's possible manifestation)
    directedness, S (of R toward M3)

… ad infinitum
```

Figure 2.2    Psillos' directedness regress of pure powers

### Stopping the Powers Regress: The Argument from Property Subtraction

The Powers Regress hinges on the premise that Q (F's directedness) is an essential but distinct power of F. However, I argue that Q and F are not distinct properties. It is metaphysically possible to take away one property at a time, slowly stripping an object of its properties.[34] I am interested in

---

[33] Psillos (2006: 141) discusses some ways to respond to the regress but argues that they are insufficient.

[34] Armstrong (1989: 72) uses this kind of tactic against Russell's bundle theory of objects, pressing that any object $x$ could have a near twin, or subduplicate $x_t$ with one less property than $x$, and so on. Schaffer (2003: 136) formulates this as the generalized subtraction principle: "it seems that for any n-propertied object, it is possible for there to be an n-1 propertied subduplicate." He uses this to argue that mass could be a free or solo property – not pinned to any object or combined with any other properties (a conclusion Armstrong eschews). Although Armstrong is the original inspiration for my argument against the Powers Regress, it is Schaffer's subtraction principle that I am specifically employing. Although I apply the subtraction principle to a nonobject, I do not

property subtraction as a tactic for revealing what is wrong with the claim that Q and F are distinct. My argument runs as follows. Assume properties F and Q are distinct (call this Distinctness). Suppose that we subtract all the properties of some object until only F and Q remain. If there are infinite powers conceived in the Powers Regress, then we must conduct an infinite subtraction. Suppose next that we subtract Q. So, F remains alone. The Powers Regress concludes that this is not possible. However, in principle, there *is* something (i.e., Q) that could be subtracted to get F alone (the logical possibility of inferring this hinges on Distinctness). If F is a power, then it is directed toward its characteristic manifestation. But since we have subtracted Q (F's directedness), now F is *not* directed toward its manifestation. Therefore, F is not a power and, assuming Shoemaker's thesis, it is not a property, which contradicts the assumption that it is a property. Since Distinctness generates this contradiction, it should be abandoned, thus preventing the Powers Regress.

The property subtraction argument helps reveal what is wrong with the assumptions behind the regress: F and Q are not distinct powers. Subtracting Q shows that F is not a power, for being a power or having power in *some way* requires directedness. Perhaps F and Q necessarily collaborate as components or aspects of a singular power, or perhaps upon subtracting Q we are left with some sort of primordial preproperty entity that when combined with Q yields F. But these possibilities seem obscure. The best explanation for F's disappearing (or losing property-hood) upon Q's subtraction is that F and Q are identical, that is, Power = Directedness. To be a power is to be directed toward manifestations. F does not *have* the power to bring about M or *possess* directedness toward M; rather, F just *is* the power to bring about M or *is* directedness toward M.

I will now argue for Power = Directedness. I am restricting discussion to property instances or tropes, as stated in Section 0.4. It is arguable that to be a trope is to be a "here-such," not a "this-such." The core idea is that tropes are individuated by spatiotemporal location (here fragility, there redness), not primitive quantity (this fragility, that redness) (Schaffer 2001: 247). Building on this conception of the spatiotemporal individuation of tropes (or, if one does not accept trope theory, property tokens of

---

see that it matters whether one subtracts properties from objects or collections of properties. Also, the property subtraction argument generalizes to other situations in which the property status of a purportedly distinct property is questioned: In any situation in which a property is thought to be a second-order property of another property, one can use property subtraction to intuitively test its status.

universals), I suggest a principle that property tokens G and H are numerically identical to each other if and only if (i) G and H have identical causal profiles and (ii) G and H occupy identical spatiotemporal locations.[35] Call this Property Identity.

Condition (i) of Property Identity builds in the idea that properties are defined (at least partly) by the causal or functional roles they play. The causal profile of a property consists of every one of its possible causal relations. I contend that the causal profiles for F (power) and Q (directedness) are one and the same: To be disposed toward M is to be directed toward M. We cannot subtract directedness without subtracting power, and vice versa. Therefore, condition (i) is satisfied. But since multiple property tokens can have the exact same causal profiles, individuating them also requires a spatiotemporal condition. Distinct property tokens do not wholly occupy the exact same spatial region, whereas identical tokens overlap perfectly. If F and Q perfectly spatiotemporally overlap *and* have the exact same causal profile, then they are numerically identical.[36] Regarding condition (ii), I suggest that locating a power ("here fragility") at a specific spacetime location simultaneously involves locating directedness ("here directedness towards breaking") at the exact same spacetime location. Therefore, Q and F overlap identically: If power F exists at $l$, then directedness Q exists at $l$, and vice versa. If so, then condition (ii) is satisfied. Therefore, Power = Directedness.[37]

Marmodoro (2009) also argues that power is identical to directedness but for different reasons than mine. Psillos assumes Distinctness without justification, argues Marmodoro (2009: 341–342), implying that fragility, for instance, is the power, F, of $x$ to break, and Q is, at root, F's power to

---

[35] Heil (2003: 141) proposes a similar principle.

[36] The addition of condition (ii) alleviates the worry for causal structuralism advanced by Hawthorne (2001) that two properties with the same causal profile will not have unique essences. The worry is alleviated because, although two powers might have the same causal profile, they will not have the exact same spatial location; thus, their individuation conditions will be distinct. Location partially individuates property tokens.

[37] Focusing on condition (i), one might retreat to a core idea motivating Psillos' Powers Regress and raise the following objection: Q and F have different causal roles thus they are not identical. Q maintains F, but F neither maintains Q nor itself; thus, Q and F have different causal roles, thus condition (i) is not met. In response, I make two points. First, F can maintain itself because it is its own causal basis (McKitrick 2003b) *and* its own grounds, so there is insufficient reason to think that F needs a distinct property Q to maintain its directedness toward M. Second, the contention that Q and F must have different causal roles begs the question against the pure powers theorist. On the contrary, it is equally if not more plausible that the causal role involved with being *directed* toward M is the causal role involved with being *disposed* toward M. This is, indeed, the simpler view.

manifest itself in the appropriate conditions. This implies that F is power-less: It cannot manifest itself but needs Q, whereas F is supposed to *be* a power. Marmodoro's argument is situated within an Aristotelian frame-work. Aristotle (1941a: *Metaphysics* 1031b28–1032a4) holds that it is absurd to separate an entity and its essence. For Aristotle "a thing is said to be its essence in virtue of itself" (Marmodoro 2009: 352, endnote 24), thereby rejecting the claim that an instance of an essential type (an essence) is a component of (and so "arithmetically different from") the thing that has that essence (2009: 348). In this light, Distinctness is mistaken. So, when unmanifested, a power "is an instance of readiness for action, of pure directedness toward φ-ing, and only that" (2009: 349).[38] It is a ben-efit of my argument against the Powers Regress that it does not require the Aristotelian framework but only general logical points. Nonetheless, Marmodoro's argument provides extra support for Power = Directedness.[39] If this is correct, it clears the way for pure powers to be self-grounded.[40]

## 2.8    The Self-Grounding of Pure Powers

If a pure power is self-grounded, it has neither a distinct grounding prop-erty nor a distinct causal basis. It is metaphysically self-sufficient, so to speak.

I claim that the self-grounding of pure powers is metaphysically possible, that it is the simplest explanation for pure powers' grounding, and that at least some pure powers are in fact self-grounded. I am not claiming that

---

[38] For example, we cannot separate an instance of a human being from the essence of a human being (Marmodoro 2009: 352, endnote 24).

[39] Power = Directedness is the most plausible strategy for stopping the Powers Regress. But there is another way to account for F's directedness without assuming either Distinctness or Power = Directedness. Campbell (1981: 137) suggests that having shape is not a property instance but a condition for being a property instance. Committed to the trope theory of properties, Campbell (1981: 137) suggests that "geometric figures [i.e., shapes] are doubly special; they are essential to ordinary tropes [property instances] and in themselves insufficient to count as proper beings. Form and volume are therefore best considered not as tropes in their own right at all. Real tropes are qualities-of-a-formed-volume." This suggests a principle we might call Existence Condition: C is not a property but an existence condition for a property, F, if and only if F cannot exist without C simultaneously obtaining. Based on this, my suggestion is that directedness, Q, fills the role of C for powers. Therefore, Q is not distinct from F, because Q is not a power at all. Rather, Q is a necessary condition for the existence of F. Just as tropes require shape, but shape is not a trope itself, power tropes require directedness, but directedness is not a trope itself. Thus, a regress is avoided.

[40] See Jaworski (2016: 73–75) for critical discussion of Psillos' other arguments against the possibility of self-grounded powers. I focus on the regress argument because my evaluation of it reveals more about the directedness of powers – a central theme in Part II – than other antipowers arguments.

all pure powers are necessarily self-grounded, for some might be grounded in other ways. Mass, for example, might be extrinsically grounded (Bauer 2011).[41] Even if we allow multiple ways of grounding pure powers, my main claims – the need for powers (Chapter 1), the rejection of powerful qualities (Sections 2.1–2.4), and my 3d account (Part II) – still hold.

So, assuming that pure powers can be and in some cases are self-grounded, the problem is *how*. We might want to accept pure powers' self-grounding as a basic metaphysical fact. However, reasonable hypotheses can be advanced. I develop Point Theory to explain the self-grounding and therefore the being of pure powers.[42]

*Point Theory*

I assume the following principle of Ontological Dependence: for any nonobject entities (property tokens, events, units of spacetime, etc.), one entity, $E_1$, intrinsically ontologically depends on another entity, $E_2$, if and only if $E_1$ cannot exist at $t$ without $E_2$ also existing at $t$, where $E_1$ and $E_2$ are both intrinsic to an object O, or a spacetime location $l$, such that O or $l$ instantiates both $E_1$ and $E_2$. This excludes the possibility that a power is an extrinsic property of O or $l$, which would require that the power be

---

[41] Although mass is, perhaps, extrinsically grounded, thus not self-grounded, it is arguably not funda-mental. It *is* a pure power and it *is* a sparse, natural property, but it is not necessarily fundamental. This is because the generation of mass requires some sort of premass property (a pure power) of a particle plus some property (a pure power) of the Higgs field. It is these properties – or perhaps some further properties – that are self-grounded and thus that Point Theory applies to.

[42] I have previously developed two different accounts of the being of pure powers: Point Theory (Bauer 2013) and the Minimally Sufficient Occurrence (MSO) account (Bauer 2012). The MSO account is more of a *dynamic* or process-oriented interpretation of powers' being, according to which their being resides in their constant becoming, whereas the Point Theory is more of a *static* interpretation of powers' being. Since I adopt Point Theory here, some explanation is necessary. First, the two accounts are not inconsistent because a pure power's continuous instantiation can consist of a causal profile at successive spacetime points per Point Theory, while also undergoing a "minimally sufficient occurrence," that is, the continual manifestation of a power along one track of its multitrack directedness (see Bauer (2012: 161–162)) for response to the worry that in making powers necessarily "occurrent," they become categorical). As I see things now, the MSO account is a possible add-on to the Point Theory. I do not disavow the MSO account here – it is on the table, and indeed might better explain the continuous instantiation of higher-level, nonfundamen-tal powers. However, I think the Point Theory is simpler and allows for periods of nonmanifestation (periods of complete latency), satisfying what appears to be a widespread assumption concerning the metaphysics of powers. Besides being explanatorily simpler, the Point Theory fits with the assump-tions behind the Physical Intentionality Thesis (that powers need not manifest, analogous to how desires need not be fulfilled) and the Informational Thesis (especially that information *for* need not realize or bring about what it is for) to be defended in Part II.

grounded in properties of objects or locations other than O or $l$, because for purposes of Point Theory I aim for an account of powers' being that is consistent with their having an intrinsic nature. The principle permits but does not require grounding in property-less objects or substrata, so although $E_1$ might be grounded in $E_2$, where they are both properties of O, $E_1$ need not be grounded by O itself, because property tokens might float free of objects.[43]

Assuming Ontological Dependence, my proposal is that a pure power's being consists of a causal profile at a spacetime point.

> **Point Theory**: The continuous instantiation of any pure power token onto-logically depends exclusively on (i) the existence of a spacetime point, $s$, and (ii) and a causal profile at $s$, $C_s$.

The causal profile of a power is characterized by counterfactual informa-tion specifying how the power is directed at various possible manifes-tations (this is part of the Informational Thesis that I will develop in Chapter 6).

The placement of counterfactual information at the root of reality fol-lows Lange (2009), who holds that subjunctive facts are fundamental.[44] However, unlike Lange, I contend that powers embody these subjunctive facts (or, on my interpretation, counterfactual information). For Lange, it seems, the subjunctive facts themselves are sufficient – no need for pow-ers. Lange (2009: 136) "reverses the standard picture of laws 'supporting' counterfactuals." According to the Universal Model and the Neo-Humean Model, counterfactual truths are true in virtue of laws in conjunction with qualities; so, *if the glass were hit by a hammer, it would shatter* is made true by qualitative properties of the glass plus laws of nature specifying relations between events. But Lange rejects this account. He argues instead that there are subjunctive facts – characterized by counterfactual truths which have objective truth-values (2009: 137) – that ground the laws' neces-sity: "with these subjunctive facts, we have reached ontological bedrock"

---

[43] As Schaffer (2003: 125) argues, "lone properties such as free masses are metaphysically possible – the clustering of properties is merely a contingent fact." Schaffer's argument from free-floating proper-ties is based on general property-subtraction principle, that is, for any object, we can keep taking away properties one at a time until we are left with one property: "no one specific property seems necessary for being an object," so each is subtractable, all the way down to, for example, free mass (2003: 136). Given that properties might float free, it is not necessary that properties be grounded in objects.

[44] For critical discussion of Lange's view, see Demarest (2012).

(2009: 136).[45] Point Theory modifies Lange's account by interpreting these subjunctive facts specifically as counterfactual information that forms the content of powers. If one is committed to a powers ontology, as I am, they provide a natural vehicle for embodiment of counterfactual information.[46]

According to Point Theory, subjunctive facts – interpreted as counterfactual information – constitute $C_s$. $C_s$ consists of one or more subjunctive facts: one per power, if single-track powers are preferred, or many for each power, if multitrack powers are preferred as I maintain.[47] This counterfactual information is information for, thus directed at, various possibilities. Although the counterfactual statements specifying $C_s$ are true, this does not entail that all truths about a power are counterfactual truths. For example, it might be true of a power that it is a property of an object and this is not a counterfactual truth (Bostock 2008: 148). If the instantiation of the power does not require an object – for example, if properties can float free of objects – then it will be true that the power is instantiated at a spacetime point, which is not a counterfactual truth.

I will now examine three aspects of Point Theory important to understanding its plausibility, mitigating Level 1 worries, and establishing the viability of pure powers over powerful qualities. The three aspects discussed here pertain to the relationships between space and powers, including: the

---

[45] In further detail, Lange (2009: 136) argues (i) that the necessity of the laws is "what *makes* them laws" (setting them apart from accidents), (ii) that "necessity consists of membership in a nonmaximal sub-nomically stable set," and (iii) therefore that a law "is a law in virtue of belonging to a nonmaximal sub-nomically stable set." He holds that "a set of sub-nomic truths is 'sub-nomically stable' if and only if whatever the conversational context, the set's members would all still have held under every sub-nomic counterfactual (or subjunctive) supposition that is logically consistent with the set – even under however many such suppositions are nested" (2009: 29). So, then, the question is what makes true the subjunctives that make the set of laws subnomically stable? The answer is *nothing* – because the subjunctive facts are fundamental. Given my interpretation of these subjunctive facts as counterfactual information, this information is fundamental. This is tantamount to saying powers are also fundamental, given my claim (see Chapter 6) that a power is a directed entity whose content consists of counterfactual information; the power and its information are co-necessary and co-fundamental.

[46] Powers theorists of all stripes should agree with Lange that laws are not fundamental. They argue either that laws supervene on the powers of things (Bird 2007a) or that the laws themselves are not ontologically real (Mumford 2004). So, there is nothing too radical for the powers theorist in Lange's proposal regarding laws of nature. But it is Lange's idea of fundamental subjunctive facts that helps open the possibility of Point Theory.

[47] I assume that powers are multitrack, so that any instance of a power is capable of being triggered and manifesting in variety of similar ways. Ryle (1949) introduced the idea of multitrack powers. For example, if fragility is a multitrack power, then an instance of fragility can manifest in multiple ways: cracking, breaking, shattering due to different causes such as a hammer blow, high-pitched singing, and so on. For further discussion and defense of multitrack powers, see Williams (2011), Vetter (2015: 51–59), and Corry (2019: 55–58).

relation between pure powers and spacetimes points, whether pure powers occupy space, and the movement of pure powers through spacetime.[48] Hence, these concerns (especially the latter two) pertain more to external aspects of powers (powers "from the outside"), whereas the concerns in Chapters 3–6 pertain more to internal aspects of powers (powers "from the inside").

### Pure Powers, Locations, and Spacetime Points

On Point Theory, what is the nature of the locations (including either spacetime points or sets of spacetime points, i.e., regions) where a causal profile exists?

Some friends of powers argue that while many types of fundamental properties are powers, locations (and perhaps other fundamental properties) are qualities.[49] However, locations do not seem to have any qualitative nature to them. So, it is not clear what their being qualitative means. Furthermore, there are reasonable ways to interpret locations as powers. For example, Mumford (2004: 188) observes that the force exerted by gravitational mass – a power – is sensitive to locations. It is sensitive to locations because, per Newton's law of gravity, the force on two massive bodies $x_1$ and $x_2$ is proportional to the product of their mass and inversely proportional to the square of the *distance* between them, where distance is a function of the distinct locations of $x_1$ and $x_2$. Molnar (2003: 164–165) recognizes the importance of the location-sensitivity of forces but argues that the locations of objects are not powers – they only help determine how powers are exercised. However, Mumford reasonably asks: If gravitational force is location-sensitive, why is location not gravitation-sensitive, and therefore capable of powerful manifestations? In support of Mumford's

---

[48] Esfeld and Deckert (2018) propose that the fundamental entities of reality are spacetime points and that relations between these can explain the physical world. Their account is a Neo-Humean account of reality and properties (2018: 8), so for them these points are qualitative. But if the arguments in Chapter 1 are correct, that Neo-Humeans are implicitly committed to powers over qualities, then spacetime points should be considered powerful.

[49] I assume that locations are properties, as do the major disputants in this debate. The question is, are they qualitative or powerful properties (or, perhaps, powerful qualities)? Amongst the major disputants, for example, Ellis (2010a, 2010b, 2012) maintains that locations are paradigm examples of fundamental qualities (categorical properties). Molnar (2003) also argues that locations are qualities (for him locations are, more specifically, "non-powers"); see Livanios (2017a) for an insightful critique of Molnar's argument. By contrast, Bird (2007a, 2017) and Mumford (2004) argue for a dispositional (or powerful) interpretation of locations, as I will explain below.

observation, it would seem that gravitational mass and location are powerful partners, according to the mutual manifestation model (Heil 2003, 2012; Martin 2008). Gravitational force is equally a function of mass and location.

Bird (2007a: 161–162), largely agreeing with Mumford, argues that it is much more natural for us to regard displays of gravitational force as the effects of masses, not locations.[50] This is because locations are assumed – falsely, according to Bird – to be background features, not active participants in physical events. Bird (2007a: 164) argues that the best way to accommodate a powers interpretation of spatiotemporal properties and relations, and structures requiring such, is by assuming that physical theories should be background-free.[51] If the universe is background-free, such that space and time are *not* background, then space and time are positioned to play active roles in physical processes. Locations can then be given a powers interpretation, for example, in instances of gravitational force.

Granting the background-free requirement, one option is to eliminate space and time from our theories. This would eliminate the question of the qualitative versus powerful nature of spatial and temporal properties. However, although conceivable, eliminating space and time from our theories is not a plausible option (Bird 2007a: 164). Therefore, we are left with accepting either some version of substantivalism (i.e., absolutism) or relationalism about space and time. But the background-free requirement challenges substantivalism about spacetime. This is because that view, at least on its strictest interpretation, implies that spacetime is but a container – a background – for events, implying that spacetime does not cause anything and is not affected by anything. Therefore, substantival spacetime is not amenable to a powers interpretation (2007a: 165–166).

Assuming that space and time are not mere background features, they have the potential to be affected. This implies that – combined with the

---

[50] Bird focuses specifically on *displacement* of objects relative to each other in Newton's law. However, displacement is a function of locations. Besides his worry about the proper assignment of gravitational power (to objects or to locations), he also worries that since displacement occurs in other physical laws (e.g., Coulomb's law), displacement might be considered multitrack (Bird 2007a: 161) and hence not a fundamental power (2007a: 21–24). Still, he thinks we should privilege one disposition in the total set of displacement dispositions: "given the general theory of relativity it is natural to see gravitational force as participating in the essence of spatial properties and relations" (2007a: 162).

[51] For support for the claim that physical theories should be background-free, see Baez (2001), Smolin (1991), and Rovelli (1997).

"action-reaction" principle (Anandan and Brown 1995; Brown and Pooley 2006), that is, that something is only capable of cause if it also capable of effect – space and time are potential causes too (Bird 2007a: 162, 168). Now, if space and time are "capable of acting and being acted upon," they can be given dispositional interpretations (2007a: 164) compatible with the spatiotemporal dynamicity implied by Einstein's General Theory of Relativity (GTR) (2007a: 166).[52] On Einstein's GTR, time can slow and space can warp, thereby affecting gravitational force and the travel of light. Spacetime is a dynamic, interactive participant in physical events, not a mere background container in which events happen.[53]

In addition to the location sensitivity and background-free arguments, there is another way to argue that locations have a dispositional essence, which I will briefly sketch. The basic idea is that locations are powers to be occupied. Powers are directed at being occupied, where occupation is the manifestation that is triggered when an entity (object or property) enters the boundary of a location (a region or a single spacetime point). Bird's and Mumford's accounts have some emphasis on distance and spatial separation *between* locations (Bird 2007a: 162; Mumford 2004: 188), vis-à-vis gravitational effect, whereas my "power to be occupied" hypothesis solely emphasizes the power of single locations. Additionally, this proposal is compatible with both relational and substantival interpretations of the nature of spacetime. So, it does not require a background-free conception of the universe, unlike Bird's account (though I am sympathetic to that conception). So long as there are spatial locations – however they come to be, either as fundamental background requirements or through relations between objects; either as part of a spacetime fabric or not – they have the power to be occupied.

While a comprehensive discussion of the debate concerning locations as powers or qualities is not my aim here, I have sketched some possibilities to make the locations-as-powers thesis more plausible. If the Pure Powers Model and the Point Theory are correct, then it looks like spacetime points must be powers. So, what can they do? What are their manifestations? One option is that locations are active participants – not mere background features – in the dynamics of the physical world. They are causally active in

---

[52] GTR is, *prima facie*, more compatible with relationalism over substantivalism, though the exact implications of GTR for this classic debate are not settled.

[53] In later work, Bird (2017) further explicates his reasoning for interpreting spatial and temporal relations dispositionally.

displays of mass, charge, and other fundamental powers. Or, in line with the hypothesis I sketched, any spacetime point will have the power to be occupied by some object or property token such as mass.[54]

### Pure Powers and Spatial Occupation

Point Theory holds that a pure power is an actual, continuously instantiated property. Just as with a powerful quality, a pure power is an actual property, ready to manifest when triggered. But a power's actuality requires a spatiotemporal condition of some sort. Point Theory provides that but denies the claim that a pure power requires spatial *occupation* as a quality might require.

I assume a distinction between *being instantiated at a point in space* versus *being instantiated in a region* of two or more points (thus occupying space by creating an extension or distance). A pure power can be instantiated at a point which is not extended – per Point Theory – and thus does not occupy space in that sense. Consider a world with infinite spacetime but no extended objects: Space is empty or nonoccupied. Infinite counterfactuals might be true of a single point in space, yet nothing *occupies* space.

This is important because a possible objection is that if a pure power is instantiated, then during nonmanifestation periods it should occupy a spatial region $R$, where $R$ consists of a set of two or more simultaneous points immediately neighboring each other.[55] If this conditional claim is true, the problem for pure powers seems to be that there is nothing to occupy $R$ in the way that an object or a structural property token (like shape) occupies space; thus, pure powers cease to exist when latent. In response, Point Theory implies that the spatial occupation objection is a pseudo-problem because a pure power can be instantiated at a point, where a point with a causal profile does not need to be extended in, or occupy, space. Spatial occupation in terms of extension is, perhaps, a condition for powerful qualities or pure qualities, but not for pure powers.

---

[54] If Point Theory is correct, and if we are to maintain the possibility of a one-power world, then there is a possible world with only one spacetime point (it would be a point with a single pure power). This assumes that any additional spacetime points would require powers because for any additional point that exists, it would necessarily have some causal profile – such as a power to be occupied, to enter certain relations with other points, and so on – thus negating the possibility of a one-power world.

[55] I assume that during manifesting periods, a power might present itself qualitatively (to at least *appear* to be a quality) or be involved in some spatially occupying event.

Suppose, however, it is true that if a stimulus occurs in $R$, then a manifestation will occur. Thus, it appears that a pure power is spatially extended because it is instantiated throughout $R$. However, at any point in $R$, all the counterfactuals specifying $C_s$ will be true because $C_s$ holds at every point in $R$. Therefore, what appears to be a single pure power spread throughout $R$ consists of a set of many tokens of pure powers instantiated at all the points in $R$. This can potentially account for fields of force spread through spacetime regions.

Williams (2009: 17–18) objects to pure powers based on concerns about spatial occupation. But he is mainly interested in showing that if a subatomic particle $x$ has pure powers, then $x$ must still be some "way" at all times, which requires spatial occupation and some qualitativity; therefore, since purportedly pure powers appear to be grounded in qualitativity, they are not really pure.[56] But these concerns are somewhat tangential to my discussion, given the assumption that any pure power can float free of and thus exist (i.e., remain instantiated) independently of objects, as discussed previously (see footnote 43 of this chapter). Therefore, a pure power's occupation of space, via its object bearer in some way, is not necessary.

Furthermore, Molnar (2003: 133–134) contends that fundamental particles are simple and completely lacking structure, which suggests the possibility of point particles, since to be physically extended – a nonpoint – is to have some structure. So, assuming point particles count as objects and pure powers can be properties of point particles, as contemporary physics suggests, if a pure power is borne by an object this does not necessitate that the power occupies space. That would only be true if particles necessarily occupied space in the extensional sense identified above. Therefore, on Point Theory, the instantiation of a pure power by a particle can reasonably avoid any of the qualitative nature that supposedly comes along with spatial occupation.

### The Movement of Pure Powers through Spacetime

Assuming a relativistic conception of spacetime on which space can warp, then pure powers and the points they are pinned to move, in a sense, as the spacetime fabric warps (also, points and their associated powers will move as spacetime expands). But this concerns more large-scale spatial structures. What about local frames of reference in which ordinary

---

[56] Precedent for this type of worry is found in Blackburn (1990).

movements of properties and objects take place? A pure power can move or shift between distinct points, thus accounting for the movement of pure powers, and the objects bearing them, through spacetime. This occurs either (i) as a pure power's bearer moves (e.g., a particle with mass moving through spacetime), or (ii) if property tokens can float free, then as the power itself moves. On either option, as the power moves between points, $C_s$ shifts between those points. Causal processes involving multiple powers can be accounted for this way, by a series of shifts in the location of $C_s$.

These contentions can be developed along lines consistent with one of the axiomatic systems for topology and physics developed by Carnap (1958).[57] An extensive development of this might be worthwhile, but my modest aim here is to point out the basic features most relevant to Point Theory.

Carnap (1958: 197) uses a logic of relations "to treat topological properties of space and time by a *purely topological method*" and thus with no use of concepts with a "metric (non-topological) character." He provides three distinct logical systems for describing the nature of world-points within the framework of Einstein's GTR. One of these systems, the *Wlin*-System (1958: 207–209), appears tailor-made for the conception of pure powers (or any kind of functionalized property) given by Point Theory. In the *Wlin*-System, "world-points are [...] taken as individuals – however, world-points not as particle slices, but as the spacetime points corresponding thereto" (1958: 207). That is, the world-points that make up a world-line of an individual (e.g., a particle) just are spacetime points. The world-line of a particle consists of a class of time relations that specify the temporal moments of the particle along its path, and coincident world-points are identical (1958: 207).

Supposing these world-points are spacetime points per Carnap's *Wlin*-System and these are fundamental individuals or "particles," they should possess some fundamental properties. If these are pure powers, then it follows that they are pure powers of world-points. That is, particles bearing pure powers just are spacetime points (the world-points) on the *Wlin*-System, consistent with Point Theory. These particles need not be substrata existing independently of their properties, for they might be just bundles of power tokens existing at spacetime points; alternatively, perhaps the individuals or world-points are simply property tokens.

---

[57] Thanks to Gary Merrill for suggesting this.

On the *Wlin*-System, a signal relation holds between points: "An effect reaches from a world-point $x$ to a world-point $y$ if and only if $x$ is connected to $y$ by a signal" (1958: 201). A signal can occur between a single individual (a world-point on the *Wlin*-System) at an earlier time and a later time on its world-line, or a signal can occur between distinct world-points, thus linking particles or individuals by linking their world lines, as when one particle's momentum or energy is transferred to another. The signal relation is comparable to the relation of a power to its manifestation. So, the relevance of this to pure powers on Point Theory is this: In the case of a single world-point, $s$, the status (as defined by $C_s$) of $s$ at $t_1$ affects its later status at $t_2$ (i.e., this is just a relation between spatiotemporal stages of a pure power). In the case of signals between two world-points, $s^1$ and $s^2$, $s^2$ might receive the stimulus from $s^1$ and thus manifest, connecting the two world-points by the manifestation relation (by analogy, consider one billiard ball striking another, causing it to accelerate, thus a signal relation obtains).

If these contentions are correct, the *Wlin*-System can provide an axiomatic system for fundamental physics that is consistent with Point Theory. A power's movement is a shifting of $C_s$ between points along a world-line. Since $C_s$ holds consecutively along the points of a particular world-line, this accounts for a power's identity along its world-line.[58]

As a theory of pure powers' self-grounding, Point Theory does without mysterious qualities, powerless natures that are somehow identical to powerful natures. Point Theory maintains that pure powers consist of causal profiles at spacetime points. For any given pure power, when it is not manifesting, it exists or is instantiated *qua* power because there remains an actual causal profile and an actual spacetime point that stands in being. Pure powers need not occupy space in the sense of being extended like a quality is expected to be. They can move (or shift) through spacetime per the mechanisms detailed in Carnap's *Wlin*-System. Based on these considerations, I conclude that Point Theory mitigates Level 1 worries about pure powers (especially the problem of being), thus effectively neutralizing the explanatory advantage the Powerful Qualities Model appears to have over the Pure Powers Model.

---

[58] Every metaphysical account of objects and properties must allow for the movement of these entities through space and time, to the extent that motion is not illusory. And all objects and properties are located at points or clusters of points. Therefore, pure powers theorists are not exclusively burdened to explain the movement of properties.

## 2.9   Further Questions

Key questions remain. I argued for Power = Directedness. But more exploration of directedness – and the Physical Intentionality Thesis it is part of – is needed, as Chapters 3–5 will provide. What about the informational content of a power? A causal profile of a power should be interpreted in terms of counterfactual information, as Chapter 6 will explore further. Lastly, how do qualities, or at least the appearance of qualities, come to be out of pure powers? That is a Level 2 issue concerning systems of powers, which Chapter 7 will address.

Now we are ready to see powers from the inside.

## PART II

## *What Are Powers Like?*

CHAPTER 3

# *Powers from the Inside*
## *Physical Intentionality*

## 3.1 The Physical Intentionality Thesis

### *Avoiding Mysterianism about Powers*

Some philosophers are mysterians about phenomenal consciousness. They claim that although each of us individually knows what consciousness is like from the inside, we cannot ever understand why it is like this or how it originates.[1] By analogy, we could be mysterians about matter: We might know (or be justified in believing) that matter exists, but we cannot know what it is like. For example, empiricist philosophers avoid positing any kind of raw substance or substratum underlying observable property instances. At least, they avoid saying anything positive about substance or the internal nature of matter: Although we might suppose that it has or needs an internal nature, we are epistemically cut off from its deep structure.[2] Therefore, we have to remain mysterians about the internal nature of

---

[1] See, for example, McGinn (1989).

[2] Russell (1927: 163) suggests a mysterian view about the ultimate nature of matter when he argues as follows: "Modern physics, therefore, reduces matter to a set of events which proceed outward from a centre. If there is something further in the centre itself, we cannot know about it, and it is irrelevant to physics [...] What we know about them is not their intrinsic character, but their structure and their mathematical laws [...] Physics is mathematical, not because we know so much about the physical world, but because we know so little: it is only its mathematical properties that we can discover. For the rest, our knowledge is negative. In places where there are no eyes or ears or brains there are no colours or sounds, but there are events having certain characteristics which lead them to cause colours and sounds in places where there are eyes, ears and brains. We cannot find out what the world looks like from a place where there is nobody, because if we go to look there will be somebody there; the attempt is as hopeless as trying to jump on one's own shadow." On this view, humans are simply not cognitively equipped to discern the ultimate nature of matter. Gamez (2018: 23–24) uses this line of reasoning to support the notion that physical objects are "black boxes" from which our brains receive signals for processing. I tend to agree, but I advocate two points in response: First, these "black boxes" *must have powers* to affect us if we are to have information about them (here I invoke the necessity of powers as concluded in Chapter 1); and second, we can make reasonable (albeit speculative) claims about the nature of these powers, as I attempt to do in this book.

matter. In this vein, we could be mysterians about physical properties: We cannot know – or perhaps even have reasonable insight into – what powers or qualities are like from the inside.

Neo-Humeans eschew a powers interpretation of properties partially on grounds that we have no knowledge or perception of powers. They hold that powers are mysterious and therefore better left out of one's ontology.[3] They also tend to be mysterians about qualities (although they certainly do posit them) for they hold that qualities are quiddities whose nonpowerful essences are inherently unknowable.[4] However, a mysterian view of powers should be a last resort. Indeed, I think that there are substantial, defensible claims regarding the internal nature of powers. And if powers are the fundamental properties of matter, then a plausible theory of powers' internality could be seen as a window into the internality of matter itself.

Powers, in appropriate circumstances, recognize and collaborate with each other to produce manifestations. They are responsive to each other. In seeking to provide identity and individuation conditions for powers, many accounts of powers (mine included) recognize their networked existence and the relations they have to each other for possible manifestations. Yet the drivers of all events are the powers themselves: the nodes in the network. Hence, each power should have some sort of internal nature that explains its modality and grounds its role in a power network. By analogy, to apply the frequently used phrase from Nagel (1974), I am after a sense of "what it is like" to be a power. However, I am neither assuming nor suggesting that powers actually have qualia; far from it. Rather, it is a metaphorical suggestion intended to invite reflection concerning the inherent nature of powers.

My theory of powers from the inside, the **3d** account, combines **direct**edness (i.e., intentionality) and **data** (i.e., information) as essential ingredients of **d**ispositions (i.e., powers). In this chapter, I will begin arguing for PIT (the Physical Intentionality Thesis), that powers and thoughts share the marks of intentionality, thus supporting one of two key theses in the 3d account.

---

[3] The same cannot go for mysterianism about consciousness, since we intuitively know that consciousness exists. The mystery regarding consciousness is not whether it exists but understanding its origin and nature.

[4] Jaworski (2016: 82) remarks that quiddities are akin to haecceities, the hypothetical primitive individuating essences of objects.

## Two Arguments for PIT

My primary argument for PIT is the Argument from the Marks of Intentionality, which runs as follows. The marks of intentionality (especially directedness, intentional inexistence, and intentional indeterminacy) plausibly identify when a state or property is intentional. These marks apply equally well to physical powers as they do to mental states. Therefore, physical powers are intentional. This argument will be developed over the course of this chapter and (especially) Chapters 4 and 5.

I have an additional argument for PIT, the Argument from the Unity of Nature. If intentionality runs throughout nature from physical powers to minds, then nature is more unified than it otherwise would be. Without such an intentionality continuum there would be two metaphysical realms, one with intentionality and one without. Being metaphysically unified is a theoretical virtue. The desirability of such unity gives extra motivation to posit physical intentionality. The Argument from the Unity of Nature need not be taken in isolation from the Argument from the Marks of Intentionality. The latter assists the former argument by confirming that intentionality does indeed run throughout nature, thus that unity is obtained.[5] Moreover, the Informational Thesis (to be discussed in Chapter 6) bolsters the Argument from the Unity of Nature. Finally, the full implications of the metaphysical unity implied by PIT will become clear in Chapter 8 when I defend the Intentionality Continuum Thesis.

Now, let us begin examining PIT.

## 3.2   Historical Precursors to the Physical Intentionality Thesis

There is a long history of thought about intentionality. Though this history largely concerns mental (or psychological) intentionality, some philosophers have discussed matter having intention, purpose, directedness, and the like. A couple of examples will demonstrate the historical interest in extending something like mental intentionality into the material world.

Aristotle (1941b: *Physics* 199a10-199b33) maintained that natural substances have a *telos*, an end toward which they are directed. In effect,

---

[5] Taken apart from the Argument from the Marks of Intentionality, the Argument from the Unity of Nature independently has abductive plausibility: Since unity is desirable as a theoretical virtue, we have reasons to posit the Physical Intentionality Thesis. So, the possibility of gaining unity through intentionality could persuade those who are more reluctant to accept PIT to tentatively accept it.

natural substances have an internal principle governing their activity (Johnson 2005: 6). This internal principle specifies what a teleological state is directed toward, that is, its end, thus governing its capacity to change and be active in the world of becoming. Similar to Aristotelian teleological states, powers are natural, directed states. The two types of states at least have some conceptual overlap. Thus, Aristotle's teleology can be viewed as a historical precedent to PIT. There are, however, crucial differences. First, teleological states have an *end*, whereas powers have a manifestation. Second, Aristotelian teleology is a stronger claim than PIT since the former is usually understood in axiological terms and not just scientific cum metaphysical terms. Still, both ideas are in the family of views that hold that "X is directed toward Y."[6] Kroll (2017) presents a contemporary teleological account of powers, but his reference to directedness is not supposed to involve goals or purposes (Kroll's view is discussed in Section 3.4).

Leibniz invokes ideas akin to physical intentionality in speaking of the internal principle of things. In explaining his concept of the monad, he asserts that "The action of the internal principle which brings about the change or the passage from one perception to another may be called *appetition*" (Leibniz 1991: 18, para. 15). And monads are the "sources of their own internal actions" (1991: 19, para. 18).[7] Schrenk (2017: 274) suggests a similarity between monads and powers. But there are differences, foremost being that monads are substances whereas powers are properties. Additionally, monads do not causally interact with each other; they are "windowless" (Rescher 1991: 59) and follow preset patterns whereas powers are inherently causally productive (at least, that is a view largely shared by powers theorists, me included).

---

[6] Open questions include, "How exactly is teleology related to intentionality?" and "Is teleology a species of intentionality, or vice versa?"

[7] Ellis (2002: 149) – examining the debate over the source of activity in nature – notes that according to Leibniz "inanimate things have, or can acquire, causal powers" ("living forces" or *vires vivae*). Compared to Newton, who viewed forces as external to things, Leibniz thought that things were intrinsically animated (Ellis 2002: 149). The dispositional essentialist's (and more broadly the powers theorist's) response to Newton's claim that gravity requires an external agent constantly acting in accord with law is as follows: We know that things can and do "stretch out beyond their visual boundaries" and get involved in causal processes at a distance, for instance, electromagnetic fields have fuzzy boundaries (Ellis 2002: 153). Therefore, gravity in principle is no obstacle to dispositional essentialist metaphysics. The "distortion of space-time," according to the General Theory of Relativity, is created by an object not as "an effect of its presence, but an integral and essential part of its being, without which the object could not exist" (Ellis 2002: 153). Therefore, no external agent or force is required, as Newtonianism holds, suggesting that the impetus for causal actions comes from within things.

Yet, as Rescher points out, each monad follows a kind of "inner programming" (1991: 59) that allows the individual monads in a system to constitute a "harmonious whole" (1991: 200). This is similar to how powers can form harmonious networks. Intentionality is closely tied to the internal nature or "programming" of anything that has intentionality, because it implies instructions or informational content that is *for* something. Thus, the same would seem to hold true of physical intentionality, and therefore powers, if we suppose that physical and psychological (or mental) intentionality are equivalent (as I will argue). If that is so, physical intentionality can plausibly be claimed to be closely tied to the "internal principle" or "programming" of a power. But whereas monads are programmed to *act*, powers are programmed to *interact*: that is, they are intrinsically directed toward causal interactions with each other.

## 3.3 Brentano's Thesis and Overview of the Physical Intentionality Thesis

In *Psychology from an Empirical Standpoint*, first published in 1874, Brentano set himself to discover a positive feature possessed by all mental phenomena but not by any physical phenomena. He thought he found it when he declared that "Intentional in-existence is characteristic exclusively of mental phenomena. No physical phenomena exhibits anything like it" (Brentano 2015: 93). The "aboutness" of mental sates is necessarily tied to intentional inexistence: a state can be about something that does not exist. Since arguing that intentionality (and especially intentional inexistence) definitively distinguishes mental and physical states, philosophers seemed to fall in line, yielding a default assumption that mental phenomena are essentially about things that might not exist, whereas physical phenomena do not have such aboutness.[8]

Brentano (2015: 89–92) considers other ways to distinguish mental and physical states. For instance, he discusses the Cartesian hypothesis that physical phenomena are extended while mental phenomena are not. The problem with the extension criterion is twofold. First, it is a negative conception of mental phenomena (mental states are *not* extended) whereas a positive conception is preferable. Second, it is controversial because while some thinkers claim that sounds and smells lack extension

---

[8] After his 1874 work, Brentano continued to investigate the nature of intentionality. For example, Brentano (1911) argues that intentionality is nonrelational. See Kriegel (2016) for a fascinating discussion of Brentano's "mature theory of intentionality."

or spatial location (2015: 90), others claim that "that sensory appetites appear localized" in the body (2015: 91) and are therefore, apparently, spatially extended.

Aboutness stood out to Brentano as a positive characterization of mental states. However, these thoughts about aboutness did not issue solely from the mind of Brentano. Earlier psychologists in the Scholastic tradition "already pointed out that there is a special affinity and analogy which exists among all mental phenomena" but not physical phenomena, focusing particularly on the "intentional (or mental) inexistence of an object," "reference to a content," and "direction toward an object (which is not to be understood here as meaning a thing)" amongst other related aspects (2015: 92). In sum, "Every mental phenomenon includes something as object within itself [...]" (2015: 92).

Furthermore, only mental phenomena are "perceived in inner consciousness" – however, "That feature which best characterizes mental phenomena is undoubtedly their intentional in-existence," which "clearly" distinguishes mental and physical phenomena (Brentano 2015: 95). Therefore, intentionality provides a strict distinction between mental and physical states of existence. Thoughts (beliefs, desires, etc.) are about something other than themselves: They have a content. Intentionality might be the most fundamental feature of cognition (Priest 2005: 5).

Nonetheless, I intend to challenge the view that intentionality decidedly distinguishes mental from physical states. In recent decades, some metaphysicians have argued that powers exemplify all the necessary marks or characteristics of intentionality. Since powers adhere in ordinary physical objects, not just minds, it is suggested that *physical* intentionality is real. Hence, we get PIT: Powers, like thoughts, are intentional states.

If it can be shown that powers, including fundamental instances such as charge and mass as well as nonfundamental instances such as elasticity and flammability, possess intentionality, then it follows that intentionality is not borne exclusively by mental phenomena. Intentionality would be a pervasive feature of all of reality and – contrary to Brentano's thesis – insufficient to distinguish the mental from the physical realms of existence. That alone is a significant implication. But my primary purpose for making this argument is to show how intentionality is a part of a coherent, informative account of powers from the inside.

PIT comes in two versions: PIT (Identity) and PIT (Analogy). PIT (Identity) claims that physical and mental intentionality are identical. In this case, mental and physical intentionality would perfectly share all the relevant marks of intentionality to be discussed in Chapters 4 and 5. PIT

(Analogy) claims that physical and mental intentionality are strongly alike but not identical in all respects. In this case, mental and physical intentionality would differ to some degree along one or more of the relevant marks of intentionality but remain sufficiently similar to make for an interesting metaphysical thesis.[9] It is not always clear which version of PIT metaphysicians have in mind when they support or criticize physical intentionality.

For example, Molnar (2003: 61) seems to voice support for PIT (Analogy) when he claims that physical intentionality "is in fundamental respects analogous to *mental intentionality*" and "that something *very much like* intentionality is a pervasive and ineliminable feature of the physical world." However, he also asserts that "that the directedness of dispositions to their manifestations *is* the directedness of intentional properties" (Molnar 2003: 81; my italics). I think the latter is the correct way to interpret Molnar's position[10] and examining why helps reveal that PIT (Identity) should be the default view. The apparent reason for Molnar asserting PIT (Analogy), not PIT (Identity), is that states of mental intentionality are in some cases conscious and representational, whereas states of physical intentionality are neither representational nor conscious (2003: 81). However, since they do sometimes coincide in the case of mental intentionality, physical intentionality can only be analogous, not identical to, mental intentionality. However, this is the wrong way to look at the phenomenon of intentionality. Whether or not instances of intentionality, be they physical or mental, coincide with consciousness or representation is irrelevant to whether two specific types of intentionality are in fact simply one type (therefore, identical or the same in all respects). If we just focus on the marks of intentionality (directedness, intentional inexistence, and so on), while keeping in mind that consciousness and representation are not marks of intentionality but rather phenomena that can be correlated with intentionality, then in assessing whether either version of PIT is correct we can set aside questions of representation and consciousness

---

[9] For example, Jaworski (2016: 57–58) stops short of commitment to PIT (Identity) and seems to affirm only PIT (Analogy), although he is committed to powers being directed. He holds that mental states are a species of powers, which I agree with, rather than the intentionality of powers being a species of mental intentionality.

[10] Moreover, according to Molnar (2003: 81), directedness is an undefined, fundamental feature of powers. If such an essential feature of powers is fundamental to them, as it also is to mental states, and powers share the other marks of intentionality, this also suggests – beyond the reasons given in the passage this footnote accompanies – that Molnar can be interpreted as supporting PIT (Identity). Bird (2007a: 120–126) also interprets Molnar's view as PIT (Identity), that is, that physical intentionality = mental intentionality. Although he mainly focuses on Place (1996), who clearly affirms PIT (Identity), Bird seems to lump Molnar and other PIT proponents together.

(although, in Chapter 4, I will argue that physical intentional states *are* in fact representational). Intentionality per se is the same in both the physical and mental cases. Therefore, PIT (Identity) should be the default view.

Henceforth, when I refer to PIT (Identity), I mean only that the relevant marks of intentionality are fully satisfied by powers, including (most fundamentally) that the directedness of mental states is the same phenomenon as the directedness of physical states. When I use the term "PIT" going forward, I mean PIT (Identity) unless otherwise indicated. Nonetheless, PIT (Analogy) remains a viable and interesting thesis. If my arguments fall short of demonstrating PIT (Identity), PIT (Analogy) is not a bad fallback position.

I argue in Chapter 4 that PIT is correct because powers share all the essential marks of intentionality. Some marks that I believe are not essential will be discussed in Chapter 5 since they still illuminate the nature of powers. However, in the remainder of this chapter I will discuss some views related to PIT, which will help to understand physical intentionality.

## 3.4   Views Related to the Physical Intentionality Thesis

There are several views related to PIT. Taken together, these form a family of views that attribute something mind-like or teleological to powers. Exploring these will deepen our understanding of PIT.

### An Epistemic Interpretation of PIT

One view is that although intentionality is useful for understanding the nature of powers, it does not involve a metaphysical commitment, unlike PIT. For example, Borghini (2009) thinks that intentionality is relevant to individuating powers (an epistemic matter, as he sees it) but not in providing identity conditions (a metaphysical matter), thus taking a kind of "intentional stance" (Dennett 1987) toward powers. Borghini (2009: 215–216) claims that it is difficult to individuate powers because they are potentially hidden for the duration of their instantiation. Furthermore, one would have to identify all the properties they relate to in order to single them out.[11] To help individuate powers, we can invoke the manifestations

---

[11] That is why Borghini thinks that conditional analyses are not viable; I take him to mean that, if a conditional analysis were successful, it would have to specify all the properties that need to be included – triggers, and so on – and excluded – masks, finks, and so on – if the power is to manifest.

they are directed toward, that is, *intended toward* – Borghini talks of powers having intentions but makes clear this does not mean a conscious plan or anything like that. For him, "Intentional talk is a conceptual ladder used to individuate dispositions" (2009: 215). How is this supposed to work? The "intentional character" of a power permits us to focus on those properties that are relevant to picking out what the power is for (2009: 216). But intentional talk does not affect the metaphysical identity conditions of powers – it simply allows us to single out powers by referencing their intentional object.

In response to Borghini, it is not clear why talk of intention provides any help in individuating powers if all it does is direct our attention to the manifestations that the power is for. We do not really need talk of intentionality to individuate powers. We can instead individuate powers by their behavior, that is, their record of manifestation processes. In this case, we would not invoke intentions but would simply pick out the range of possible manifestations a power could produce (or a set of powers could produce) as a way of individuating powers. In contrast to Borghini, intentionality is a real metaphysical feature of powers that determines their identity. If some condition, $c$, individuates a power, it does so because $c$ picks out conditions that are essential to the power's behavior: It establishes the power's possible actions or causal profile, that is, its *identity*. In other words, a functional-operational definiens – represented by a causal profile – specifies the power's nature.

## Teleological Views of Powers

A second view related to PIT emphasizes teleological aspects of powers. A teleological reading is actually suggested by the very idea of physical intentionality. For example, Oderberg (2017) argues that PIT has more to do with finality than intentionality, and that mental and physical intentionality possess important differences. I will save further discussion of Oderberg's argument for Chapter 5 (where, in Section 5.6, I discuss objections to PIT). However, there is another view of powers emphasizing teleology. Kroll (2017) presents an interesting and well-developed teleological account of powers with a non-Aristotelian understanding of directedness. While discussion of Kroll's worries about PIT might also fit in a discussion of objections to PIT, I discuss them in this section because his criticisms are intrinsically related to his positive account of powers and they provide a useful context for exploring PIT.

Kroll (2017: 20) maintains that a disposition (power) "*just is* the property of being in a state directed at a certain teleological end."[12] This is what distinguishes powers from qualities: The latter are not directed toward teleological ends. Kroll's sense of "directedness" is a generalized teleological notion "that outstrips talk of goals, purposes, design, and function" (2017: 24). This might seem contradictory – that it is teleological and nonteleological at the same time. But to support this nonpurposive teleological idea of directedness, Kroll appeals to a teleological account of events in progress. In order to be an "event in progress" it must be "directed at the end that it cause the resultant state" of such an event to obtain at a later time (2017: 26). The idea seems to be that the "end" is not the purpose or goal but that which happens to occur, because it is disposed to occur, as a result of some process. Still, what is it to be teleologically directed at an end, if that end is not somehow privileged as a goal? Despite Kroll's intention, it seems to me that he builds purpose or goal into powers in specifying an "end" of directedness. After all, it is not as if a given power can result in any manifestation; powers are directed toward specific types of manifestations.

In contrast to Kroll's teleological account, I suggest that we pursue an intentionality-based interpretation of powers, viz. PIT. However, Kroll (2017: 32) advances what he calls an "obvious objection" to PIT, discussion of which foreshadows a key argument in Chapter 4. The objection is that mental states are directed at their objects because they represent those objects; assuming that representationality is essential to intentionality, and that powers do *not* represent their manifestations, powers cannot genuinely be intentional states. Hence, only some nonintentionality-based – and thus nonrepresentation-based – interpretation of powers is warranted. Kroll's account aims to provide a viable nonrepresentational account of powers' directedness, thereby avoiding the ontological burden of adding representationality to powers that PIT seems to imply.[13]

---

[12] Why not just "property of being directed"? Why "property of being in a state directed"? McKitrick (2017: 43) worries that, if a state is a state of affairs (e.g., a particular instantiating a property, as Armstrong (1997) maintains), it suggests that a power is a second-order property and requires (non-self) grounding. Setting aside this worry about a power being a second-order property, what really matters for my purposes is Kroll's sense of "directedness."

[13] Generally, Kroll (2017: 32) agrees with advocates of PIT that we should look beyond conditional analyses and that the parallel between mental and physical intentionality need not be perfect to accept that there is "a more general notion of intentionality" that covers both (2017: 32). Perhaps he would be willing to accept PIT (Analogy) if not PIT (Identity). He says that if his notion of directedness is shown to fall under a general notion of intentionality, he would join that camp (2017: 33).

Kroll (2017: 32) argues for his preferred sense of directedness by contrasting differing senses of directedness, exemplified as follows:

(i)   "Steve driving to Boston is directed at its culmination."

(ii)  "a vase's disposition to break when struck is directed at its manifestation."

(iii) "Johnny's belief that Santa has red cheeks is directed at Santa."

Examples (i) and (ii) are similar, but (iii) is different, suggests Kroll (2017: 33). Example (iii) is an instance of mental intentionality and requires representationality, a feature which Kroll's teleological account of powers does not allow (justifiably, by Kroll's lights). To maintain PIT against Kroll's account, PIT supporters need to show that Kroll's account of directedness is insufficient, while some appeal to an account that unifies (ii) and (iii) (i.e., shows their similarity) is plausible and sufficient to explain the directedness of powers.

Kroll offers a belief state in (iii) but he does not specify whether this is a latent or occurrent belief. This is an important distinction. Some beliefs are occurrent: They are presently active in the mind of the believer. However, some are latent: They are not occurrent but disposed to become occurrent in appropriate triggering conditions.[14] Suppose Taylor is disposed to believe that there is a mouse in the attic but currently has zero information supporting that belief. He is disposed to believe it if presented with relevant information. This is a dispositional belief in a weak sense: It is something Taylor is disposed to believe (although he might still not believe it when presented with relevant information if some cognitive bias causes him to deny the supporting facts). A strong sense of a dispositional belief would be something you already believe but are not consciously thinking about now. On either the strong or weak sense of a latent belief, the belief is dispositional – and it is representational. So, latent beliefs are a phenomenon where representationality and power (dispositionality) converge.

What about other types of mental states beyond beliefs? Desires, in particular, seem more relevant than beliefs to the question of PIT's veracity. Compare the following examples (mine) to (iii):

(iv)  "Johnny's desire that Santa bring gifts is directed at Santa bringing gifts."

---

[14] There is a larger debate concerning whether beliefs are exclusively dispositional or categorical properties of the mind. For example, see Schwitzgebel (2001, 2002). This debate is separate from the issue I am raising vis-à-vis Kroll's examples; I am merely suggesting that beliefs can be either latent or occurrent, that is, disposed to manifest or manifested.

Or, as an example of an individually achievable desire (supposing there are objective criteria for getting on Santa's good list):

(v)   "Johnny's desire to get on Santa's good list is directed at Johnny getting on the good list (i.e., manifesting in Johnny being on the good list)."

Now, (iv) and (v) are similar to (iii) simply because they are mental states. Although desires and beliefs have different directions of fit – desires being world to mind and beliefs being mind to world – they are equally mental, intentional states. Importantly, (iv) and especially (v) are more similar to (i) and (ii), than (iii) is to (i) and (ii). Focusing on (v) and (ii), it is natural to say that Johnny's desire and the vase's fragility are directed at their respective outcomes. Their directedness is toward specific realizations: the vase breaking and Johnny being on the good list. I am not claiming that the vase consciously *wants* to break as Johnny might consciously *want* to be on the good list. Consciously wanting is not necessary to the directedness of Johnny's desire, although it is necessary for Johnny's phenomenal experience of that desire (what it is like to have a desire, or the feeling of wanting). The key point is that (v) is more similar to (ii) than (iii) is to (ii). This is because, among other things, (v) and (ii) exemplify objects being directed toward future possible outcomes. The belief in (iii) is also directed but it seems different because the belief does not "work" toward bringing about a new reality, whereas desires and powers do, in a sense, work toward bringing about the reality they are for; they are productive of their outcomes. In sum, there is more similarity between the directedness of powers and desires than there is between powers and beliefs.

Positing a telos might help explain the directedness of powers, but Kroll denies that it involves the notions of goal, purpose, or function that are central to Aristotle's teleology.[15] So, what is it? It is supposed to be a "general notion of teleological directedness" (Kroll 2017: 27). But when divorced from goal, purpose, and so on, a "general notion" seems too vague and unhelpful in explaining directedness.[16] By contrast, physical intentionality – based on the concept of mental intentionality, with which we have some immediate grasp owing to our subjective experience – offers a more specific sense in which a power is directed: It is

---

[15] See Johnson (2005) for detailed discussion of Aristotle's teleology.
[16] For further critical discussion of Kroll's analysis, see McKitrick (2017) and Manley and Wasserman (2017).

simply for that toward which it is directed, its possible manifestations that the power "intends" to realize.

Furthermore, if powers carry counterfactual information, as I suggested in Chapter 2 and will explore further in Chapter 6, this information *represents* possible manifestations. I will argue that powers' directedness is in fact representational. This contrasts with the categorization of physical powers as nonrepresentational intentional states in the influential analysis given by Molnar (2003). A large part of my discussion in Chapter 4 will focus on my proposed modifications to Molnar's analysis.

### Other Views Related to PIT

The views discussed thus far are related to but ultimately reject PIT. There are two other views to mention. These views, one having to do with information and the other with agency, seem largely to coincide with the basic tenets of PIT although they do not explicitly accept the thesis. If a view suggests that intentionality resides in basic physical, non-psychological systems, then I count it as accepting that physical intentionality is real.

First, some views give information a central explanatory role in fundamental metaphysics. In developing an epistemology based on information transmission between the world and mind, Dretske (1981) postulates an informational view of physical reality that ties informational structures directly to intentionality. He distinguishes orders of intentionality, from physical nonsemantic intentionality found in basic informational structures to higher-order, cognitive intentionality (1981: 171–173). Intentionality is found in the flow of information between physical states due to "nomic regularities" that underpin "the transmission of information" (1981: 76). Dretske's perspective on intentionality will be discussed more in Chapter 6 because it provides elements relevant to the Informational Thesis. More directly related to powers theory, Williams (2010, 2019) argues that powers carry informational structures (blueprints) which allows all powers in a system of powers to "fit" together metaphysically. That is, he accepts powers holism. He does not appear to accept PIT, yet many elements of his view suggest an intentionality-based interpretation of powers. I also save further discussion of this view for Chapter 6.

Second, some views ascribe a limited kind of agency to physical powers. Ellis (2002: 152) states that "It is evident that the causal powers of things stretch out somehow beyond their boundaries." His commitment to the claim that powers have limited agency – and that more complex agencies, including human agencies, are built out of powers (Ellis 2013) – is not a far step from physical intentionality. Commitment to agency arguably implies commitment to intentionality. Indeed, Armstrong (2002: 169) recommends that Ellis follow Molnar's path and accept that powers possess intentionality. Ellis' view will be discussed further in Chapter 8.

### 3.5    The Powers Model, the Physical Intentionality Thesis, and Modality

PIT is compatible with any version of the Powers Model, including the Pure Powers Model and the Powerful Qualities Model. PIT claims that powers, however conceived, share the marks of psychological intentionality to include, most importantly, directedness and intentional inexistence. The basic insight supporting PIT is that just as mental states are directed toward objects that might not exist, powers are directed toward their manifestations that might not occur. As long as a property is inherently powerful, it has physical intentionality.

The Powers Model holds both that powers are the primary building blocks of reality and that they are inherently modal. PIT reaffirms the claim that powers are modal properties because intentionality itself is a modal phenomenon. For instance, beliefs can be possibly (i.e., contingently) true or necessarily true; desires can be possibly (i.e., contingently) fulfilled or necessarily fulfilled. So, the intentional character of powers reveals why powers are modal properties: They are directed at possible interactions with other powers and thus they are directed at possible manifestations. Powers are already considered inherently modal properties – one of the reasons, alongside their unobservable nature, they are so contentious – regardless of whether PIT is true or not. I am suggesting that PIT sheds explanatory light on the internal, modal character of powers. But to more clearly see why, we must examine the marks of intentionality.

# CHAPTER 4

# A Defense of Physical Intentionality
## Essential Marks

## 4.1 Introducing the Marks of Intentionality

The previous chapter differentiated the Physical Intentionality Thesis (PIT) from similar views but gave little positive support for PIT. In this and the next chapter, I will defend the Argument from the Marks of Intentionality: Since powers plausibly share relevant marks of intentionality with mental states (or "thoughts," broadly speaking), we can confidently conclude that PIT is correct.

Many philosophers have debated whether the marks apply to powers.[1] They have also debated whether, if PIT is correct, it implies that a new criterion should be developed to distinguish physical and mental states. Whereas Martin and Pfeifer (1986) took the assimilation of physical powers to the realm of intentionality to show the need for a new differentiating line between physical powers and mental states, Place (1996) accepted the implication that there is no distinction between the two kinds of states from an intentionality point of view. Powers might not be conscious states, but they *are* fully intentional. As Marmodoro (2009: 339) observes, Place's "influence is widening in the circle of powers-ontologists who define a power in terms of its directionality toward its manifestation." A prime example is Molnar (2003: 60–81) but many other powers theorists accept at least some aspects of PIT as discussed in Chapter 3.[2]

---

[1] Many analyses of PIT vis-à-vis the marks of intentionality have been conducted since the seminal paper of Martin and Pfeifer (1986), some in support of physical intentionality (Bauer 2016; Molnar 2003; Place 1996) and others against it (Bird 2007a; Borghini 2009; Mumford 1999; Oderberg 2017).

[2] Even if one does not accept PIT entirely, one could accept the centrality of directedness. For example, Vetter (2015: 25) posits "a potentiality-based" structuralism, akin to causal structuralism (Shoemaker 1980, 1998 and Hawthorne 2001). Whereas causal structuralism holds that the identities of properties are determined by their role in a causal structure, Vetter's potentiality-based structure replaces the "causal" aspect with potentiality. Therefore, the core relation is not "… causes …" but "… is a potentiality to …" which she terms "the *manifestation relation*" (2015: 25). Importantly, this manifestation relation "is directed: it goes from potentiality to manifestation" (2015: 25). What is the nature of this directedness? I contend that it is the directedness of intentionality. So, in effect,

In the first discussions of PIT and the marks of intentionality, Martin and Pfeifer (1986) and Place (1996) identified five marks of intentionality: directedness, intentional inexistence, intentional indeterminacy, and two linguistic marks (referential opacity and lack of truth import). Molnar (2003: 66–70) and Bird (2007a: 125–126) each introduce two further marks. Bird introduces what he calls the extrinsicness of the intentional object as well as the direction of causation, whereas Molnar introduces both unique and impossible intentional objects as possible marks to differentiate mental states from powers. Finally, we should include direction of fit (Searle 1983, 2004, 2010). These ten marks of intentionality are summarized in Figure 4.1 below.[3]

| Essential marks of intentionality (X = the intentional state, Y = the intentional object) | |
| --- | --- |
| Directedness | X is directed toward Y. |
| Intentional inexistence | Although Y might not exist, X remains directed toward Y. |
| Intentional indeterminacy | Y might be ontologically indeterminate or vague. |
| **Additional marks of intentionality** | |
| Referential opacity (first linguistic mark) | Within an intensional context, there is referential opacity concerning X, that is, lack of truth-preservation between co-referring phrases. |
| Lack of truth import (second linguistic mark) | The truth or falsity of an embedded declarative sentence ascribing X to someone does not depend on whether one denies or asserts that ascription. |
| Impossible intentional objects | X could be directed toward Y although Y is impossible. |
| Unique intentional objects | X could be directed toward Y, where Y is unique (one of a kind). |
| Extrinsicness of intentional states | Y is an extrinsic property. |
| Direction of causation | Y causes X, not the other way around. |
| Direction of fit | X has a direction of "fit" in relation to Y (Y-to-X, or X-to-Y, or both). |

Figure 4.1   The marks of intentionality

I accept an intentionality-based structure. This is compatible with both Vetter's potentiality-based structuralism and others' causal structuralism.

[3] Martin and Pfeifer (1986) used the original five marks in arguing that intentionality is the mark of the dispositional, not the mental, to the effect that we need a different conception of intentionality to distinguish the mental from the dispositional. By contrast, Place (1996) and Molnar (2003) argue that we should simply accept intentionality as the mark of the dispositional. The original marks are culled from a variety of sources, as Place (1996: 92) clarifies, to include Anscombe (1965), Chisholm (1957), and Searle (1979), among other sources.

I suggest that the first three marks are essential – or at least the most important – marks of intentionality. The essential marks appear to be more foundational because the additional marks imply or assume the essential marks, but not vice versa. Further discussion will bear that out. Although the additional marks are not essential for intentionality, they do reveal interesting aspects of intentional states and when applied to powers they illuminate various aspects of their nature.

## 4.2   Directedness and Intentional Inexistence

Directedness is crucial to my account of powers from the inside. Therefore, I will give it significant attention.[4] Directedness is sometimes suggested as metaphorical.[5] However, I will clarify it and provide a plausible interpretation of what it means for a power to be directed. Along the way, I will pay significant attention to intentional inexistence since it goes hand in hand with directedness given that a state can be directed at a nonexistent state. Specifically, I will incorporate discussion of the mark of intentional inexistence into my criteria for evaluating interpretations of directedness.

If $XRY$ is the relation between X, the intentional state, and Y, the object of X's intentionality, then the directedness criterion says that X is directed toward Y (Bird 2007a: 119). This represents how both a thought is directed toward the object of the thought, and a power is directed toward the manifestation of the power (see Figure 4.2). If there were just one mark of PIT, it would be directedness. Directedness is an asymmetric, irreflexive, and intransitive relation between X and Y. Concerning asymmetry, X is directed toward Y, but Y is not directed toward X. Concerning irreflexiveness, although the directedness relation is generally irreflexive, there could be an exception if some powers are directed at their own stability.[6] Yet even then the manifestation might be interpreted as separate from the power itself. Concerning intransitivity, just because X is directed toward Y, and Y toward Z, does not entail that X is directed toward Z.[7]

---

[4] Directedness is not only essential to the Powers Model, but perhaps to the Neo-Humean Model as well because it is not clear that Neo-Humeans can avoid implicating notions of directedness. Not implausibly, the fundamental quiddities are disposed to gain different powers in different nomic environments (Chapter 1); and being disposed is being directed (Chapter 2). Furthermore, the description of the process of dispositional manifestation by the most famous Neo-Humean (Lewis 1997) is, surprisingly, teleological – and, therefore, directed in some sense (Kroll 2017: 15). It seems that we must posit directedness in some form in our theory of properties.

[5] See, for example, Coates (2021: 8349).

[6] This could be the case if there are "static" dispositions (Williams 2005).

[7] This compares favorably to Vetter (2015: 25) on the intransitivity of the potentiality relation that she posits as core to her account of modality (which is tightly connected to her account of powers).

$$X: \text{thought}_{\text{MIND}} \rightarrow [Y: \text{object}]$$
$$X: \text{power}_{\text{OBJECT}} \rightarrow [Y: \text{manifestation}]$$

Figure 4.2    The "objects" of directedness in thoughts and in powers ($\rightarrow$ represents directedness, [Y] represents Y's possible inexistence)

The terms "intentionality," "directedness," and "aboutness" are often used interchangeably. Although directedness is given as one mark among many, several philosophers emphasize it over the other marks, perhaps explaining why "directedness" is sometimes used synonymously with "intentionality" and "aboutness." Directedness is the major point of dispute in the debate between Place (1996, 1999) and Mumford (1999). Searle (1983: 3) seems to equate intentionality and directedness. Molnar (2003: 63) claims that just as mental states are directed to something "beyond themselves," physical powers possess "direction toward something outside themselves" – their proper manifestation – thus to reveal their full nature we must find what they are directed toward.

So, directedness is readily accepted as an especially important mark of intentionality. But the concept of directedness goes hand in hand with intentional inexistence, as Figure 4.2 indicates. Directedness is supposed to be "outcome-independent" (Manley and Wasserman 2017: 58) – implying that the manifestation need not exist – if it is to be a suitable concept for analyzing powers. To illustrate this, consider an example provided by Martin (1996: 74). There could be particles in our local region of spacetime that would interact with particles in some very distant region of spacetime if the distance were diminished sufficiently. Owing to the distance between them, these particles never meet in the course of cosmic history, so they never produce the manifestations they are capable of producing. The manifestations are inexistent. Yet these particles retain their potential to interact: They are directed toward various (merely possible) outcomes.[8] "Dispositional readinesses are for what might not exist or what might be blocked or spatiotemporally unavailable" (Martin 2008: 29). Being ready, in Martin's sense, is being directed toward possible outcomes.

The criterion of intentional inexistence says that though Y might not exist, X is still directed toward Y. This forms the heart of Brentano's thesis concerning what distinguishes mental from physical states, as discussed in Chapter 3. However, I contend that directedness is the more important

---

[8] See Jaworski (2016: 57) for further discussion.

criterion, for the following reasons. Provided we have an intuitive sense of directedness, then we know what it means for the object of that directedness to not exist. But the same does not hold true of intentional inexistence; just because we have a sense of the object's (or manifestation's) inexistence does not mean that we understand that something is directed toward that possible object. Moreover, if X could exist while Y does not, recognizing this as a case of intentional inexistence requires X's being directed toward Y. Therefore, the mark of directedness deserves the foremost attention in the evaluation of PIT.

Notice that directedness is a distinct phenomenon from direction of fit. Direction of fit concerns how mental states relate to or "fit" the world. Beliefs have a mind-to-world direction of fit: A belief aims to capture facts about the world. Desires have a world-to-mind direction of fit: A desire aims to make the world conform to the agent's wishes.[9] Directedness, by comparison, refers to the fact that these states – regardless of their specific direction of fit – are directed toward that which is to be "fitted" to the directed state. Powers are directed states, but they also have a direction of fit. In particular, powers more readily fit the model of desires with their world-to-mind direction of fit, because powers have a world-to-power direction of fit. I will address powers and direction of fit in more detail in Chapter 5.

One might object that directedness is too ambiguous to use as a mark of intentionality, therefore we cannot reliably infer that powers satisfy it. This objection is a call to construct a fair and reasonable interpretation of what "X pointing toward Y" is. Toward that end, I examine what it means for one state to be directed toward another state; the term "state" here is used broadly to include properties, state of affairs, events, and the like.

To aid in the quest for a theory of directedness, I propose four criteria: inexistence; broadness; informativity; and temporality. First, the notion of directedness should accommodate inexistence, as already discussed. Whatever notion of directedness is adopted must not require (but should allow) the existence of the state, Y, that X is directed toward. Second, the interpretation of directedness should accommodate directedness across a broad array of intentional states. The interpretation should not restrict directedness to psychological phenomena, thereby begging the question against physical

---

[9] More generally, cognitive states such as memories and perceptions (in addition to beliefs) have a mind-to-world direction of fit, while volitional states such as intentions-in-action and prior intentions (in addition to desires) have a world-to-mind direction of fit (Searle 2004: 170–171).

intentionality.[10] Third, the interpretation should be sufficiently informative, thus deepening our understanding of directedness and perhaps raising new questions about directedness and intentionality. Fourth, the interpretation should accommodate past, present, and future orientations of X toward Y. Directed states can be directed toward things in the past, present, or future; for example, beliefs about events occurring yesterday, today, and tomorrow. Likewise, powers can be directed toward manifestations now and in the future. Whether dispositions can be directed toward manifestations in the past is an open question; but if time can be reversed, objects can travel to the past, or backwards causation is possible, then it would appear that powers can be directed toward manifestations in the past.[11]

My plan going forward in this section is, first, to say what directedness is *not*. In particular, it is not spatial orientation. This might seem rather obvious but explaining why will reveal interesting aspects of directedness and represent a step forward in the dialectic. Then I will come to my positive view, which builds on and modifies the intentionality landscape explored by Molnar (2003). In short, I argue that directedness involves representationality. That is, directedness is a kind of representational state. Given that most if not all types of mental states are representational, this supports the claim that physical and mental directedness (and by extension, physical and mental intentionality) converge and should be considered identical when we compare physical powers to the relevant class of mental states. Ultimately, I argue that powers are a kind of nonconscious, representational state, equivalent to computational states or unconscious, representational mental states, that is, tacit beliefs and desires. So, physical intentionality = (a particular type of) mental intentionality.[12]

### What Directedness Is Not

Spatial orientation is both the least abstract and least metaphorical interpretation of directedness. According to this interpretation, X is spatially

---

[10] Furthermore, the interpretation should allow disposition-laden terms, for directedness might necessarily involve dispositionality. Although the purpose of the interpretation is to characterize directedness, not dispositionality, if some directed states are already dispositional states (e.g., dispositional beliefs) – and vice versa – this would strengthen the case for PIT.

[11] Powers could be directed toward past manifestations if time is asymmetrical, as Price (1996) argues. If so, this would increase the similarity between mental and physical forms of directedness.

[12] By analogy, if we claim that some hypothesized physical force is, in actuality, identical to the strong nuclear force, we are not claiming that the hypothesized force is identical to all of the standard four physical forces, just that it is identical to one type of physical force.

oriented toward Y. However, directedness should not be understood in terms of spatial orientation.

While dismissing animistic interpretation of directedness as implausible, Mumford (1999: 221) considers the spatial interpretation (although he rejects it).[13] It is worth examination to draw out important lessons for a plausible view of directedness. Mumford gives two examples of X being "directed toward" Y without X having a mind, which is important if we are going to apply directedness beyond the bounds of psychology. One example involves an arrow directed toward a particular target. Another involves a falling rock directed toward a road below it. In both cases, X is directed toward Y in a spatial sense: directedness is a spatial relationship grounded in the locations of X and Y and the physical orientation of X relative to Y. Is the mere spatial orientation between X and Y sufficient as an understanding of directedness? It is not.

The spatial orientation interpretation is applicable neither to mental states nor physical powers. In the former case (mental states), it is too narrow. There are clearly mental states that are not spatially directed toward their intentional objects in any sense. For instance, a general fear of snakes is not spatially oriented (though it might be when snakes appear in your view), and a belief in love's redemptive power is not either. In the

---

[13] Mumford (1999: 221) understands animism "as a purely physical thing striving towards some desired goal" such that physical objects act "in the way things with minds" do. (Some powers theorists, contra Mumford, are willing to attribute agency – if not animism per se – to powers. For example, Ellis (2013: 191) attributes a basic, limited, and naturalistic agency to fundamental particles, which I will discuss in Chapter 8.) To explain the appearance of directedness, Mumford (1999: 217) develops a functional theory of powers that avoids any sense of animism and preserves intentionality as the mark of the mental. The functionalist theory says that powers (or characterizations of such, at least) are a subset of the set of functions (or characterizations of such) and makes two main claims (1999: 223): first, it is a conceptual truth that powers causally mediate from stimuli to manifestations, and second, the type of power some property is consists in it having the relation specified in the first claim. In other words, a power is a *function from stimulus to manifestation* (my phrase). A power is an actual property that is functionally linked from a variety of stimuli to possible manifestations. Unlike the functional theory of powers proposed by Prior (1985), which sees powers as causally inefficacious, Mumford's functionalism maintains that powers are causally relevant to their manifestations. However, his functionalist account avoids reference to directedness, aims, strivings, or similar concepts (1999: 224). So, on this account, a power's functional nature is not an explanation of or support for it being directed, but I have doubts about that. Being directed and having aims in the agential sense – which Mumford conflates – are two different things. Agency is one feature of some mental states (or systems of mental states), not a definitive mark of intentionality. Intentionality or directionality might be required for agency, but not vice versa. Moreover, functions seem to have the very directedness that PIT attributes to powers. They are states directed toward their outcomes (manifestations). A function is, I suggest, a kind of directedness toward an output. Although Mumford intends otherwise, I suspect that he implicitly proposes a theory that assumes the directedness of powers.

latter case (physical powers), the interpretation is not informative enough. Although power-bearing objects might be spatially oriented – for example, a hammer (with the power to break glass, among other powers) might be spatially oriented toward a glass to the hammer's north – it is not sufficient to explain the nature of the power's directedness, that the hammer is disposed to break a glass *wherever* the glass is. It is not sufficient to explain why powers are generally *for* their manifestations, akin to how an algorithm is for a certain kind of output.

Moreover, spatial directedness does not capture the mark of intentional inexistence (Mumford 1999: 221), an essential feature of intentionality. That which the rock is falling toward (the ground) and that which the arrow is pointed toward (the target) exist. In fact, it seems necessary that these intentional objects exist, for if they did not, then the rock and arrow would not be spatially directed toward them. If X is spatially directed toward Y, intuitively Y should exist, otherwise X is not genuinely directed toward Y. However, the sense of directedness at play with intentional relationships of all sorts – whether they are powers or mental states – implies that the object of directedness might not exist.

Additionally, the spatial interpretation suggests only a present relationship between X and Y, so it does not satisfy the temporality criterion. An arrow is spatially directed only toward a present object, not an object of the past or the future. Although an arrow might be directed toward a future target, this is not spatial directedness and actually comes closer to the sense of directedness at play with powers and mental states. An arrow cannot be spatially directed toward a target existing in the past. So, this interpretation does not capture the idea that an intentional state can be directed toward past or future objects. In the case of mental states, you can desire some future state (something you expect) or something from the past (something you wish were still around). In the case of powers, a power is typically directed toward a future manifestation (that seems to be the essence of a power). But, interestingly, a power could perhaps be directed toward a past manifestation – supposing that there is no preferred direction of time (Price 1996).

Spatial directedness is, at best, only contingently and partially relevant to understanding directedness. While believing that the moon is full, I might be looking up at the moon – which is, suppose, part of the cause of my belief – but my *belief* itself is not spatially directed upward. Rather, my belief is directed toward the moon in the sense of trying to correctly fit or match a state of affairs in the world. Or my belief that tigers exist is not spatially directed toward any location, for I might not be thinking about tigers existing anywhere – just *that* they exist. I might, however, believe there is a tiger behind a curtain, and in some sense my belief is directed there, but this is only part of its directedness. Directedness has to do with the belief being about the tiger, the curtain, and a specific relation between the two, not only – and maybe not at all – about the spatial relation between the believer and the object. Similar comments apply to powers. Although powers might be directed toward outcomes at specific spatial locations, this is not essential to powers and not what they are essentially directed toward. A glass is disposed to break, not necessarily break at some given location or time, although that might contingently be the case. There is (or, at least, can be) a sort of indeterminacy about the *where* and *when* of directedness.

In sum, the spatial interpretation of directedness does not respect the intentional inexistence, broadness, or temporality criteria. It is relatively clear and somewhat informative because we have a secure grasp of what it means to be spatially oriented. However, spatial orientation is neither sufficient nor necessary to understand the directedness of intentional states.

### Directedness and Representationality

I will now argue that we should interpret directedness as a representational phenomenon: X is directed toward Y because X represents Y. Given that intentional states can represent features or objects in the world (as is the case with beliefs) or ways that an agent wants the world to be (as is the case with desires), we should take seriously the idea that directedness simply is a representational phenomenon. If this is correct, then to maintain PIT we need to accept that powers represent their manifestations. Let us explore this hypothesis.

X can represent Y without Y existing. Representation does not imply the existence of that which is represented. Therefore, this interpretation of directedness has no problem respecting the criterion of intentional inexistence. Furthermore, X can represent Y whether Y exists in the past, present, or future, just as directed states can be oriented toward past, present, or future objects (in the case of beliefs) or manifestations (in the case of powers). Therefore, the temporality criterion is respected. Intuitively we have a good sense of what it means for something (e.g., pictures, maps, words) to represent other things, despite the exact nature of representationality being a contentious point. Therefore, the informativity criterion is satisfied.

Although the representational interpretation of directedness respects intentional inexistence, is informative to the extent that we have a rough and ready grasp of representationality, and allows past, present, and future temporality, it might be somewhat narrow and thus not respect the broadness criterion. This is the case if there are nonrepresentational types of intentionality, a possibility which is discussed below. However, I will argue that the directedness of powers should be characterized in terms of representationality. I think this proposal illuminates PIT and dovetails nicely with the Informational Thesis (IT).

I will now take a close look at the categorization of intentionality developed by Molnar (2003: 81). Doing so provides a window into different ways of thinking about directedness. Molnar divides intentionality into two broad types, representational and nonrepresentational. Representational states are those, he thinks, that are subject to semantic evaluation because they convey information that can be accurate or inaccurate. Representations, at root, have semantic content or properties – that is, they have truth conditions or are truth evaluable. But representationality is not essential in general to intentionality on Molnar's view; it is a further feature that intentional states can have. Moreover, Molnar subdivides each of these types of intentionality into conscious and nonconscious intentionality.[14]

Given this schema, nonrepresentational conscious states include epiphenomenal states (if such states exist) and efficacious (nonepiphenomenal) mental states such as bodily sensations like pain. Nonrepresentational nonconscious states includes physical (nonmental) powers, including fundamental powers (such as mass and charge) and nonfundamental powers (such as fragility and elasticity). Representational conscious states include epiphenomenal states (if such states exist) and efficacious, conscious mental states *of humans*, such as beliefs and desires. Finally, representational nonconscious states include physical states like thoughts, memories, and calculations *of robots*. A summary of these categorizations can be seen in Figure 4.3.[15]

---

[14] Searle (1983: 2) also distinguishes intentionality from consciousness: there are conscious states without intentionality (e.g., elation) and intentional states without consciousness (an unconscious belief or tacit belief, i.e., "beliefs one has that one normally doesn't think about"). By contrast, Molnar only thinks that the latter states are possible; there are no conscious states without intentionality (although he thinks there are conscious states without representationality, e.g., pain).

[15] My table of Molnar's analysis replicates the most important content of Molnar's own diagram (2003: 81) but uses simpler formatting. Molnar divides conscious intentionality – whether representational or nonrepresentational, as seen in the first row ("Conscious") of Figure 4.3 – into

| | Representational | Nonrepresentational |
|---|---|---|
| Conscious | Conscious mental states of humans | Bodily sensations |
| Nonconscious | Thoughts, memories, calculations of robots | Physical powers |

Figure 4.3   Molnar's categories of intentionality

I propose several modifications to Molnar's categorizations as summarized in Figure 4.4.

| | Representational | Nonrepresentational |
|---|---|---|
| Conscious | Conscious mental states of humans **and animals** | Bodily sensations **(possibly)** |
| Nonconscious | Thoughts, memories, calculations of robots, **computers, and AI** **Tacit mental states of humans and animals** **Physical powers** | **(empty category)** |

Figure 4.4   Revised categories of intentionality (changes to Molnar's analysis are bolded)

Under "Representational Conscious" states, we should include nonhuman animals as well as humans since there is substantial neurobiological, behavioral, and evolutionary evidence that animals not only have representational states such as desires, but that in many cases they are consciously aware of these.[16] For example, cats sometimes consciously desire attention from their human friends (not as often as dogs do, because cats are more self-respecting than dogs). Cats do not think of their desires in linguistic terms, but neither do infants yet I am not prepared to deny that infants consciously desire attention from their parents or caretakers.

Under "Representational Nonconscious" states, I make several changes. First, I include not only nonconscious computational states of robots but also those of computers and artificial intelligence (AI) more

---

the *epiphenomenal* (which he leaves empty, and I leave out as an organizing category since it is not important to my discussion) and the *efficacious*. Since he leaves the epiphenomenal category empty, he seems to think all conscious states are efficacious. Also, concerning "Representational Nonconscious" states, it is easy to understand what Molnar means by "memories" and "calculations" of robots, but a little harder to understand exactly what he means by the term "thoughts." I believe he is simply referring to functional, causally relevant states of robots (and computers) aimed at various outcomes, akin to tacit (nonconscious) desires.

[16] Although it should be noted that there remains, and likely will always remain, debate about animal consciousness – including especially self-consciousness – amongst philosophers. However, I have no significant doubts that most kinds of animals are conscious beings.

generally – computer programs of various sorts, in both computers and robots, represent features of their environments[17,18] – as well as those of single-celled organisms whose computational states[19] arguably have representational content.

Continuing with changes under "Representational Nonconscious" states, I add tacit, nonconscious mental states. Humans (and probably nonhuman animals) have tacit, nonconscious mental states. In appropriate circumstances, these tacit states can become conscious. A tacit mental state is an intentional, representational state that, like a conscious mental state, is about something (e.g., the object of a belief or desire). At the same time, tacit mental states are powers (dispositions) because they are directed toward their possible manifestations, which are of two types: the state becoming conscious or the state becoming directly relevant to one of the agent's present actions. These two types of manifestations can occur together but that is not necessary. For one could become consciously aware of a desire without acting upon it, or a desire could affect one's actions without one becoming consciously aware of it. Furthermore, a belief *qua belief* (whether tacit or occurrent) is clearly for something beyond itself, just as the tacit (dispositional) belief *qua dispositional state* is for something beyond itself. In other words, tacit beliefs might be directed in two ways: The *contents* of tacit beliefs and desires are for something else (the object of belief or desire) and so directed like all other psychological intentional states; and they are *dispositional* states, and so directed toward their manifestations like other powers. So, in the case of tacit mental states we see the synthesis (indeed, identity) of psychological and physical intentionality: tacit mental states are clear cases of intentional (and representational) states that are simultaneously dispositional.[20] Since tacit mental states are simultaneously representational and powerful, it follows that at least *some* types of powers – tacit mental states – are in fact representational.[21]

---

[17] Tom Powers (2013: 230) argues that computers (and AI, robots, etc.) can have moral agency, which requires that they possess intentional states.

[18] It is not clear why Molnar lists robots specifically, given that computers in general have nonconscious computational states. It is true that "robots" acquire perceptual information from sensory devices as they move about their environments, thus they have nonconscious perceptual states, but computers in general can also have such states if connected to the appropriate input devices (e.g., cameras, microphones).

[19] Ehrenfeucht et al. (2004) provide a detailed analysis of the computational nature of gene assembly in ciliates, a type of single-celled animal possessing cilia.

[20] For discussion of mental states as dispositional, see Schwitzgebel (2001, 2002) and Gozzano (2020).

[21] In other words, in tacit mental states, representationality and dispositionality definitely converge. The contents of a tacit mental state S signify a (possible or actual) state-of-affairs outside S. And

I aim to show that physical (nonmental) powers are also representational. Since, contra Molnar, I argue that powers are representational, this leaves the "Nonrepresentational Nonconscious" category empty and groups powers together with tacit mental states and computational states. Powers are similar to computational states in two ways: First, they are entirely nonconscious; second, they represent their possible manifestations or outcomes akin to how computational states represent outcomes (i.e., the outcomes of sequences of instructions).

The powers-as-representational claim, I argue, better aligns powers and mental states in the landscape of intentionality. But is this a better approach than Molnar's claim that powers possess a primitive directedness and occupy a unique place in the landscape? While all theories have some primitive elements and accepting them is certainly not incoherent, in this case I think it is better to avoid accepting directedness as primitive.[22] Doing so unnecessarily creates a fundamental divide in reality between physical and mental intentionality, which runs counter to the motivation behind PIT. There are already divides between physical and mental phenomena, including consciousness, perception, and metacognition. If we can avoid carving out another divide – regarding how intentionality, and more specifically directedness, are conceived – that would help unify our conception of nature.[23] My powers-as-representational claim eliminates the need to climb some rungs of the ladder from physical intentionality to mental intentionality.

Before examining the relationship between representationality and directedness (and intentionality more generally), a further clarification is

---

the dispositional nature of S is directed toward manifesting: If it is a belief, the manifestation is either the belief becoming conscious or otherwise becoming subconsciously active in one's decision-making (or both); if it is a desire, the manifestation is the desire becoming conscious or otherwise motivating one to seek the object of said desire (or both).

[22] It is useful to distinguish "primitive" from "undefined." By the former I mean metaphysically irreducible or basic; if X is primitive feature, it is not grounded by further features. But it might yet be definable because it can be usefully described or characterized in order better understand it. Something undefinable means it is not subject to further conceptual analysis. In this light, my characterization of physical intentionality is not undefined since I take the marks of intentionality to, in effect, define the notion (if the marks do not fully define physical intentionality, they at least partially define it). At the same time, I also do not necessarily think it is primitive, as Molnar does, given that I argue it can be assimilated under representationality, a phenomenon I assume (along with, apparently, Molnar) is not primitive.

[23] Moreover, we have little grasp of intentionality except as found in philosophy of mind, therefore the idea that physical intentionality is "*an undefined primitive* of the theory of properties" (Molnar 2003: 81) is unhelpful in understanding the relation between a power and its nonexistent manifestation (McKitrick 2021: 291). It is better, because more informative, to characterize powers' directedness as representational.

needed. It is possible (though far from certain) to have intentionality and directedness without representation, as exemplified under "Nonrepresentational Conscious" by bodily sensations in Figures 4.3 and 4.4. Molnar (2003: 81) argues that, like bodily sensations, physical powers are nonrepresentational intentional states. But since I categorize powers as representational – though, as I will show, nonpropositional – this means that the category "Nonrepresentational Nonconscious" is empty and might as well be eliminated. This is conceptually beneficial because creating a special subcategory of intentionality for powers makes them outliers and more mysterious. The same could be said for bodily sensations like pain, however we already have good reason to suppose that pains (even if not representational) are indeed conscious, intentional, mental states.

On my view, physical powers – "physical" meaning nonmental – are intentional, nonconscious, representational yet nonpropositional states. They represent and are thus directed toward their manifestations; their informational content represents possible stimuli and circumstances of manifestation, as I will explain in Chapter 6. This means that, if we restrict the domain of mental states to tacit, nonconscious representational states, physical and mental intentionality share all relevant features – except that mental representational states are typically considered to be propositional in nature, which I will explore in due course.

Again, it is instructive to consider Molnar's discussion of representation and meaning.[24] Perhaps, he suggests (2003: 71), the only way to maintain a naturalistic explanation of directedness is for the directed state to represent what it is directed toward. If representation requires reference to something beyond the representation, does this mean that a theory of meaning is needed? If so, this could defeat PIT (2003: 72): "Clearly a theory of meaning cannot be stretched to cover physical powers because it is impossible to see physical powers as semantic properties. Solubility has no *intelligible content* that represents dissolving. An electric charge is not *about* its manifestation" (if "about" indicates propositional aboutness). Therefore, according to the representational cum semantic point of view – according to which semantically evaluable representationality is the limit of intentionality (thus directedness) – powers cannot be intentional.

---

[24] One way of understanding representations is pictorially. However, the pictorial view of representation – as presented, for instance, by Wittgenstein (1922) in his *Tractatus Logico-Philosophicus* – is no longer seen as plausible (Molnar 2003: 71). Furthermore, the pictorial view implies that representationality requires phenomenology, which is highly implausible and, when applied to powers, begs the question against any view that powers have representational directedness.

One way around this problem is to drive a wedge between representationality and intentionality. Molnar (2003: 72) attempts to do this by arguing for "states or properties that are (a) mental, (b) non semantic, that is, not representational in the relevant sense, but (c) intentional." In other words, some mental states are "intentional but meaningless (nonrepresentative)" (2003: 72). Therefore, powers can be assimilated into the class of nonrepresentational, yet intentional, states. This implies that powers are directed but not in virtue of being representational in the semantic sense. Molnar is equating meaningfulness – understood to require propositional content – and representationality, something I will question. But first let us follow Molnar's reasoning.

There is conceptual room to argue that perceptual states – which are quite clearly intentional states – are not wholly representational. Molnar (2003: 72) suggests that the intentionality of perceptions cannot be fully explained by representational content. If the exact same informational content can come from two different types of perception (e.g., seeing and touching) yet there is something distinctive about those two ways of perceiving, they must involve more than representational content. For example, touching and seeing a round object can equally inform *you that the object is round* (other information might of course be transmitted as well) yet there is something inherently distinctive about the intentionality of seeing compared to the intentionality of touching the object. Molnar does not assert what this distinctive feature is. But it should have something to do with what makes vision, audition, touch, and so on the distinctive sensory modalities that they are. For instance, they issue distinctive sensory information: visual information, auditory information, tactile information, and they do so with a distinctive raw feel of what it is like to see or hear or touch something. Despite this argument, Molnar (2003: 73) acknowledges that "perception is overwhelmingly representational" and remains subject to "semantical or quasi-semantical evaluation" despite having some extra-semantic properties. I tend to agree. Perception seems so strongly representational that the burden of proof lies with those who claim that perception is not fully explainable in representational terms.

Moreover, Molnar (2003: 74–80) suggests that bodily sensations are intentional yet nonrepresentational states. He argues that although pains are intentional states, they are not representational because they are not semantically evaluable.[25] Most importantly, "The directedness of sensations

---

[25] So, for Molnar (2003: 80), there are two kinds of intentionality: that of the rational mind (representational) and that of the sentient mind (nonrepresentational).

to their intentional object cannot be understood in terms of meaning at all" and "*In this respect* there is no difference between sensations and purely physical powers" (2003: 80).[26] Therefore, we should group pains and powers together as nonrepresentational intentional states (the former mental, the latter physical).

Whether or not representationality is essential to intentionality – and whether or not Molnar is correct about bodily states being nonrepresentational[27] – I think that there is a solid case to make for the claim that the directedness of powers *is* representational. This, I contend, should be the default view about powers' directedness.[28] I take representationality to illuminate the fact of a property's directedness. More specifically, if powers are representational, this helps explain their directedness. Otherwise, along with Molnar we might take powers' directedness as primitive. But if we do so, it makes powers' directedness more mysterious. This, in turn, conflicts with the explanatory motivations for PIT. Why do powers do what they do? As I am arguing, part of the explanation is that they are physical intentional states directed at their manifestations. The other part has to do with their informational content (discussed in Chapter 6).

### Is Representationality Propositional?

One might argue that if powers' directedness is representational, then powers have propositional content; however, powers do not have propositional content; therefore, they cannot be representational. In response, I

---

[26] Specifically, the directedness of sensation is not explainable by reference to either natural or nonnatural meaning. Molnar employs a distinction between natural and nonnatural meaning made by Grice (1989: 213–215). Natural meaning is exemplified, suggests Grice, by "those spots mean measles." The idea of "means" here is that there is a real, ontological relation between spots and measles. Nonnatural meaning is exemplified by terms in ordinary uses of our language. The most important distinguishing feature is that natural meaning cannot misrepresent whereas nonnatural meaning does allow misrepresentation. Grice (1989: 215) claims that the distinction covers "most cases" of meaning.

[27] Perhaps bodily sensations such as pains and hungers *are* representational. One might argue that pains represent the cause or source of the pain, even if the cause is not real (thus satisfying intentional inexistence) due to some sort of psychophysical manipulation. Their representing (or misrepresenting) is their pointing or being directed toward the cause(s) of the sensation. However, in defense of Molnar's claim, although pain has a cause, so do beliefs (classic representational states) yet beliefs need not represent their cause. For example, if one believes that extraterrestrials exist, the belief represents "that extraterrestrials exist," but their existence did not cause this; rather, too many science fiction films did. I remain ambivalent about the representationality of bodily sensations for now. Since it is not crucial to my project, I let them stand as possible nonrepresentational conscious states.

[28] In his characterization of PIT, Kroll (2017: 32) implies that this should be the default view as well.

suggest that there is logical and metaphysical room for nonpropositional representationality. If so, we can assimilate powers to the class of nonpropositional representational states.

So, is all representationality propositional? That is, is all representationality of a kind that requires the existence of a proposition of the form such as "that *x* is P" or "that *x* exists"? This view, propositionalism, tends to assume that "intentional attitude" (where such attitudes are traditionally classified as representational) and "propositional attitude" are interchangeable (Grzankowski and Montague 2018: 1). But this is not necessarily the case.

Brentano (1966) did not hold propositionalism about paradigmatic representational states such as beliefs and judgments. Rather, such intentional attitudes are *objectual* attitudes, not propositional attitudes (Kriegel 2018: 198). A belief state, which represents a state of affairs, is not a belief-that *x* but a belief-in *x* (this is Kriegel's way of formulating Brentano's idea). In particular, "Judgments are always directed at some sort of individual object, but present-as-existent/nonexistent that object [...] It is never any entity of a different ontological category, such as a proposition or a state of affairs" (2018: 198). Consider the common paraphrasing of "S believes that *x* exists" into "S believes in *x*" (2018: 198). According to Kriegel's interpretation, this gets the order wrong: "S believes in *x*," the objectual formulation, is primary. So, what does this mean for powers? The objectual view is akin to the intuitive understanding of powers as "power *for* such-and-such manifestation" not "power *that* such-and-such manifestation occurs." I am not, however, suggesting that powers should be modeled exactly on Brentano's objectual view of intentional states. The point is that there are viable options beyond propositionalism in the debate about the nature of representationality. If belief states can be nonpropositional yet representational, then powers can be too. The objectual model provides one possibility, where the "object" is the manifestation.

Moreover, it has been suggested that some mental states are nonpropositional yet representational. Searle (2018) argues that although large classes of intentional states such as desires and perceptions are propositional – where a proposition is not essentially linguistic but could be, for instance, visual (2018: 263) – some intentional states have no propositional content. His example is boredom: although sometimes boredom can have propositional content, as when you are "bored by such and such a fact about" something (a person or object), sometimes you find a "person or object boring *tout court*" (2018: 270). You are simply bored by a particular movie, with no related beliefs or desires that give the state of boredom propositional content. Yet it is an intentional state because it is directed at the thing that bores you. If some select mental states are intentional yet nonpropositional, this makes room for powers to occupy the same space – intentional yet nonpropositional states – on the physical side of reality.

Still, it is not clear whether boredom, in its nonpropositional instances, remains representational, which is crucial to the position I am carving out for powers. Searle's (2018: 266) general position seems to be that propositions are what represent: to represent is to be propositional, whether linguistic or visual or some other sense of propositional. So, although Searle's example shows that directedness (as the key feature of intentionality) can be nonpropositional, if this implies that it is also nonrepresentational then it does not help my argument. However, I think that it is plausible that being in a state of boredom *tout court*, though nonpropositional, still represents the object of boredom; it just does not represent any specific fact or property of that object. The state of boredom is directed at the boring movie and represents that movie, but there is no propositional content involved (that is how boring you find it).[29]

A further possibility comes closer to the kind of representationality I suspect powers' directedness exemplifies. Camp (2018) suggests that maps are representational but not propositional. They represent various geographical or related features but do not carry propositional content. They show relationships between locations on the map and indicate possible routes (e.g., you can take this or that road to get from point A to B) as well as necessary restraints (e.g., if you are at A, you must go East to arrive at point B, provided you avoid the ocean), thus capturing modal considerations. The representations carried by maps can be interpreted propositionally for epistemic purposes, as any representation can, but maps are not inherently propositional. If this is correct, it opens logical room for physical states like powers to be representational.

I contend that physical powers carry representational, nonpropositional, nonconscious, map-like information for their potential manifestations. Although this representational information can be captured by counterfactual statements, this does not mean that it is inherently propositional. So far, I have shown that the representational thesis about powers' directedness is coherent; in Chapter 6, I will further address how powers represent.

---

[29] Readers can insert a movie that they find particularly boring in order to make the example compelling.

I have argued that powers share the essentials marks of directedness and intentional inexistence with thoughts. In the rest of this chapter, I discuss what I consider the third and last essential mark of intentionality: intentional indeterminacy.

## 4.3   Intentional Indeterminacy

Intentional indeterminacy is the idea that Y, which X is directed toward, might be ontologically indeterminate or vague. You might believe that there is a beer on the table without thinking about or knowing the kind of beer (IPA, porter, etc.) or its ABV (alcohol by volume) percentage. You can be thinking of Napoleon at the moment of the first shot at Waterloo without thinking of the number of hairs on Napoleon's head, although there is a definite number at that moment (Bird 2007a: 120).

This mark has the potential to mislead if it is characterized in terms of the indeterminacy of Y. To see why, consider cases where Y exists and cases where Y does not exist. In cases where Y exists (i.e., where intentional inexistence does *not* hold), Y is not ontologically indeterminate. Even though Y is not ontologically indeterminate in these cases, intentional indeterminacy might still occur. Despite Y's existence, X (the intentional state) might indeterminately represent Y. For example, one's representation of Napoleon is indeterminate as to the actual number of hairs on his head. Now, consider cases where Y does not exist, such as false beliefs or unfulfilled desires. In these cases, X represents Y as being some way, but the representation might be incomplete and therefore indeterminate – just as is possible in the cases where Y exists. The upshot is that indeterminacy, if it occurs, lies in *how* the intentional state, X, represents Y. That is, vagueness is representational vagueness; it is not on the side of the thing represented but on the side of the thing that represents – the mental state or the physical power.[30]

The implication of PIT is that physical powers also display indeterminacy or vagueness toward their manifestations. That is, the manifestation of a power can be indeterminate in situations when the manifestation has not yet occurred – keeping in mind that a power's manifestation might not ever occur. For example, consider a glass pane. Just because the pane is disposed to break and this must occur at a specific time and place in a specific way, does not imply that the glass pane is disposed to break at any

---

[30]  I am not denying, however, that there can be ontologically indeterminate states.

specific time and place; that depends on a number of situational factors (Place 1996: 104). So, there is some indeterminacy in where, when, and how it will break and the pane's fragility – the power – does not represent just one specific time, place, or method of breaking. Yet the pane remains directed at breaking (among other types of manifestations toward which the pane is directed – for example, permitting light to enter, dampening sound waves). When, where, and how this breaking will occur, if it does, depends on environmental factors and the cooperation of the relevant mutual manifestation partner.

Some argue that the parallel between the indeterminacy of mental states and that of powers is illusory (Bird 2007a: 124). The illusion is explained by the fact that when the stimulus conditions and circumstances of a power's manifestation are fully specified, the power's manifestation is fully determinate. There might be infinitely many determinate ways for a vase to break but it is indeterminate which way it will break when the stimulus and circumstances are unspecified (or underspecified). However, when fully specified, the power's "intention" toward its manifestation is determinate. To prove the intentional indeterminacy of powers, there would have to be a power directed toward a single, indeterminate manifestation, not a power directed toward multiple determinate manifestations (one of which is to be determinately selected by the circumstances of manifestation) (2007a: 124). Otherwise, there is no vagueness in the power's directedness: it remains directed toward its various potential instances of breaking. If powers are multitrack, then each power determinately and equally represents all of its potential manifestations. Which one occurs depends on many factors. This is unlike mental states; even though mental states represent their objects, they do not always determinately, precisely represent them.

Despite Bird's criticism, some powers display indeterminacy. Molnar (2003: 64) calls attention to a specific class of powers, propensities, and argues that the parallel to intentional indeterminacy here is stronger; but to work, the example needs to be a "physical analogue" to the fuzziness sometimes found in mental states. We should bear in mind that the fuzziness should be independent of description since we are inquiring about vagueness in the representation, not the linguistic description of said representation. Molnar claims that the propensity for atomic decay is indeterminate. For example, a radium atom is disposed to decay in one year with probability .04. The implication is that there is "no definite moment within the ensuing 2,130 years" when the power to disintegrate will occur, therefore "The manifestation-outcome is *de re* indeterminate as to timing"

(2003: 64). This is a promising example because it intuitively feels indeterministic and it concerns a fundamental (or near-fundamental) physical power.

In describing the example, Molnar speaks of the object – the manifestation – being fuzzy. But I emphasize that, keeping consistent with my point at the start of this section, that the directed state, X, can be indeterminate in its representation of Y. Whether the manifestation itself of a propensity is fuzzy or not, the representation (the state of directedness) is fuzzy because it does not pick out a specific time or place for the decay, just as one's thought about Napoleon is fuzzy or incomplete.

However, does Molnar's example genuinely support the case for PIT? Bird (2007a: 124) thinks not. Unlike the vagueness of thoughts – if I *expect* a phone call "soon" this indicates "a vague time-span" (Molnar 2003: 62–63) – physical propensities are not vague at all, just indeterminate, argues Bird. In response to Bird, I do not see a significant difference between vagueness and indeterminacy. Vagueness is lack of precision. And if a time, location, or conception are imprecise, then they are indeterminate, and vice versa. The vagueness of the timespan referred to by "soon" simply reflects its indeterminate nature. Likewise, the timespan of atomic decay is vague due to its indeterminacy. If one expects the phone call *soon* and if the radium will decay *sometime* in the next 2,130 years, when exactly those events happen is indeterminate and vague. Although only some powers are propensities, this at least shows that powers can display intentional indeterminacy, thus clearly showing the applicability of this mark.

Expectation (as in expecting a phone call soon) is a kind of prediction, thus a *belief* about the future, which displays indeterminacy. However, *desires* are better analogues to powers, as I have already argued in Section 3.4, and they better display the kind of indeterminacy found in powers: a desire can be for some outcome without being for a specific outcome.[31] For example, suppose you want dark chocolate; sometimes you care only that you get dark chocolate, not a specific brand or style (70 percent or 80 percent will do equally well, thank you). Similarly, a power can be for some manifestation without being for a specific outcome. In the desire case, a specific outcome is determined by various specific circumstances

---

[31]  Place (1996: 103) also suggests that desires are a better case of mental intentional states to compare with physical powers – for the object of desires is "something which positively does not yet exist and may never do so," yet the directed state (intentional state) remains directed toward its object, that is, the manifestation of the desire.

outside the control of the agent; a similar point holds for powers, that is, the outcome is determined by powerful partners as well as environmental circumstances outside the "control" of the power in question.

This concludes my application of what I consider to be the essential marks of intentionality – in order of priority: directedness, intentional inexistence, intentional indeterminacy – to physical powers. Now I turn to additional marks of intentionality as well as some implications of, and objections to, PIT.

# CHAPTER 5

# A Defense of Physical Intentionality
## Additional Marks and Objections

## 5.1 Linguistic Marks: Referential Opacity and Lack of Truth Import

In the previous chapter, I discussed the essential or most central marks of intentionality: directedness, intentional inexistence, and intentional indeterminacy. Now I will discuss some additional marks: linguistic marks, unique intentional objects, impossible intentional objects, extrinsicness, direction of causation, and direction of fit (see Figure 4.1 in Chapter 4 for all of the marks). The nonlinguistic additional marks carry significant implications for understanding powers so I will spend considerable time with these, whereas the linguistic marks carry less significance so I will spend little time with these (in the rest of this section). Later in the chapter, I will address several objections to PIT.

A pair of linguistic marks are part of the original set of five marks. The first is the mark of referential opacity, that within an intensional (with an "s" not a "t") context, there is referential opacity concerning X (an intentional state), that is, lack of truth-preservation between co-referring phrases.[1] The second is the mark of lack of truth import, that the truth or falsity of an embedded declarative sentence, ascribing X to someone, does not turn on whether one denies or asserts that ascription. These features concern what we can call S-intensionality to clearly distinguish it from T-intensionality (Place 1996). S-intensional features of language have a long discussion in the history of the philosophy of mind and language.[2]

I maintain that the linguistic marks are derivative and not essential to intentionality. That is, the intentionality of sentences – sentences being the object of concern for the S-intensionality criteria – are not intrinsic but derived forms of intentionality (Searle 1984: 5, 27). Therefore,

---

[1] The term "referential opacity" derives from Quine (1980).
[2] For example, see Quine (1980) and Chisholm (1957).

T-intentionality is what matters to evaluating PIT, not S-intensionality. Language is a derivative form of intentionality because its source is in the T-intentionality of the mind. Beliefs, perceptions, desires, judgments, and so on are the original intentional states from which language acquires its intentionality. Furthermore, sentences are representations of states that are themselves representations of their conditions of satisfaction (Searle 2004: 176). Therefore, S-intensional phenomena, which strictly pertain to symbolic representations such as sentences, are derived from intentional features. For these reasons, S-intensionality is not an essential mark to consider in making the case for PIT.

These points minimize the importance of the linguistic marks for evaluating PIT's veracity, where the concern is whether powers are intrinsically intentional in the way that mental states are. One could still utilize the S-intensional criteria to distinguish psychological intentionality as a different *subtype* of intentionality – one that can underpin and create S-intensional states – compared to physical intentionality. But they are not fundamentally different. If both physical and mental intentionality meet the essential marks of intentionality, as I have argued, then PIT prevails.[3]

## 5.2   Unique and Impossible Intentional Objects

There are two marks of intentionality that neither PIT supporters nor critics usually address: the claims that there can be unique intentional objects and impossible intentional objects. These criteria can potentially demarcate physical and mental intentionality while adding further depth to the discussion of PIT.[4]

### Unique Intentional Objects

Martin and Pfeifer (1986: 551–552), searching for a criterion beyond the standard marks of intentionality, suggest that mental intentionality permits unique intentional objects whereas physical intentional states do not.

---

[3] For further discussion of the linguistic marks, see Place (1996), Molnar (2003: 64–66), and Bird (2007a: 121–123). Place effectively rejects the linguistic marks as legitimate guides to T-intentionality because they involve only S-intensionality. Molnar and Bird both think that the marks are relevant, but whereas Molnar argues that physical powers satisfy these marks, Bird argues that they do not. I side with Place and Molnar.

[4] Molnar (2003: 66) explores these as a potential objection to PIT: If the standard marks of intentionality (the original five) do not delineate powers from intentional states, then perhaps there is some further mark, such as unique or impossible intentional objects.

An intentional agent might perceive and thus form a representation of a particular object at a particular time and place. The agents see or hear this particular, unique object, presented in exactly this way, such that only that particular object can satisfy the intentional object's conditions of satisfaction.

However, a purely physical device can have unique intentional objects as well. Molnar (2003: 69–70) suggests that a palm print recognition device, which possesses a power to recognize a particular palm, has as its unique intentional object the very hand that has imprinted on the device. We might also envision a fingerprint recognition device, like the ones many smartphones have. The question of consciousness is irrelevant: In Martin and Pfeifer's example, the causal work is done by "strictly causal elements (memory traces, recall, reidentification)" (Molnar 2003: 70). Besides, there are nonconscious, mental, representational states – that is, tacit mental states (see Section 4.2).

Given that a physical system can be directed at a particular, unique palm, I conclude that unique intentional objects do not provide a road-block to PIT.

### Impossible Intentional Objects

What about impossible intentional objects? Mental states can be directed toward impossible or contradictory objects. For example, one can have a (false) belief that square circles exist (either as abstract or concrete objects) and one can wish for impossible things (that it would rain and not rain right here and now). But – the argument goes – while mental states can have impossible intentional objects, physical states cannot, thus physical and mental intentionality are different.

Is this a good way to defend Brentano's thesis? Molnar (2003: 66–68) argues not, but in my estimate does not go far enough. He claims that some – perhaps most – types of psychological states *cannot* have impossible intentional objects. For instance, one cannot hear notes that are simultaneously above and below some pitch value, and one cannot feel a pain of quality Q and intensity 1 in a location, while also feeling a pain of quality Q but intensity 2 in the same location (2003: 67). Despite these instances of intentional states that cannot have impossible intentional objects, Molnar worries that the general phenomenon of impossible intentional objects indeed suggests that mental and physical intentionality are not identical, only analogous (as discussed in Section 3.3, there is some ambiguity in Molnar's discussion as to whether he accepts PIT as a claim of identity or analogy between mental and physical intentionality). Although I agree with Molnar that the criterion of impossible intentionality objects is not a sufficient line of demarcation, I disagree with the suggestion that it blocks PIT (Identity).

There seem to be various nontrivial, *un*manifestable powers belonging to ordinary objects. Jenkins and Nolan (2012: 743–747) discuss several plausible cases.[5] For example, in scientific reasoning we often idealize conditions to study and establish fundamental principles. It can be useful to know how a car will skid on a frictionless surface or how predator populations will change in response to ideal prey populations (2012: 746). Even if these idealizations represent nomically impossible situations (because there are no actually frictionless surfaces and rabbit populations do not increase by .1), the powers posited behind these idealizations are still epistemically useful. Indeed, Jenkins and Nolan suggest, and I am inclined to agree, that they are true: that the car *is* disposed to skid on frictionless surfaces even though this is a nomically impossible manifestation, or that that a rabbit population *is* disposed to increase by .1 rabbits even though this is metaphysically impossible (2012: 746). (The former example is more intuitive to me, however.) Given PIT, I would claim that these powers are directed toward impossible intentional objects: They are unmanifestable because their manifestations could not ever occur, yet these powers *are* directed toward the relevant manifestations. Therefore, the mark of impossible intentional objects does not block PIT.

It should be noted that most intentional states – mental or physical – do not have unique or impossible intentional objects, and some of the cases discussed seem somewhat fringe. So, I do not hold these marks to be essential to physical intentionality. Yet, given that there are plausible cases of unique and impossible manifestations that powers are directed toward, physical intentionality keeps pace with mental intentionality on these marks.

## 5.3    Extrinsicness

Bird (2007a: 120) uses two additional marks of intentionality to challenge PIT: extrinsicness and direction of causation. Are these marks essential to intentionality? I think that they are of less concern than the three marks

---

[5] They also discuss cases of unmanifestable agential powers, but since physical intentionality is the focus here only the powers of ordinary objects are relevant.

discussed in Chapter 4 but of more concern than the marks discussed in Sections 5.1 and 5.2. Either way, I will have strong criticisms as I evaluate extrinsicness in this section and direction of causation in the next section. These criticisms, I believe, reveal fascinating facets of the metaphysics of powers.

The first of Bird's two additional marks is that the objects of direct-edness are extrinsic properties.[6] Call this mark *extrinsicness*. It is taken from externalism in the philosophy of mind – that the relevant inten-tional objects are often outside or external to the mind, hence are extrinsic properties – although this is a controversial thesis (Mendola 2008). The extrinsicness mark says that the property picked out by *RY* in the X*RY* relation – where X is the directed, intentional state – is extrinsic (Bird 2007a: 120). In response, I argue that powers can qualify as extrinsic in some cases. And they do so in two senses of "extrinsic," thus covering two interpretations of Bird's point.

Some background first. Bird (2007a: 29–30) holds that sparse powers (or "potencies" as he calls them) are necessarily intrinsic,[7] while allowing that abundant (nonnatural) powers can be extrinsic as McKitrick (2003a) argues. The sparse powers include, at least, all the fundamental powers.

In contrast to his view that all sparse powers are intrinsic, Bird (2007a: 120) assumes that the "external/extrinsic property of thought is irreduc-ible" (i.e., he accepts externalism in the philosophy of mind). Alluding to famous externalist cases, he observes that

> I may be thinking of Napoleon but my swamp-man molecular twin is not. The semantic value of Oscar's water-thoughts differ from the semantic value of Twin-Oscar's twater-thoughts even though those persons are internally identical. Their thoughts are directed onto different kinds. Since the two subjects are intrinsically alike but their thoughts have different intentions, it follows that in such cases the intentional character of thought is an extrinsic property of the subject. (Bird 2007a: 120)[8]

---

[6] A property token, F, is intrinsic just in case object *a*'s possessing F is ontologically independent of any property or property-complex of another distinct, existent object *b*. A property token, F, is extrinsic just in case object *a*'s possessing F ontologically depends on some property or property-complex of a distinct, existent object *b*.

[7] Bird (2007a: 29) affirms the claim of Lewis (1997: 148) that "If two things (actual or merely possible) are exact intrinsic duplicates (and if they are subject to the same laws of nature) then they are disposed alike."

[8] Putnam (1973, 1975) forms the twin-earth thought experiment and Davidson (1987) forms the swamp-man thought experiment. It is assumed here that externalism is true. Although it is more popular than internalism (Bourget and Chalmers 2014), it has faced substantial, deserving criticism (e.g., Mendola 2008).

The property picked out by *R*Y is extrinsic (2007a: 120). For any agent, S, if X is one of S's beliefs (to focus on a particular type of thought), then X itself is internal to S's mind but X is directed toward, or about, Y. Since a physically identical duplicate, S*, might have beliefs directed onto different kinds and objects than S, the content of the belief is extrinsic (let us ignore cases where X is directed onto itself). If PIT holds, then (sparse) powers should possess a similar extrinsic character, which according to Bird is false. Before evaluating Bird's argument, I will explain two senses of extrinsicness.

There are two ways to conceive of extrinsicness in evaluating PIT. First – what Bird seems to have primarily in mind – X might be extrinsic in the sense that the property Y toward which X is directed is external to or not contained by X itself, thus the contents of X are extrinsic. Second, X might be extrinsic in the sense that the property picked out by Y serves as the ontological grounds for X, thus the grounds of X do not consist entirely of intrinsic features of the agent that bears X.[9] It will be shown that Bird intends both conceptions of extrinsicness, that there is an important difference between the two conceptions, and that it is plausible that powers and beliefs display remarkable similarities on *both* conceptions.

The swamp-man and twin-earth examples suggest that beliefs are directed toward things in an agent's environment (Y is part of the agent's environment), indicating that Bird intends to capture at least the first conception of extrinsicness. However, he also affirms the reality of extrinsic, abundant powers (Bird 2007a: 125). This elicits a different sense of extrinsicness having to do with the ontological grounds of a property's instantiation. Some powers of objects are extrinsic because their instantiation depends on, or is grounded in, properties of the objects' environments: for example, the weight (power to depress a scale) of an object depends on its surrounding gravitational field (Yablo 1999) and a key's power to open a door depends on the door's lock being for that key (McKitrick 2003a).

Although Bird agrees with McKitrick (2003a) that there are extrinsic powers, he does not think that there are any extrinsic *sparse* powers, thus preserving his defense of sparse powers against PIT. Nonetheless, he apparently assumes that if any sparse powers exemplify McKitrick's parameters for extrinsicness, then the mark of extrinsicness would be

---

[9] See Bauer (2011: 82–86) for discussion of the distinction between a property being extrinsic and being extrinsically grounded (in a nonintentionality context).

satisfied. Moreover, in accepting the possibility of the extrinsic grounding of powers, Bird effectively accepts that X might be grounded by properties extrinsic to that which has X, where the extrinsic grounding properties might or might not be the state Y toward which X is directed.

I will assess PIT in terms of both conceptualizations of extrinsicness, as summarized below.

Extrinsic-D: That toward which a power is *directed* is an extrinsic property.

Extrinsic-G: A power is *grounded* extrinsically.

Extrinsic-D and Extrinsic-G occur together in some cases but in other cases come apart. Extrinsic-G obtains when powers are extrinsic because their instantiation requires a property, or set of properties, residing in the environment of the power-bearing object. Yet these grounding properties are *not* necessarily Y toward which X (the power) points, as in Extrinsic-D.

For example, in environment 1, a key, K, is directed toward opening a door; but in environment 2, K is not so directed because the lock in the door is replaced. The lock grounds K's power to open the door, and that is why the power is extrinsic. But K is not directed toward opening the lock, or at least not *only* toward opening the lock; for it is also directed toward opening the *door*, one of its other possible manifestations. It is also directed toward many other possible manifestations: fitting on a key ring, scratching a car, breaking a thread, and so on. A second example: The weight of an object, *a*, is extrinsically grounded by *a* residing in its gravitational field, yet *a*'s weight is not directed toward the gravitational field; it is directed at depressing weight scales, and so on.

Turning to thoughts, when Extrinsic-D holds, the property, Y, that a belief, X, is directed toward might not be the grounds of X if, for instance, the agent comes to have the belief based on inferences concerning data not directly connected to Y. For example, a scientist might come to believe that some entity exists based on consequences of an accepted theory, although the entity does not in fact exist (consider the history of phlogiston, for instance). As a second example, an agent acquires a belief that she wants to travel in space, caused by stargazing or dreaming. This belief is not directed toward stars or dreams but is directed toward traveling in space.

Given these examples, it is possible that an agent makes an inference or, through experience of external things, comes to believe something, yet the object of the belief is not itself the grounds for the belief. This is similar to a power being grounded in something in its environment, yet directed toward something else, as in the cases of the key and weight discussed above. Thus, there is a distinction between Extrinsic-D and Extrinsic-G.

Now I will argue that powers indeed satisfy Extrinsic-D. If X points or is directed toward its intentional object, Y, which X does not contain in itself, then Extrinsic-D holds. In other words, X must "reach beyond" itself. This is true in all cases of intentionality, including cases where Y exists or does not exist, is in the future of X, is fictional or real, abstract or concrete. Because this is true of powers in general, it is true of sparse powers too. First, it is important to emphasize that the manifestation of a power is the proper entity of comparison to the object (or property) that a belief or desire is about. A power is directed toward its manifestation, which is extrinsic to the object bearing the power. The manifestation of a power, like the object of a thought, is not contained in the power (or thought) itself.

The very concept of power is of a property that can manifest when properly triggered. The manifestation itself is not intrinsic to the power and is not contained by the power. The manifestation is extrinsic to the power in the power's latent, unmanifested state. The manifestation is a future possibility. Consider fragility: The breaking is extrinsic to the power to break, a power which will cease to be instantiated once the breaking occurs. Fragility is directed toward something other than itself, the event of breaking. A key is disposed to unlock the door and the manifestation (the door being unlocked) is extrinsic to the key.

In further support of the claim that powers satisfy Extrinsic-D, as with thoughts, the object of directedness might not ever exist. If something possesses an intentional state, X, yet the object Y does not exist, Y itself could not be considered intrinsic to that which possesses X, for Y is not actual though X is. This is implied by the mark of intentional inexistence discussed in Section 4.2.[10]

To conclude the discussion of extrinsicness, I will argue that some (sparse) powers satisfy Extrinsic-G. Some preliminary remarks are in order. When Extrinsic-G holds for beliefs, the agent does not possess the belief X solely in virtue of intrinsic features. For example, if an agent S, in an environment containing a tree, perceives the tree, then S will form

---

[10]  However, X will still contain the content that Y is what X is directed toward, or information representing Y. That is why, following the interpretation of Brentano's theory of intentionality set forth by Kriegel (2016), intentional states themselves are nonrelational, for (among other reasons) they do not existentially depend on their intentional objects.

a belief about the tree. If S's physically identical duplicate, S*, were in a nontree environment, S* would not (assuming other factors are equal) have a belief about a tree (although if other factors are not equal, they could easily hallucinate a tree and the intentional state itself would be identical to the one caused by a real tree). Thus, environmental conditions ground some (perhaps most) beliefs. The parallel for powers would be a situation in which a power of an object *o* is extrinsically grounded by a property of a second object in *o*'s environment, or a property of the environment itself. Two arguments will be presented showing that some sparse powers satisfy Extrinsic-G, the Arguments from Priority Monism and Particle Physics.

The Argument from Priority Monism is relevant to the extrinsicness of all powers, but here it is developed in terms of sparse powers. According to Schaffer (2010b), the whole World (or cosmos) is a fundamental, individual concrete entity unto itself, ontologically prior to all the parts of the world (including stars, planets, organisms, particles, etc.). On this view, Priority Monism, the World's parts are genuine concrete individual objects (part-objects, as they will be called here) but they have a derivative or secondary being relative to the World. The being of the World comes first. The competing view is pluralism, the seemingly more common view that there are multiple fundamental objects (the parts of the world). First, I will distinguish Priority Monism from Blobjectivism, a similar but distinct view. Then, I will argue that Priority Monism supports the case that powers satisfy Extrinsic-G. Finally, I will give reasons for thinking that Priority Monism is true.

Priority Monism contrasts with Blobjectivism (Horgan and Potrč 2008), which holds that the whole world or the Blobject is the *only* genuine concrete individual object. Derivatives such as stars, planets, organisms, and particles are objects in name only, ontologically mere confluences of properties of the Blobject. If Blobjectivism is true, it would appear that all properties are intrinsic, if properties are properly possessed only by objects. By contrast, Priority Monism posits the World as a genuine object as well as ordinary, everyday objects as genuine objects (part-objects), despite their derivate status. So, Priority Monism is committed to more objects in its ontology, although it should be kept in mind in comparing it to Blobjectivism that the latter must posit confluences of properties to account for the appearance of everyday objects.

Priority Monism implies that some property of the World partially ontologically grounds all of its part-objects and thus also the properties of those part-objects. The World is fundamental, such that part-objects of the

World ontologically depend on the World. This implies that a property or property-complex of the World ontologically grounds its part-objects, thus also the properties of its part-objects, where some of these part-objects are subatomic particles.[11]

It follows that any property, F, borne by a part-object, *a* (such as a subatomic particle), of the World, is partially grounded in a property or property-complex of the World. Although F is a property instantiated by *a*, part of F's ontological grounds or basis for being is the World qua World, a non-*a* object. Thus, F of *a* ontologically depends partially on the World for its being. But F also depends partially on the part-object *a* that bears it, because F is a property of that object. But properties that ontologically depend on properties of objects other than their object bearers are extrinsic properties. Therefore, if Priority Monism is true, then any property F, borne by *a*, is an extrinsic property. This applies to all powers that are properties of part-objects of the World. It is also worth noting that although F's instantiation requires the World, this should not obscure the fact that F is a property of *a* (not the World) and that *a* – a particular kind of particle with essential properties – bears a sort of primary ontological responsibility for F's instantiation. In short, *a* itself has a lot to do with why F is instantiated. This contrasts with many ordinary extrinsic properties, for which the object gaining the extrinsic property does so by happenstance and has very little to do with the nature of the object (e.g., any concrete object has the property of *being on a rug* when the object is so positioned).[12]

One possible objection to the Argument from Priority Monism is developable on the thesis that any duplicate of *a* will also possess F (Langton and Lewis 1998: 338). So, for example, the duplicate of a given electron will also possess charge, and the duplicate of a given vase will also be fragile. If this is the case, then these properties (charge, fragility) are intrinsic properties, thus contradicting Extrinsic-G. In duplicating the object, intuitively we bring along its properties.

The problem with this duplication objection is that it begs the question against Priority Monism. If Priority Monism is granted, then the properties of duplicates of objects, including electrons and vases, will be extrinsic.

---

[11] The object bearing a property might be a substance or a bundle of properties (which have the power to bundle together). I assumed a bundle theory of objects in Sections 0.4 and 2.6. So, if bundle theory is correct, then "objects" in the above argument are bundles of properties that bears further properties.

[12] So, there remain many interesting questions concerning *a*'s properties from an "internal" point of view.

They will be duplicated against the background, so to speak, of the World as the fundamental object. In effect, the World changes the conditions that determine whether properties of part-objects are intrinsic or extrinsic properties of those objects. Therefore, the World partially grounds the existence of F borne by *a*, thus making F extrinsic and thus satisfying Extrinsic-G.[13]

Another objection to the Argument from Priority Monism is that the World and *a*, bearing F, are not distinct objects. To be "extrinsic" (in the sense of Extrinsic-G), the grounding duties for F must be shared by two distinct objects for the required ontological dependence of F to obtain. But is *a* really distinct from the World? The objector says no: *a* is not distinct from the World because *a* is merely a part of the larger whole that is the World, and thus the required dependence relation does not obtain.

Contrast the question of distinctness between *a* and the World with the question of distinctness between two ordinary objects, *a* and *b*. If one were to make a claim about a property F, of *a*, at location $l_1$ being dependent upon a property of *b* at location $l_2$, then F would be extrinsic because *a* and *b* are distinct from each other. By contrast, regarding *a* and the World, we do not have one object at $l_1$ and another object at $l_2$; rather, *a* is a part of a larger whole such that the required distinctness does not obtain. Or so the objector suggests.

The force of this objection depends on what is meant by "distinct." Considering this, I have two related responses to the objection. For the first response I will assume "distinct" means spatially distinct and employ the following analysis in order to refine the objection: Two objects, *a* and *b*, are distinct if and only if *a* and *b* occupy spatially distinct locations. Call this Spatial Distinctness. The objection thus states that *a* must occupy a spatial location distinct from the World for *a* and the World to be distinct, such that the proper dependence relation holds for F to count as extrinsic. Thus, the refined objection is that the World and *a* are not spatially distinct since *a* is just a part of the World – that is, *a* is spatially contained in the World. This means that F of *a* cannot properly depend on properties

---

[13] Where does this leave the duplication test of intrinsic properties? It remains a reliable indicator of intrinsicness if Priority Monism is false; indeed, I will employ it in making the Argument from Particle Physics (for Extrinsic-G) further below in this section. But if Priority Monism is true, then the duplication condition is not a reliable guide to the intrinsic/extrinsic status of properties. Instead, in each case we must examine the ontological dependence relations to see whether a given property is extrinsic or intrinsic. On Priority Monism, the only intrinsic properties will be properties of the World qua World. All nonfundamental properties (properties not borne by the World qua World), will be extrinsic properties.

of the World because $a$ is not sufficiently distinct from the World such that the required dependence relation obtains. Therefore, according to the objector, F is not an extrinsic property of $a$.

I respond by first noticing that although $a$ is located somewhere, the World does not technically have a location. Therefore, Spatial Distinctness does not apply and so cannot reliably be used to argue against F's extrinsicness. The World does not have a location because it encompasses all of spacetime. Supposing spacetime is relational, not substantial, the World provides the necessary relational framework against which the part-objects of the World have locations; but the World itself does not have a location because it is not located anywhere in relation to something else. Supposing spacetime is substantial, not relational, then spacetime is a part or property of the World; the World itself would provide for, or contain, locations but would not itself have a location. Thus, on either a substantial or relational interpretation of spacetime, the World is not located somewhere and thus Spatial Distinctness does not apply to the question at hand, that is, whether F is an extrinsic property of $a$.[14]

My additional response to the second objection begins by conceding that the World and $a$ share space or overlap, so there remains a strong sense in which they are not distinct in the sense implied by Spatial Distinctness. In general, because parts and wholes spatially overlap to some degree, they are not completely spatially distinct. So perhaps the real question behind the second objection is whether a part of a whole can properly be thought of as a distinct object from its whole.

I will defend the claim that although parts and wholes are not completely spatially distinct, they might be sufficiently (indeed, more than sufficiently) spatially distinct for a property of a part-object of a whole to be extrinsic because it is partially grounded by the whole of which it is a part. Suppose a page of a book has the property, P, of being the last page of the book. The book and the page spatially overlap and thus are not completely spatially distinct. In the merological sense, the book and the page are distinct objects: there is a book and there is a page that is part of the book. But in the spatial sense, they are not completely distinct because they overlap to some degree. However, the lack of complete spatial distinctness of

---

[14] To put my first response differently: can we reasonably assign the World a location? In some sense it is everywhere, yet anywhere one could point is not where the World is, but just a part-object of the World, that is, that which has a location. In a way, the World is everywhere its part-objects are simply because they are parts of the World. However, this also implies that just one small part of the World is there, not the World itself. Although the World is not *entirely* spatially distinct from $a$, it is largely distinct from $a$.

the book and the page does not prevent P from being an extrinsic property of the page. That is, the page possesses P partially in virtue of being part of the book. Although the book and the page overlap spatially to some degree, P remains an extrinsic property of the page.

To summarize the Argument from Priority Monism, since F ontologically depends not only on the object *a*, which bears F, but also on the World, F is an extrinsic property of *a*. If so, the World grounds sparse powers but what those powers point toward (their intentional objects) is not the World itself. This parallels the case of extrinsically grounded beliefs (satisfying Extrinsic-G) that do not point toward their grounding objects (not satisfying Extrinsic-D), a possibility discussed above. Priority Monism is a logically coherent theory on which all sparse powers are extrinsically grounded. Thus, if Priority Monism is true, Extrinsic-G plausibly represents a parallel between beliefs and sparse powers.[15]

Is Priority Monism true? One advantage that Priority Monism has over pluralism is that it entails that all of existence is unified and integrated (Schaffer 2010a: 350). This contrasts with the Humean model of the world on which "All events seem entirely loose and separate. One event follows another; but we never can observe any tie between them. They seem *conjoined*, but never *connected*" (Hume 2003: Section VII, Part II). The Humean model is clearly a pluralist view of the world's fundamental ontology. And it is one on which the parts and properties underlying events could be freely recombined in different ways to create entirely new structures. There is nothing tying everything together. The Neo-Humean model of the world updates and develops Hume's model but shares its core tenets. The internal relatedness of all the parts and properties of the universe, inferred from the premise that the free recombination of elements is *not* viable (contrary to what Humeans think), supports Priority Monism. Schaffer (2010a: 341–342) argues that "that all things are internally related in ways that render them interdependent," and "the substantial unity of the whole universe is inferred from the interdependence of all of its parts." In sum, Priority Monism has an ontological advantage because it entails that all parts of the universe (properties, events, etc.) are unified by the World, an all-encompassing object on which everything else depends.

Another advantage of Priority Monism over its competitor, pluralism, is that it gives a better metaphysical explanation why the universe obeys

---

[15] Even though I do not categorically accept Priority Monism, there are considerable reasons in support of it, as I will explain below. But the possibility of Priority Monism shows that powers can be extrinsic just as mental states can be extrinsic if externalism in philosophy of mind is true.

principles of symmetry in physics. Symmetry is the idea that the properties (physical, mathematical) of particles and systems remain unchanged despite undergoing various transformations or operations. To take a simple example, an object possesses symmetry if rotating it 180 degrees generates no observable difference. This is a spatial symmetry. But there also exist what physicists call internal symmetries. These have to do with the laws that govern or describe properties and forces of particles in the Standard Model of particle physics, the dominant quantum theory positing various subatomic particles (quarks, leptons such as electrons, and gauge bosons) and the physical forces that direct their interaction. These internal symmetries treat fields and the particles they generate as interchangeable (Randall 2005: 195). Symmetry indicates that the world at its roots is unified – that there is a fundamental unity under all the apparent differences we observe in the universe. And this is exactly what Priority Monism provides: If the World is interconnected and essentially unified, it would be no surprise that the world exhibits the symmetry it does and that it reliably guides physicists' investigations.

One might object that the phenomenon of symmetry breaking indicates a lack of unity. "The secret of nature is symmetry, but much of the texture of the world is due to mechanisms of symmetry breaking," as Gross (1996: 14257) observes. One example of symmetry breaking is the much-discussed Higgs mechanism by which particles gain their masses (more on this below). Nonetheless, in instances of symmetry breaking the laws themselves remain "symmetric but the state of the system is not" (1996: 14257). According to Randall (2005: 207), "underlying symmetries must be broken, although they remain implicit in the physical laws describing the world." If the universe is to have the physical structure it actually has, symmetries will be broken. However, the fundamental symmetries themselves are real and necessary for symmetry breaking to occur. With the reality of these fundamental symmetries intact, the unity implied by Priority Monism is retained.

Priority Monism is more plausible than pluralism, because the former but not the latter renders plausible the principles of symmetry, provided that symmetry requires the kind of unity and integration that Priority Monism brings to the table. With pluralism everything is loose and separate, fundamentally lacking unity, so it is difficult to see how symmetry obtains. There are other reasons to favor Priority Monism but these considerations regarding integration, unity, and symmetry motivate the view and thus enhance the idea that powers satisfy Extrinsic-G.[16]

---

[16] Thanks to an anonymous reviewer for recommending these lines of reasoning for Priority Monism.

Continuing the physics theme, the Argument from Particle Physics plausibly shows that mass, conceived as a sparse power, is an extrinsic property.[17] The argument issues from the Standard Model of particle physics, as explained above, which classifies all the known fundamental particles and three of the four fundamental forces (gravity is not included). Physicists Peter Higgs and François Englert predicted the existence of what came to be called a Higgs field (consisting of Higgs boson particles). Observational data from supercollider experiments at CERN provided confirmation of the existence of the Higgs boson; later investigation and interpretation have convincingly shown that the long-sought Higgs boson is real.[18] The key premise is that the interaction between the Higgs boson and other subatomic particles generates the property mass in non-Higgs particles (except photons, which have no mass). This is the so-called Higgs mechanism.

Mass is arguably a sparse power.[19] Intuitively, it appears to be an intrinsic property.[20] If mass is in fact intrinsic, then a particle's having mass does *not* depend on its environment or any other objects or particles. However, the fact that a particle's mass depends on its interaction with the Higgs field implies that whether it obtains *does* depend on its environment. This is because the Higgs field is part of a particle's environment. Therefore, mass is an extrinsic power.[21]

It is due to the fact that a given particle, *p*, is embedded in an environment permeated by the Higgs field that *p* gains mass; if *p* were not in the Higgs field, then *p* would not possess mass. Two electrons otherwise identical to each other might differ with respect to having mass as a result of being situated in different environments (one with the Higgs field, the other without), therefore mass is not intrinsic. This gains support from the duplication test for intrinsic properties (Langton and Lewis 1998: 338): The properties that a duplicate of an object shares with its original are its

---

[17] I develop this line of argument in much more detail in Bauer (2011) where I also speculate – but do not commit to the claim – that other sparse powers, such as charge and spin, are also extrinsic. A similar but less detailed argument that mass is extrinsic is presented by Balashov (2002: 469–471).

[18] For more information, visit the CERN page: http://home.web.cern.ch/topics/higgs-boson (accessed June 6, 2022).

[19] For example, see Ellis (2001: 114–115), Ellis (2002: 47), Isaacs (2000), Martin (1993: 184), and Molnar (2003: 131–137).

[20] For example, see Bird (2007a: 30), Ellis (2001: 28), Molnar (2003: 102–107), and Mumford (2006: 471–480).

[21] This conclusion applies to both inertial mass and rest mass since these are physically equivalent according to Einstein's equivalence principle.

intrinsic properties. Therefore, mass parallels the case of physically identical agents having different mental states based on different environmental conditions. (In defending the Argument from Priority Monism, I argued that applying the duplication test for intrinsicness begs the question against Extrinsic-G. But this does not require that we abandon the duplication test altogether, just that it does not prove intrinsicness or extrinsicness if Priority Monism is true.)

Comparing mass and weight is instructive. Assume that having weight is particle $p$'s power to register an exact quantity on a weight scale. The exact quantity registered by $p$ depends on the strength of gravitational field $p$ occupies (Yablo 1999). Since $p$ will have different exact weights in different gravitational fields, weight is therefore an extrinsic power. Similarly, $p$'s having any mass depends upon $p$ occupying a Higgs field environment.

It might be true that $p$ intrinsically has the power *to gain mass* when stimulated by interaction with the Higgs field, given the field's power to generate mass in particles. But such interaction does not cause $p$ to display (manifest) mass. Rather, the interaction generates $p$'s possessing mass; further forces acting upon $p$ trigger a manifestation of mass by $p$, for instance if $p$ is accelerated by an external force. Thus, $p$ having mass depends on $p$'s environment. If the Argument from Particle Physics is sound, then at least one sparse power, mass, satisfies Extrinsic-G.

The Arguments from Priority Monism and Particle Physics show the plausibility of the claim that, as with beliefs and desires, at least some sparse powers meet the Extrinsic-G mark of intentionality because they depend upon features of the environment (the Higgs field) or other objects (the World as a whole). Thus, Extrinsic-G represents a further parallel between mental states and sparse powers regarding intentionality.

Consider again the last sentence of the passage from Bird (2007a: 120) but substitute "powers" for "thoughts," and "objects" for "subjects."

> Since the two **objects** are intrinsically alike but their **powers** have different intentions, it follows that in such cases the intentional character of **powers** is an extrinsic property of the **object**.[22]

Is this true? It is not only metaphysically possible but plausible, I have argued, for some sparse powers such as mass.

---

[22] "Objects" could be "particles"; "intentions" or "intentional character" could reasonably be "aboutness" or "directedness."

## 5.4   Direction of Causation

This mark holds that when X is directed toward Y because Y has caused X, the direction of the causation is, naturally enough, from Y *to* X (Bird 2007a: 120). So, Y causes X while X is directed toward Y. That is, when an intentional relation obtains in virtue of some causal relation, the object of the intentional state is what causes the intentional state. No particular account of causation is assumed. Direction of causation is different from direction of fit (to be addressed in Section 5.5) because direction of causation does not concern the match or fit between thought and world; it concerns which one (thought or world) causes the other to occur or exist.

While the direction of causation from Y to X might not be true in all cases, Bird (2007a: 120) contends that it is a plausible part of many instances of intentionality. Bird's example is of Napoleon, the man, causing a thought about Napoleon, not the other way around. There are exceptions to this phenomenon in which the intentional object is not the cause of the relevant belief. For example, if Y itself is a belief of an agent, S, Y might cause another belief X in S. Napoleon's own belief that he is a superior military commander, Y, causes him to believe that he will be victorious in battle, X, in which case one intentional state (with its own intentional object) at least partially causes S to have a further intentional state (with its own intentional object). Furthermore, the object of thought (the intentional object) need not always be external to the agent's mind. Suppose Napoleon believes, Y, *that* he believes he is a superior military commander, X; in this case, Y is a metacognitive state, and X is both an intentional state and an intentional object. (In the case of metacognition, one might wonder if it is not only that the intentional object is intrinsic to S, but intrinsic to the intentional state itself.) The discussion here will focus on intentional states that are caused by events or objects external to the agent's mind, thereby avoiding the kinds of complexities involved in the cases mentioned.

If the direction of causation is from Y to X in many cases of intentionality, then we should expect a parallel with respect to powers. However, Bird (2007a: 125) claims that the parallel does not hold. The parallel would be a power's manifestation – that is, the intentional object toward which the power is directed – causing the instantiation of the power.[23] But

---

[23] If the arguments in Section 5.3 show that sparse powers satisfy Extrinsic-G, then something extrinsic to the object bearing a sparse power grounds the power. This grounding relation is similar, but not identical, to something external *causing* the object to have a sparse power; Schaffer (2016) argues that the concept of grounding is strongly analogous to that of causation. Despite this similarity, in

powers (plus their stimuli) cause manifestations, not the other way around. Therefore, the direction of causation involved with powers is opposite to that involved with thoughts. Nonetheless, Bird's argument has two inter-related problems that, upon examination, reveal parallels between powers and mental states.

> First problem: Intentional states, partly in virtue of their very intentionality, are sometimes causes of their intentional objects, similar to how powers are causes of their manifestations.
> Second problem: In cases of intentionality involving a power, there are two causal relations, one from the intentional object to the intentional state and one from the agent to the intentional state.

These problems provide evidence that the relation picked out by this mark does not fully capture the causal relations involved in intentionality. Once the totality of the causal relations involved in intentionality is brought to light, it will be seen that intentionality and powerfulness are closer in nature in terms of directionality of causation than Bird's assessment reveals.

Turning to the first problem, Bird (2007a: 125) suggests that although some intentional states such as desires do cause their objects – if Elizabeth intends to eat chocolate, this causes her to eat chocolate – this has "nothing to do with intending being intentional and *everything to do* with its also being a disposition of a certain kind, a disposition to make it the case that Y" (my emphasis).[24] But is the intentionality component really causally irrelevant as Bird suggests?

Taking a step back, desires certainly qualify as intentional states. The desire to eat chocolate is about eating chocolate, where consuming chocolate is the intentional object that need not exist. But that does not mean, Bird contends, that everything resulting from a desire is thereby caused by the desire being intentional; the desire's power explains why the desire is causally relevant to Elizabeth eating chocolate. So, the desire to eat chocolate causes the eating of chocolate, not because it is intentional, but because it is powerful. When this power manifests, Elizabeth eats chocolate.

---

this case it would still not be the manifestation, Y, causing the power, X, and thus it would not fit the form of the mark of direction of causation. In the arguments in Section 5.3, the point of interest was the parallel between sparse powers and thoughts in which something extrinsic, not necessarily the object of the intentional state, grounds the intentional state (or power).

[24] There are many examples in which an intentional state and a power are closely associated, as in the chocolate example.

The desire appears to have a powerful component in addition to an intentional component, for the desire can be triggered in the presence of chocolate (or the thought of chocolate) and consuming chocolate is a manifestation that need not occur. The similarities between the powerful and intentional components of S's desire are apparent, as Figure 5.1 shows.

| Components of desire | Object of the component | Primary effect of the component |
|---|---|---|
| Intention | Eating chocolate | Actual eating of chocolate |
| Power | Eating chocolate | Actual eating of chocolate |

Figure 5.1   Parallels of intentionality and powerfulness (Originally printed in Bauer (2016). Reprinted by permission.)

Both the power and the intention are essential, inseparable components of the desire to eat chocolate. And both play a causal role. If Elizabeth's desire were not intentional, she would not be disposed toward eating chocolate; and, if she were not so disposed, why should we posit that she has a desire (and thus the associated intentional component) to eat chocolate at all?

For these reasons, it is plausible that the intentional nature of the desire causally factors into eating chocolate. More precisely, the intentionality (not just the power or disposition) of a subject's desire is a necessary causal component of an overall sufficient condition for the desire being fulfilled. Therefore, the chocolate example is a case of an intentional state (a desire) at least partly causing what it is for, contrary to Bird's claim. This runs parallel to how powers cause what they are for, that is, their manifestations.

In sum, Bird's concern is to show that Y causes X. Although Bird recognizes desire as a potential counterexample to the direction of causation criterion, he argues that the apparent reversal of directionality in the example (from Y to X, to X to Y) is due to the desire being powerful. I offered an alternative interpretation of the example according to which intentionality is at least a necessary part (along with powerfulness) of the cause of the desire being fulfilled (eating chocolate in the example given).

Therefore, the direction of causation from Y to X is not universal; sometimes X causes Y similar to how powers cause their manifestations. Despite this evaluation, I recognize that the intentionality of some mental states (particularly desires), although causally necessary, is not causally sufficient to realize the object of the desire, since their powerful component is also necessary. By contrast, nonmental (physical) powers, once triggered, might in fact be causally sufficient for their manifestations.

Turning now to the second problem with Bird's evaluation of direction of causation, no thought is caused *solely* by the intentional object. Thoughts – beliefs and desires included – that have as their content some external object or property are arguably caused by mutually manifesting powerful properties, one coming from the world (the intentional object) and one from the mind.[25] Powers require powerful partners (except spontaneously manifesting powers, if any exist). In Bird's example, supposing that an agent is responding to an actual piece of chocolate, the desire in the agent is caused by some power of the chocolate *and* some power of the agent's mind to respond to the chocolate, such as a latent desire for chocolate, a belief that chocolate is good, and so on. (I assume here that the intentional object is the chocolate piece itself, rather than the *eating* of the chocolate, and that the chocolate has a power to cause an agent to desire it.)

There exists both the agent's power and intention to fulfill an occurrent desire to eat chocolate (discussed as part of the first problem above), and at deeper cognitive level, the agent's latent capacity (a power) to have an occurrent desire to eat chocolate upon perceiving chocolate (this is part of the second problem). But this goes against Bird's claim that Y causes X, at least if that is taken as a complete description of causation in intentional relations. For Y is *not* the whole causal story here. In general, the object of a thought is not a sufficient cause for the instantiation of the thought because some property of the agent's mind (the latent capacity) is also part of the total cause. Therefore, to conclude that the direction of causation is only from object to thought ignores the causal role of the agent who has the thought.

There is, plausibly, a network of intentional contents and a background set of preintentional capacities necessary for any thought to be instantiated (Searle 1983: 65–66 and 2004: 172–174). Whereas some thoughts might be caused solely by internal machinations (e.g., dreams, hallucinations) no thought is ever caused *completely* by external factors. If externalism is true, the *content* of a thought might be completely set by external factors when the external object exists, but in this case it would still be true that some property of the mind in conjunction with the object is needed to cause the

---

[25] I assume here that powers are causally relevant or can play causal roles in events. Martin (2008) defends the idea that all causes reduce to powers – a cause is just a power or set of intersecting powers. McKitrick (2005) argues that dispositions are causally relevant. Mumford and Anjum (2011) extensively defend causal dispositionalism, the idea that effects are the products of manifesting powers.

thought to exist. Even if one accepts a theory of the cause of mental states in which the mind plays a strictly passive role, the mind must still exercise passive powers, such as the powers to receive content and form individual thoughts.

To further specify the second problem, it is useful to focus on the concept of powerful partners (Heil 2003: 122 and 2012: 120–121; Martin 2008: 60). On this model of powers' manifestations, a power $P_1$ meets its partner $P_2$, resulting in a mutual manifestation. So, there are two causal relations involved. The cause of the manifestation (excluding peripheral events and conditions) is the partnering of the two powers. Applying this model to the case of thoughts, a belief about some external-world object requires two powers: $P_1$, a power in the mind, grounded perhaps in neural machinery plus a concept pertinent to beliefs of a certain type (e.g., a concept about chocolate), and $P_2$, a power in the world (a chocolaty object prone to cause the relevant desires in agents) partnering to manifest in a desire within the agent to eat chocolate.

Figure 5.2 presents the primary causal factors typically involved in producing an intentional state (many other factors will also be necessary):

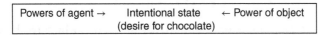

Powers of agent →     Intentional state     ← Power of object
(desire for chocolate)

Figure 5.2    Powers involved in producing an intentional state (Originally printed in Bauer (2016). Reprinted by permission.)

Neither the agent's nor the object's power must be a single power token; it could be a complex set of powers. The intentional state might be any type of thought, belief, or desire. Figure 5.2 represents the case in which the object of the desire in fact exists, but this need not be the case. In the case of intentional inexistence, the desire will not be caused by the object of the desire directly. It could be an imagined object in which case there are still two powers (or power complexes) at play coming from different directions; but in many cases one of the causes will be a power of an actual external object.

Given these observations, I infer that Bird's direction of causation criterion insufficiently captures the causal relations involved in intentionality. The direction of the power of the object is *from* the object *to* the thought (or intentional state); and the direction of the power of the agent is *from* what we might call a proto-thought to have the intentional state, *to* the manifestation which is actually having the intentional state.

My discussion of the second problem has so far emphasized what goes into the production of the intentional state. But there is another question regarding whether the intentional state, once it exists, actually causes to come about that which it represents, such as *eating* chocolate. This event, like the production of the intentional state to begin with, also has two directions of causation as represented in Figure 5.3 (notice that the left side of Figure 5.3 is the middle part from Figure 5.2).

| Intentional state → | Realization of the intentional object | ← Power of object |
|---|---|---|
| (desire for chocolate) | (actual eating of chocolate) | (power of chocolate) |

Figure 5.3   Realization of an intentional state   (Originally printed in Bauer (2016). Reprinted by permission.)

Once the agent has a desire for chocolate, produced as a collective result of powers of the agent and the chocolate (as shown in Figure 5.2) this desire (plus the chocolate) will cause the intention to be realized (as shown in), provided nothing interferes in the activity of these powers.

## 5.5   Direction of Fit

There is one more mark of intentionality to discuss, which has been over-looked as an explicit mark of intentionality in the analysis of PIT. It is well known that intentional states have a direction of fit owing to their conditions of satisfaction (Searle 1983, 2004, 2010) and I suggest that powers do as well. Some states have a world-to-mind direction of fit while others have a mind-to-world direction of fit. For instance, beliefs have a mind-to-world direction of fit: A belief aims to fit or match the world, the way things stand in reality. The same holds for memories and perceptions. Desires, by contrast, have a world-to-mind direction of fit: A desire aims to be fulfilled, to get things in the world to match one's desire. The same holds, Searle observes (2004: 172), for intentions in action (the intention you have while completing or doing an action) and prior intentions (the intention you form prior to an action).[26]

What about powers? It seems that powers have a double (or two-way) direction of fit, a special concept of direction of fit. Declarations (of marriage, for instance) have double direction of fit because they create a new

---

[26] Perhaps some mental states have null fit: for example, being "glad that the sun is shining" *presupposes* a direction of fit, thus evaluating its fit as good or bad is irrelevant (Searle 2004: 169). This is why having a direction of fit is not an essential mark of intentionality.

reality, like a desire aims for, which the declaration simultaneously, automatically matches, like a belief aims for (Searle 2010: 12, 85). Similarly, "besires" – motivational states with representational content, that is, belief-like desires – arguably have a double direction of fit. Swartzer (2013) defends the reality of appetitive besires, mental states that simultaneously possess a perception of a need (mind-to-world direction of fit) plus a desire or motivation to fulfill that need (world-to-mind direction of fit). Note that double-fitting mental states, like mental states with one direction of fit, can be unconscious (particularly besires, if not declarations). Since consciousness is not a requirement for double direction of fit, powers can certainly qualify as having double-fittingness. But do they?

Powers seem to fit the desire model best (as noted in Section 3.4), although instead of "world-to-mind" they exhibit "world-to-power" direction of fit, where the "world" here refers to manifestation events that powers bring about. A given power is directed toward changing the world, that is, causing a manifestation that the power is directed toward (fulfilling a desire, so to speak).[27] However, I contend that this only captures half of a powers' direction of fit. For powers cannot be directed toward their manifestations unless they respond appropriately to the other powers in their network, that is, the system of powers in which they are members and with which they cooperate to produce manifestations. In other words, powers also have a "power-to-world" direction of fit (akin to the "mind to world" direction of fit that beliefs have), where the "world" in this case is the network of powers that serve as manifestation partners for each other. Each power must fit in with its potential manifestation partners. This suggests the "problem of fit" (Williams 2010), or how powers match up with each other to produce coherent systems capable of manifestations. This will be addressed in Chapters 6 and 7.

Direction of fit is an overlooked intentionality-related feature of powers that boosts the case for PIT, although powers are most closely related to a subclass of mental states that have double fit, as I have argued above.

This completes the Argument from the Marks of Intentionality in support of PIT. I applied ten marks, three essential (in the previous chapter) and seven additional (in this chapter).[28] Some metaphysicians complain

---

[27] Building on Searle's (2010) specific example of declarations, by analogy one might think of powers as natural, nonlinguistic "declarations." They impose themselves on reality thereby making a new reality that they necessarily fit.

[28] In Chapter 8, I will fully develop the Argument from the Unity of Nature, which complements the Argument from the Marks of Intentionality.

that PIT cannot explain much, if anything, about powers.[29] By applying the marks of intentionality, I have defended PIT and given reasons why it illuminates powers from the inside, thus indicating why we should take it seriously. PIT, I contend, serves as the centerpiece in a theory of powers.

## 5.6 Objections to the Physical Intentionality Thesis

I have evaluated various objections in the midst of my defense of PIT. Now I will briefly discuss some additional objections: that physical intentionality is mysterious, that it is not sufficiently like mental intentionality, and that powers are directed toward nonexistent manifestations.

### Physical Intentionality Is Mysterious

Some critics dismiss physical intentionality as mysterious or radical. For example, Barker (2013: 649) claims that PIT "is deeply obscure" and gives it little attention as a theory about the nature of powers.[30] However, this kind of criticism appears to be simply an expression of counter-intuitiveness. In contrast to such criticism, there are forceful reactions in support of PIT in the philosophical landscape (Molnar 2003; Place 1996). So, dismissals based on mysteriousness or counter-intuitiveness will not get us far in investigating physical intentionality. We must seriously engage with the marks of intentionality and other relevant features and implications of PIT. I contend that when we do so, we find that PIT has quite a lot going for it and should be considered a reasonable option in the conceptual land-scape where powers reside. I think we see that PIT can be framed in a plau-sible light, though of course it is far from obviously true – no interesting metaphysical claim deserves that status.

Rather than introducing new mystery, PIT helps at least partially explain other mysteries. For example, PIT makes it *less* mysterious why minds and consciousness exist. Given physical intentionality, mind-like stuff is welded into the foundations of reality. PIT is clearly neither a full expla-nation of mental phenomena nor consciousness because intentionality is

---

[29] For example, see Barker (2013: 649).

[30] Barker (2013: 649) cites Molnar (2003) as the primary proponent of PIT. However, Place (1996) is an equally strong proponent. While Barker seems to conceive of PIT as a separate way of understanding *pure* powers – briefly mentioning it as a fourth interpretation alongside his discussion of the three ways of understanding pure powers (as discussed in Chapter 1) – I see it as complementing either interpretation of the Powers Model (the Pure Powers Model or the Powerful Qualities Model).

only a necessary precondition for mind and consciousness. Yet intentionality should factor into a compete explanation of mind. Although one might say this tends to shift the burden of explaining mind to a different, more fundamental level without actually resolving the issue, at some point in every inquiry we find ourselves at the end of analysis and must accept something as a fundamental element of reality. What I am suggesting is that intentionality, in the form of powers carrying informational content for their manifestations, is found at the fundament of physical reality. The buck stops somewhere, and my claim is that it is with powers directed toward manifestations.

### *Physical Intentionality Is Too Unlike Mental Intentionality*

One might object that in some ways physical and mental intentionality are alike, but in important ways they are not (Oderberg 2017). The ways in which it is not reveal what is distinctive about rational thought (mental states) and show why claims to panpsychism, animism, and the like are inappropriate. Adopting an Aristotelian stance, Oderberg (2017: 2393) thinks that powers display finality or "action for an end." This is genuinely final causation, more similar to Aristotelian teleology than to Kroll's brand of teleology (discussed in Section 3.4). Furthermore, physical powers display specific indifference (2017: 2393–2394): They have a limited range of specific manifestations with some indifference to the circumstances of manifestation (i.e., the power will allow some variation in the circumstances of manifestation but still manifest). By contrast, token thoughts are restricted to an object but are indifferent as to how the object is considered. The finality found in thoughts, as compared to the finality found in physical powers, has a kind of freedom through abstraction: Objects can be thought of in various incomplete ways, under certain aspects. Moreover, thoughts, which are the products of mental powers, are abstract to various degrees; by contrast, manifestations, which are the products of physical powers, are concrete and particular (2017: 2422).

In response to Oderberg's stance, I contend that while there might in fact be important differences between mental and physical intentionality, including differences pertaining to abstraction, these differences are additional features beyond the essential core of intentionality itself. Intentionality exists along a continuum, with each type satisfying all the essential marks of intentionality as argued in Chapter 4 and many, but not all, additional features as discussed in this chapter. Moreover, there are supplemental features such as consciousness and cognitive abilities – perhaps added on through evolutionary processes – that help create subcategories of intentionality (e.g., conscious intentionality). Therefore, Oderberg's critique is consistent with all instances of intentionality being physical, but "mental" intentionality being a more complex form of intentionality that requires additional features such as consciousness and abstraction abilities.

## Nonexistent Manifestations

A third possible objection – one that can be leveled against any theory of powers but becomes more pointed if PIT is affirmed – focuses on powers' relations to nonexistent manifestations. If we take powers to *be*, or at least *have*, relations to manifestations and hold that powers need not manifest, then powers are directed toward and bear relations to things that do not exist.

However, PIT implies that powers need not be conceived as relations at all and so alleviates the worry about nonexistent manifestations. PIT claims that powers are not real relations (Jaworski 2016: 58) but akin to mental states directed toward outcomes. In support of this response, it is plausible that on Brentano's conception of intentionality, intentional states do not bear relations to objects. According to Kriegel (2016: 2), Brentano's mature theory of intentionality – as developed beyond but consistently with *Psychology from an Empirical Standpoint* – intentionality is nonrelational; it is "an intrinsic property of subjects," not of intentional acts. According to this view about intentionality, reasonably named "subjectism" (Kriegel 2016: 4), apparent relations to intentional objects are sort of compressed into the subject (the thing that has the intentional state). This can be captured by paraphrasing our intentional statements; for example, "'S is thinking of dragons' is paraphrased into 'S is a dragons-thinker'" (2016: 4).

I will now apply the "subjectism" approach to physical powers. Given that mental and physical intentionality are at root identical, as I have argued, it can be accurately stated that, for some power P and its proper manifestation M, "P is directed toward (or, is for) M" should be paraphrased into "P is an M-er." In other words, P has information for M regardless of M's inexistence. P represents M whether M occurs or not. P is a property that Ms.[31] When applied to powers, this approach might better be called "powerism." This emphasizes that the ontological focus in

[31] See Marmodoro (2014) for an Aristotelian view of the nonrelationality of powers.

cases of physical intentionality is the intentional state – the power – not the intentional object, that is, the manifestation. This is just as the ontological focus in cases of mental intentionality is the intentional state – the subject, not the intentional object. Both the "power" and the "subject" are the agents of intentionality, although the former in a less robust sense than any conscious agent.

The above discussion supports a nonrelational view of powers. The very idea of intentionality – which we know is a real phenomenon in mental states – entails the possible inexistence of the intentional state's object. It is just a fact about mental reality. If we should accept this about mental states, then if physical powers meet all the relevant marks of intentionality (as I have argued), we should accept the same about physical powers. It is just a fact about physical, modal reality. So, powers are best conceived as nonrelational or perhaps quasi-relational. They could be considered quasi-relational in that they appear to be relations because their nature involves directedness toward possible manifestations.[32] For these reasons, PIT helps powers theorists avoid the worry about nonexistent manifestations and avoid qualifying powers as relational properties.

Although he is a nonpowers theorist, Armstrong (2002: 168–169) suggests that powers theorists like Ellis cannot be rid of powers pointing to their unmanifested effects and this "pointing" should be classified as physical intentionality: "Perhaps one can live with physical intentionality. That is what Molnar was prepared to do, and that would be my recommendation to Ellis" (2002: 169). Although Armstrong maintains that PIT is an implausible metaphysical claim, perhaps some "can live with" it. Indeed.

### 5.7 The Physical Intentionality Thesis and the Other Models of Physical Modality

Advocates of the Universals Model think that the outcomes of interacting properties are governed by laws. I argued in Section 1.3 that the Universals Model implicitly accepts powers. It is not too much of a stretch to say that

---

[32] Given the nonrelationality of powers, there is no need to posit uninstantiated universals to account for the manifestations that powers point toward, as Tugby (2013) does in his theory of Platonic dispositionalism; however, if one finds that powers bear real relations to their manifestations, then Tugby's proposal certainly has merit. Furthermore, if one wants to avoid Platonism while preserving powers as relational, and genuinely related to their nonexistent manifestations, perhaps mere possibilia – such as possible manifestations – could be counted as nonactual, uninstantiated *existents*. They could be considered real because they have intelligible content and are not *nothing*. (Thanks to a reviewer for suggesting this.)

the laws that it posits must direct the qualities that get involved in causal action; this is implied by the governing metaphor of laws. Governing involves directing – providing directedness – toward ends. So, I suggest, something akin to physical intentionality is not totally foreign to this view. The Universals Model implies that a law is the modal force that directs F toward G. However, directedness in this case comes from outside the properties that are so directed, whereas on the Powers Model directedness comes from inside.

What about the Neo-Humean Model? Theorists accepting this model should be even more resistant to physical intentionality, directedness, and the like. For Neo-Humeans, powers (as well as metaphysical necessities, intrinsic causes, etc.) might seem to be like Leibniz's monads "with their desire or will or appetite for particular ends" (Schrenk 2017: 308), especially when PIT or some related thesis is added to the Powers Model. However, the Neo-Humean Model appears to need powers (see Section 1.2). In particular, Humean Supervenience implies that properties respond to different global conditions. So, although Humean Supervenience rejects the governing view of laws, it places something like directedness inside the "qualities" at the supervenience base. Properties, on this view, are directed toward different possible manifestations relative to their global conditions.

Therefore, there are reasons for Universals Model theorists and Neo-Humean Model theorists to be open to assigning directedness and physical intentionality to properties.

# CHAPTER 6

# Powers from the Inside
## Information

## 6.1 The Informational Thesis

Physical powers are intentional, representational yet nonpropositional, nonconscious properties, as argued in Chapters 3–5. In this chapter, I further explore powers from the inside. The Informational Thesis (IT), represented by data in the 3d account, claims that powers carry information for their potential manifestations. More specifically, powers carry representational, yet nonpropositional map-like information geared toward their potential manifestations. This information can be given a counterfactual characterization.

Why think that information has an important connection to powers? What is the need for both IT and PIT? Whereas PIT maintains that powers *are* intentional properties directed toward various outcomes, IT maintains that powers carry information specifying *what* powers are directed toward, their various potential interactions with other powers. IT concerns the content that defines a power's causal profile, or the pattern of various stimuli and manifestations that specify the directedness that each power has. While this will be explained in further detail below, for now the idea that powers and information are essentially connected needs motivation.

There are applications of the concept of information across a variety of academic fields, including many subfields of philosophy. In philosophy, information has been explicitly employed in understanding powers (Williams 2010, 2019), laws of nature (Dorato 2005), causation (Collier 1990), knowledge (Dretske 1981), mind (Chalmers 1996), and pantheism (Bauer 2019; Pfeifer 2016). Several of these accounts are directly relevant to questions of physical modality. Williams (2010, 2019: 85–95) characterizes powers in informational terms by holding that they contain instructions in the form of a blueprint (this will form a large part of my basis for developing IT). Collier (1990) argues for a link between information and causality. Dorato (2005: xi) suggests a connection between information and modality in framing the laws of nature as the universe's software or instructions; although he ultimately rejects the software metaphor, it is important enough to justify the title of his book, *The Software of the Universe*. Dretske (1981: 171–173) links physical information and intentionality. Although he favors the Universals Model of physical modality (Dretske 1977), if he were to accept the Powers Model it seems he should accept a tight connection between powers and information. In sum, there is a clear precedence for linking information and physical modality.

There is also precedent for information-theoretic accounts of the internal nature of consciousness. Such accounts, I suggest, motivate the application of informational concepts to capture the internal nature of other phenomena. For example, Tononi (2008) develops Integrated Information Theory, which proposes a measure of the amount of consciousness in a system as given by the variable $\phi$. Additionally, Graziano (2013) argues that awareness, a specific part of consciousness, is a special sort of information that the brain processes. These theories are controversial, as all theories of consciousness are. But if these informational theories help explain – or at least explore in illuminating ways – the nature of consciousnesses, then it is conceivable than an informational view of powers can do the same. If it can be somewhat plausible for consciousness, it can be at least somewhat plausible for powers, especially given that powers possess physical intentionality, a feature necessary for consciousness.

So, I want to look at powers through an informational lens. First, I further motivate the connection between information and powers via two arguments, one based on physics and one based on causation. Then I attempt to illuminate the being and modality of powers from the inside via the blueprinting metaphor (Williams 2010, 2019), which centrally involves an informational component. This prompts a more detailed discussion of the nature of information and IT, after which I examine some important implications of IT including its relation to the dispositional modality, the analysis of powers, and the power/quality (dispositional/categorical) distinction. In the chapter's conclusion, I explore how the three d's of the 3d account are interrelated and form a rich, novel account of powers.

## 6.2 Connections between Information and Powers

In this section, I present two arguments – one based on quantum mechanics and another on the metaphysics of causation – that suggest a metaphysical connection between information and powers, thus motivating IT.

### The Argument from Physics

Information plays an important metaphysical role in particle physics. To begin with, all quantum mechanical states – that is, any state of reality to which quantum mechanical principles apply – are arrays of quantum tendencies. Prior to collapse the wave function is a probability distribution of various possible states. Thus, quantum states are arrays of objective quantum tendencies or potentials toward various actualizations or manifestations (Stapp 2010: 105–106). These quantum tendencies are, quite plausibly, a species of causal powers (propensities). The pervasive use of "tendency" and "potential" in accounts of quantum mechanics implies the presence of causal powers. Thus, the inherent potentiality built into the quantum world indicates the presence of powers. Moreover, the ontology of powers fits well with certain interpretations of quantum mechanics, such as the GRW (named for Ghirardi, Rimini, and Weber) interpretation (Dorato and Esfeld 2010).

Quantum states are not only powerful, but informational – that is, they are arrays of discrete information states in a total information space of possibilities. It is quite possible that the universe literally computes information, undergoing a computational process that is subject to quantum mechanical principles (Davies 2010; Lloyd 2010). For example, Lloyd (2010: 96) argues as follows.

> Starting from its very earliest moments, every piece of the universe was processing information. The universe computes. It is this ongoing computation of the universe itself that gave rise naturally to subsequent information-processing revolutions such as life, sex, brains, language, and electronic computers.

According to this view, computation occurs on particles. Since the number of particles is finite, there is a limit to the universe's computational power. The total number of "elementary events or bit flips" that have occurred since the start of the universe "is not greater than $10^{120}$" (or, approximately $2^{400}$) (2010: 101).[1]

Arguments such as these are rooted in the "it from bit" thesis (Wheeler 1990), the claim that information is ontologically fundamental and thus prior to matter.[2] Wheeler's thesis implies that "The universe is fundamentally

---

[1] If particles and their properties ultimately constitute everything that exists in the universe, Lloyd's claims appear to assume the Church-Turing Thesis (Copeland 2020), that is, that all computations can be carried out on a Turing machine.

[2] See Dembski (2016) for further development of the thesis that information is more fundamental than matter.

composed of data, understood as dedomena, patterns or fields of differences, instead of matter or energy, with material objects as a complex secondary manifestation" (Floridi 2010: 70). Information, though not necessarily "material," is physical in the sense that it is subject to principles of physics. If information takes ontological priority over matter, then physical events – including the quantum events generated by quantum tendencies (i.e., powers) directed toward potential manifestations – fundamentally involve computation of information governed by quantum mechanical principles.

Since quantum mechanical states appear to be both powerful *and* informational, the distinct possibility arises that information and powers are metaphysically connected. We can interpret this connection between power and information through a distinction between information *for* and information *as* reality (Floridi 2010: 74, 2011: 30).[3] Given this distinction, we can reasonably assert that quantum information is *for* a set of new information states (manifestations) yet it exists *as* a set of quantum tendencies or powers. This is just one possibility for how to connect them. I will revisit the connection between information and power later (Section 6.6).

What I hope to have shown through the argument from physics is that information and powers are co-necessary features of quantum states, although I grant that this does not suffice to conclude that they are metaphysically interdependent. This is because co-necessities in general are not always (perhaps not often) metaphysically interdependent.[4] However, I suggest that they are in this case, because for any given quantum state we are dealing with a relatively small range of necessary conditions. When we have identified necessary conditions at a fundamental level, embodied by fundamental particles, it suggests that the conditions are not randomly placed but tightly interdependent.

## *The Argument from Causation*

The argument from causation, like the argument from physics, suggests a deep connection between information and powers. I will argue for this by first explaining why there is, quite plausibly, a strong connection between information and causation. Then I will explain why there is a strong connection between causation and powers. Together, these premises imply a metaphysical connection between information and powers.

---

[3] Floridi also identifies information *about* reality.
[4] Thanks to Kris Rhodes for raising this point.

There is strong precedent for connecting information and causation. For example, Chalmers (1996: 281) holds that "an information space associated with a physical object will always be defined with respect to a *causal pathway* [...] and a space of possible effects at the end of the pathway" – for example, turning on a light by flipping a light switch requires a causal pathway from the switch to the light, permitting a change in the information state of the light-switch system).[5] Gregersen (2010: 323) observes that "informational structures" play a "causal role in material constellations" or the building-up of matter, reflecting Wheeler's "it from bit" thesis discussed above. And one of the reasons Davies and Gregersen (2010: 7) give "information a central role in a scientifically informed ontology" is that it makes a "causal difference" in the world – for example, genetic information is required for tissue construction.

Building on these observations, I argue that where and when causation occurs, information transmission occurs. Physical information provides an opportunity for (though does not necessitate) causal effects. Two billiard balls on a table represent a certain information state, with specifiable differences based on billiard ball location, mass, and so on. These information states with their attendant differences partially generate the possibility of one billiard ball causing the other to move. So, physical information supports causal production. Turning to the connection between causation and powers, where and when powers are at work, causation occurs. In defense of this premise, causation arguably requires the manifestation of powers. If effects are the product of manifesting powers (Mumford and Anjum 2011), then causality depends on the action of powers. Where there is a causal effect, there is the manifestation of a power. Therefore, causation metaphysically links information and powers: where and when powers are at work, information transmission occurs.

The arguments from physics and causation mutually support each other, assuming that quantum tendencies are causally productive and involve causal powers. However, these two arguments neither individually nor collectively support any kind of reductive analysis of powers in terms of information (or vice versa). Both arguments could be explored in greater detail but that goes beyond my present purpose, which is only to motivate the idea that there is a metaphysical connection, not just a random association, between information and powers.

---

[5]  Chalmers (1996: 284–287) explores the concept of information in forming his hypothesis that information might link conscious experience and physical phenomena.

## 6.3    Powers Holism and the Blueprinting of Powers

"A physical power is essentially an *executable* property" Molnar (2003: 63). This characterization suggests a functional understanding of powers, which implies a need for differences that create the opportunity for action. On this functional characterization, two states X and Y ("input" and "output") are mapped to each other by way of a power. How do powers "know" how to execute their functions? How do they connect states X and Y? I suggest that powers carry information that indicates or represents how to get from X to Y. Williams (2010, 2019) explicitly accepts an informational characterization of powers and I will use his view as a lens to show why we should accept IT, or something like it, in any robust account of powers. Foreshadowing a key idea behind his acceptance of powers holism, Williams (2005: 313) suggests an instructional understanding of powers, contending that "An object's full set of dispositions is like an infinite set of commands or instructions for what actions the object must carry out under those conditions."[6] This insight is extremely helpful in discerning the nature of powers from the inside.

The theory of powers holism, also advocated by Mumford (2004: 182–184), holds that the identity conditions (i.e., the causal role) of any given power is determined by its relation to other powers in a system of powers. It provides a useful starting point for understanding the informational character of powers. The reason I focus on Williams' powers holism is because it is richly developed and provides a useful lens through which to discern the role of information. Here I focus on the informational element; in Chapter 7, I will return to powers holism in discussing systems of powers.

In developing powers holism, Williams (2010, 2019) suggests that powers carry information specifying how they fit together with other powers to produce manifestations – this is the "problem of fit" as he calls it. Central to his solution is the claim that each power "contains within it a blueprint for the entire universe" (2010: 95, 2019: 85–95). Each blueprint (to be understood metaphorically) contains information (to be understood literally) about how powers stand in relation to each other, ensuring that a given power will be for a certain set of manifestations by specifying how that power works with other powers in its

---

[6] This view goes hand in hand with the claim that there are, in addition to dynamic powers, static powers – instructions concerning what to do in all possible situations, even when nothing is happening to the object, such as when it is, simply, existing (Williams 2005).

holistic network.[7] Information metaphysically connects powers to each other in a network.

Powers "carry their causal potential inside them" (Williams 2017: 144). While this observation supports the "powers from the inside" point of view that is central to my investigation, it raises the question of how powers carry this causal potential. As indicated by the blueprint metaphor, powers carry their potential in the form of information. Their informational content is essential to powers being able to do what they can do.

Notice that in general we can accept a holistic view of some sort, according to which an individual thing cannot be fully understood outside of the network or system of which it is a member or part, while also accepting that each individual thing in the network must have a degree of independence. That is, *individual things* fit into the holistic network, a network which then completes the nature or identity of the thing. Applying this thought to powers, each power must be something on its own in order to stand in relation to other powers and fit with them. It is possible, I maintain, for all powers in a network but one to be eliminated. The network is eliminated, but the remaining power token stands alone. What is that lone power like, from the inside? I contend that it must still carry information about its possible interactions with other powers, whether they are instantiated or not. It must still have an informational blueprint.

The idea of an informational blueprint, or something close to it, for physical reality arises elsewhere. For example, Rovelli (2017: 242) interprets Democritean atoms as having information about each other, claiming that the way in which they "arrange themselves is correlated with the way *other* atoms arrange themselves." The world "is a network of correlations between sets of atoms, a network of real, reciprocal information between physical systems" (2017: 243). So, different possible correlations of atoms amount to different informational states of a system of atoms.

On the blueprinting metaphor, a power, $P_1$, contains a kind of blueprint $\beta$ that shows how $P_1$ relates to other powers $P_2$, $P_3$, and so on. $\beta_{P_1}$ is effectively a map of the possible behaviors of $P_1$, such that if $P_1$ undergoes a stimulus, S – in the form of interaction with another power, $P_2$, with its own particularized blueprint $\beta_{P_2}$ – then M will occur, provided the absence of conditions that prevent P from manifesting.[8] However, there are many

[7] Although in his statement of powers holism Mumford (2004) does not mention the idea of powers carrying information, I think that powers holism commits one to the blueprinting idea or something in that ballpark to explain the cooperative behavior between powers in a system.
[8] See Bird (2007a: 36–38) for a discussion of prevention conditions.

possible interactions. So, the blueprint analogy is limited, if it is taken to represent only one possible set of interactions and outcomes. The complete modality of any power needs to be part of its informational structure or blueprint. Thus, β should be conceived, I suggest, as a multilayered mapping of closely related sets of possible interactions between powers, tracking multiple possible differences in circumstances and triggers. More precisely, I contend that for a set of powers $P_1 \ldots P_n$, $P_1$ has blueprint $\beta_{P_1}$, $P_2$ has $\beta_{P_2}$, and so on through $\beta_{P_n}$. And each blueprint itself – $\beta_{P_1}$, $\beta_{P_2}$, and so on – has multiple layers, one for each set of possible interactions (see Figure 6.1). The information captured by each β structures each power's intentionality. It maps out the full range of potential manifestations that each power is directed toward. Without β, a power's directedness would be rudderless.

| $\beta_{P_1}$ | $\beta_{P_1}$ layer 1 (possible interactions with P2) |
| | $\beta_{P_1}$ layer 2 (possible interactions with P3) |
| | ... |
| | $\beta_{P_1}$ layer $l$ (possible interactions with P$n$) |

Figure 6.1   A layered blueprint for a power token

The information a power embodies is not itself a property, but the content of the power. It is content that individuates a power and determines what it is directed toward. Directedness, as argued in Chapter 4, is representational yet nonpropositional. That information carried by P helps complete this picture, for this information at the core of powers specifies, or orients, P's general directedness in a specific direction, that is, toward specific manifestations. It is instructional information, or information for, a specific range of manifestations. This is not an "it from bit" type of thesis, for I am not suggesting fundamental reality is simply informational. It is powerful. But information complements powers.

A power is a directedness that carries information for various possible outcomes. By comparison, a belief is one thing, and the (semantic) information it carries is another thing. A power, encoded with an informational structure, is directed toward its intentional objects, that is, manifestations. A belief, encoded with an informational structure, is directed toward its intentional objects.

Each power must be imprinted with the relevant information in order to do what it is capable of doing. Furthermore, each power must maintain its store of information regardless of the activation status (latent, active) of other powers. Even if the power in question is a "system" of one power – a lone power isolated from other powers (a possibility introduced in Section 0.7) – it must have information concerning its potential activities. This is certainly the case if it happens to be a self-manifesting power, a genuine possibility. But it is also the case for powers that require powerful partners to manifest: if such a power finds itself isolated (outside a system) or the last of a system (if other powers are eliminated), it still needs its blueprint to have its property identity and to be capable of interacting in the required ways with other powers, should the lone power return to a system of powers.[9]

In *A Tale of Two Cities*, Charles Dickens (1899: 12) observes "A wonderful fact to reflect upon, that every human creature is constituted to be that profound secret and mystery to every other." Powers, unlike humans, are no mystery to each other: they must "know" each other in an explicit but nonconscious sense if they are to act in unison, as part of a system, to achieve the effects that they are for. Corry (2019: 60) also argues that powers need "to 'know what to do' in all possible situations" and be "'ready' to act" in a variety of circumstances. This inherent "knowledge" that powers have about their potential partners and manifestations is owed, I argue, to their informational content embodied in β. The blueprints collectively align all of the powers to work together and ensures that each power's instructions are coherent with the instructions of the other powers. The idea of a power's blueprint might be metaphorical, but it is illuminating. And the metaphysical role for which β has been used in this argument must be fulfilled somehow: Powers must carry information relevant to their interactions and manifestations.

Although he does not explicitly accept PIT, the way Williams (2010, 2019) speaks of powers containing information and collaborating might appear to come close to positing physical intentionality – especially if the information is "for" fitting into a network. There is a close relationship between information *for*, and directedness *toward*, outcomes. That is why I maintain that IT and PIT go hand in hand (more on this Section 6.6). Before delving into that more deeply, what form does information take vis-à-vis powers? In what "type" of information do powers deal?

---

[9] One might object that each power must carry an overwhelming large store of information to account for all of its potential activities. But we must keep in mind that the need for vast amounts of information to make the world go is a problem for all models of physical modality. The laws of nature, on Neo-Humean and Universals Models of modality, must contain or carry or exhibit the same information about all the possible events (manifestations). On the Lewisian view, this information is spread over a vast space of possible worlds.

## 6.4    Powers and the Nature of Information

Information is a "polymorphic phenomenon and a polysemantic concept" – as such it can be part of several types of explanations depending on one's considerations (Floridi 2009: 13).

I am employing the concept of information as part of a powers-based theory of reality. According to my preferred conception, information consists of physically real (though not necessarily "material") primitive ontological differences (Bateson 2000: 271–273, 315, 381). This is reflected in computational representations of information as a series of 1s and 0s, "yes" and "no" answers, or "on" and "off" positions. If everything is the same in some system – complete uniformity regarding all existents in the system – then there is no information (for example, all 0s). If our concern is fundamental ontology, then ontological differences are at the heart of our information lens. Differences create possibilities for action. Powers, being directed toward manifestations, embody or carry differences relevant to those manifestations by creating specific possibilities for action.

There is a useful three-way, non–mutually exclusive distinction between information *as* reality, information *for* reality, and information *about* reality (Floridi 2010: 74, 2011: 30). Generally, information *as* and *for* reality are syntactic, while information *about* is semantic. Information *as* reality consists of nonalethic (neither true nor false) physical patterns. It is raw, natural data such as tree rings and fingerprints (Floridi 2010: 74).[10] Information *for* reality is instructional (e.g., algorithms, computer programs, genetic codes) and is the most relevant form of information to powers and IT, as I will explain shortly. Finally, information *about* reality is alethic, semantic information – it has an "epistemic value" as with a map or an encyclopedia entry (Floridi 2010: 74).[11,12]

An entity or phenomenon could contain information in more than one form. For example, a human's iris could be viewed as information *as* reality

---

[10] Wheeler (1990) takes the idea of information as reality to its logical extreme in advancing his "it from bit" thesis, which might be the most liberal view of information (Collier 2008: 765). See also Dembski (2016) for an information-centric view.

[11] In a similar fashion to Floridi, Collier (2008: 765) makes a tripartite distinction regarding information.

[12] Shannon information (Shannon and Weaver 1949), taken as "entropy" or the reduction of uncertainty, is not really a definition of information but a way to quantify how much information a system contains (Gamez 2018: 96). This could potentially be useful in quantifying the action of specific powers – for example, by specifying how the reduction of uncertainty correlates with the manifestation of a power – and therefore making predictions about their potential effects as relevant to various physical sciences. However, my purpose here is to posit information as a way illuminate the hidden nature of powers and understand their inner workings.

(the patterns it embodies), *for* reality (as used to verify the human's identity), and *about* reality (the iris represents the actual identity of the human person, that is, it is about his/her identity) (Floridi 2010: 74–75). Despite not being mutually exclusive, the three forms of information are useful for thinking about different ways information populates the world.

Syntactic and semantic information can also overlap. Semantic information is information with meaning and it piggybacks on syntactic information, also known simply as "data" (more on the data/information distinction below). Syntactic information can obtain without meaning or semantic information, but the latter cannot obtain without the former. All semantic information requires a syntactic component – it is structured.

Certain kinds of *prima facie* syntactical information, particularly instructional information (information *for* reality), are arguably not entirely free of semantic content in all circumstances – at least, they are a short step away from semantic evaluability. Consider a computer program, which is information for reality (i.e., for an output). It is not implausible to see it as having a kind of about-ness concerning reality: the program represents or "means" the current state of the system (in the way that the iris represents the identity of the person), that which contains the information, while also being directed toward – being for – a new reality (e.g., a new line in the program, the creation of a numerical value, the display of a pattern).

How does all this apply to powers? For powers to bring about potential new realities, they must "cooperate" with other networked powers. If they are to cooperate or interact effectively, powers must carry information *for* a large array of possible manifestations. Furthermore, at least in a quasi-semantic sense, it is somewhat plausible that they have information *about* each other: Each power has information about the other powers with which it could collaborate. This information helps close what Baltimore (2022: 680) calls the "interaction gap," the problem of explaining not only how powers interact with each other but why they interact in the specific ways they do to bring about *this* result and not *that* result. As well, each power's information for new realities represents the identity of that power itself, similar to the iris and computer program examples mentioned above, so could reasonably be interpreted as information about the power. Lastly, powers also have information *as* reality because each power carries patterns of differences against the network of which it is a member, patterns reflecting the actual current state (the reality) of the power and the power network.

The blueprint metaphor appropriately reflects this ambiguity regarding the overlap between information as, for, and about. Like an algorithm or instruction manual for achieving specific outcomes, a blueprint indicates what needs to be done to achieve a specific outcome (i.e., how powers will cooperate to yield various manifestations); but like a map, which is semantic (Floridi 2010: 74) but nonpropositional, it also represents the current state of the system of powers. Counterfactuals are relevant here: To be counter to fact – to be a possibility – there has to be a factual state of the system directed toward said possibility. The information carried by powers can reasonably be captured by sets of counterfactual statements, as is standard in powers theory.

In my usage of the terms, there is no ontological distinction between "data" and "information." Data are standardly defined as differences, consistent with my conceptualization of information above. Gamez (2018: 95) observes that these differences (data) can be extracted for various purposes with an interface, that is, a way of measuring and interpreting data. Some thinkers label this extracted data, when well-formed and meaningful, *information* (Floridi 2009: 16, 2010: 21). However, it is arguable that *any* measured differences are meaningful depending on the context and measurer. For example, voltages (data) are meaningful to engineers, binary numbers (data) to computer scientists, and letters (data) to the literate (Gamez 2018: 96).[13] Moreover, there exist humanly inaccessible, ontologically relevant differences lying in hidden physical realms that will remain forever uninterpreted and thus meaningless to us; as such, "information" might just be simply "*well-formed* data" (2018: 96), thus eliminating the meaningfulness criterion. So, we do not genuinely need the data/information distinction to capture the distinction between well-formed and ill-formed data. However, as a cautionary note, I suspect that Gamez is sliding between epistemic and ontological concerns, probably because "information" is closely related to knowledge, a product of human interaction with the world, whereas "data" is thought to be "out there." Again, however, what is meaningless data to one person might be meaningful to another, so the application of the label "information" is context-sensitive. The larger point is that there is no real distinction between information and data.

I want to mention an objection related to the previous discussion. One could argue that information does not really exist "*in* the physical world" (in

---

[13] We might add that not only grammatical sequences of letters, but individual letters, can be meaningful as well (e.g., "W" stands for George W. Bush).

physical powers or anything else) on grounds that it is produced partly by the world and partly by an interface, as Gamez (2018: 101) suggests, where an interface is a combination of both interpretation and measurement technique (2018: 94). Therefore, strictly speaking, powers would not themselves carry information, but only furnish information upon entering the interface – our metaphysical lenses, we might say. However, presumably any interface is part of the physical world (including our minds if physicalism is true), therefore the information *is* in the physical world: It is in the world's various powers, some of which are part of the interface. Gamez (2018: 100) admits the possibility that information could be a part of a system as a whole but he suggests that this is problematic, because then the location of the information would be ambiguous, and we would still need an external interface to determine the information. In response to this claim, first, this conflates epistemic concerns (accessing and measuring the information) with ontological concerns (the latter is my concern here). Second, if the information is part of a system – such as a powers system – then it is spread throughout that system. That does not mean that parts of the system – the individual powers – do not have their share of the relevant information in the overall blueprint. They do. And they must if they are capable of manifesting.

To summarize the thesis of this chapter thus far: powers in a network carry information for their various interactions and manifestations. This information is captured by the idea that each power has a blueprint, $\beta$. This data must be well-formed. If it were ill-formed, then powers would not fit into their network or system and could not interact with each other – they would not "know" what to do and thus could make no difference to outcomes. Their supposed powerfulness would be ineffective.

After addressing some important implications regarding IT in the next section, I will further develop IT in relation to PIT and my overall view of powers.

## 6.5   Implications of the Informational Thesis

Three implications of IT should interest powers and nonpowers theorists alike. First, IT can account for some considerations regarding the prospect of a unique dispositional modality. Second, IT (alongside PIT as part of the 3d account) helps avoid problems with the conditional analyses of powers. Third, IT can help explain the distinction between powers and qualities (i.e., dispositional and categorical properties). These discussions represent the beginning, not the end, of investigations regarding IT's implications for powers.

## The Dispositional Modality

The dispositional modality is a proposed third type of physical modality residing conceptually between metaphysical possibility and metaphysical necessity (Anjum and Mumford 2018; Mumford and Anjum 2011: 175). The idea is that causal powers neither necessitate their effects nor ground mere possibilities; rather, they *tend* toward their effects. This is a unique claim amongst contemporary powers theorists. Powers theories of modality have typically followed the traditional assumption that there are two basic modalities, possibility and necessity.[14]

Let us take a step back. What do powers theorists agree on concerning modality? Powers can produce a variety of particular outcomes depending on their interaction with various other powers. For example, when triggered, fragility does not necessitate breaking. This is because a mix of other powers are also at play (e.g., a special coating on the glass makes it less fragile). However, what if no countervailing powers are in the mix? What if the glass is fragile and perfectly situated to break, there are no factors that would prevent the glass from breaking, and the trigger is right on target, so to speak? In this case, it would be necessary that the glass breaks. This much, I think, all powers theorists agree to: If the situation is absolutely ideal, the glass will break. But normally the situation is not ideal and there are a variety of powers at play, in which case it is only possible that the glass will break (we might say it has a chance to break or will tend to break, but there is no guarantee). The same goes for other powers.

Here is where Anjum and Mumford (2018: 17–18) disagree: Even if conditions are perfect for the breaking to occur, there are no preventers at work, and the trigger is delivered right on target, there is no guarantee that the glass will break. Yet the manifestation of breaking is "stronger" or "special" or "privileged" compared to other possible outcomes (2018: 4). In other words, there is a *tendency* toward breaking. The dispositional modality is inherently tendential, a unique modality occupying a metaphysical space between necessity and possibility. The internal principle of tendency is a rejection of Leibniz's Principle of Sufficient Reason and implies that even if nothing prevents a power's manifestation, it might not manifest (2018: 18). Every power is fundamentally tendential. It should also be noted that, in addition to the internal principle of tendency, Anjum and

---

[14] For examples of powers-based theories of modality operating exclusively under the possibility/necessity dichotomy, see Borghini and Williams (2008), Jacobs (2010), Wang (2015), and Yates (2015).

Mumford (2018: 11) posit an external principle of tendency: It is always possible for some external factor to block the effect of a power – or a cause more generally[15] – such that even when a power does produce its relevant manifestation, the manifestation could have been prevented and is therefore not necessary.

I see two problems for the dispositional modality. First, it adds new mysteries to the metaphysics of powers. For instance, consider radioactivity. A radioactive nucleus is unstable and will at some point decay and emit a particle. However, this does not mean that the nucleus possesses a *tendency* to decay (Psillos and Ioannidis 2019). Rather, there is some probability at any given time that it will decay. But Anjum and Mumford (2018: 50) hold that tendencies are more fundamental; they are basic metaphysical facts that ground probabilities. If we accept the primacy of tendencies regarding the radioactivity example, then at any given time we have to posit two conflicting, equally strong tendencies: one to decay and one to remain stable (Psillos and Ioannidis 2019). But then one tendency is not stronger or privileged as the dispositional modality requires. If a power tends toward multiple outcomes, then why should we not simply hold instead that there are multiple possible outcomes, that is, that it is a multitrack power? Perhaps no one track is more privileged than the other: They are equally probable depending on external factors.

Second, consider the implication that, even if all conditions are perfect and the stimulus is applied correctly, a power might not manifest. This is a core commitment of the dispositional modality: A power's manifestation, across all possible circumstances, is not guaranteed *no matter what*. It is simply a tendency. But what is the reason that it manifests, if it happens to, in these perfect circumstances? It is not clear. There is no sufficient reason for manifesting. Imagine two identical powers, in the same circumstances with the same trigger: One manifests, one does not. Anjum and Mumford accept this scenario. But this means that the manifestation is contingent because it is simply a *possibility*. It seems that if the effect of a power is short of necessary, perhaps very close to necessary or highly probabilistic, then it is possible. So, I suggest that *tendency* is a subcategory of *possibility*. X being necessary implies that X is guaranteed. X tending to be the case, or being disposed to be the case, implies that X is not guaranteed, thus merely possible. Now, being possible can occur in varying degrees of

---

[15] For Anjum and Mumford, causes and powers are closely connected: They develop a powers theory of causation according to which effects are produced by the manifestations of powers (Mumford and Anjum 2011).

probability or tendency (whichever concept one chooses), but possibility covers *everything* short of necessity. Therefore, the dispositional modality, being inherently tendential, is a type of possibility. Maybe it is a special subcategory of possibility, but it falls under "possibility" nonetheless.[16]

Taking account of these considerations, I do not see the metaphysical need for a third modality. There might be a practical benefit in talking as if there is a third modality – perhaps to make sense of our linguistic practices and expectations – but there is no fundamental need to posit a third type of modality and therefore the dispositional modality is not a real form of modality.

Nonetheless, suppose there are good reasons to hold onto the dispositional modality. In that case, IT might be compatible with it.[17] IT can theoretically supplement the dispositional modality by providing an informational map of all the possible tendential connections between powers and their manifestations. Relevant counterfactuals identifying links between triggers and manifestations would have to leave room for tendencies. For example, "If $x$ received the relevant stimulus for manifesting in appropriate circumstances, $x$ would tend to manifest" where "tend to" is understood as a unique third modality between possibility and necessity. So even if all conditions are satisfied and all the powers in a system carry the relevant information to fit together appropriately, a triggered power might not manifest. But there is no telling why; the information carried by the powers is simply insufficient to guarantee all manifestations.

If the dispositional modality is not real, as I suggest, then we are left with only the traditional modalities of possibility and necessity. Now, IT maintains that every power carries an informational structure (captured by its β) of all possible connections between it and other powers in its network. This, perhaps, accounts for what appears to be a unique dispositional modality: The "tendential nature" of a power is just its sensitivity to a large array of possible conditions and interactions with other powers. Some manifestations are more likely than others, but these probabilities reduce to possible combinations of interactions specified by the βs of the relevant networked powers. However, in select circumstances, the possibilities are necessities: If the situation is perfect, the power is guaranteed to manifest. That is what it means to be a power. Short of perfect conditions

---

[16] See Corry (2019: 45–50) for further critical discussion of the dispositional modality.

[17] PIT is also compatible with the dispositional modality if Mumford and Anjum (2011: 186–189) are correct that intentionality is explainable in terms of the dispositional modality. But that contradicts my view, which makes intentionality (directedness) identical to powerfulness.

for manifestation, in which case a power's manifestation would be guaranteed, a power's manifestation remains possible.

## The Analysis of Powers

In advancing PIT, IT, and the 3d account as a whole, I am giving an account, not an analysis, of powers. An account of some phenomenon should be informative, explanatory, and raise new questions; it does not have to be reductive and can leave room for additional necessary but currently unforeseen features. There is a further difference between analyses and accounts specific to powers theorization: Analyses of powers, including the many well-known conditional analyses (Choi 2006, 2008; Lewis 1997), are not obviously about the ontology of powers. They are first and foremost conceptual analyses. Even if these analyses can withstand scrutiny and prove counterexample-free, I worry that they do not address the metaphysical nature of powers and, therefore, do not yield an ontological account of the power/quality distinction (Livanios 2017b: 4–5). At most, conditional analyses seem only partially relevant to metaphysical questions about powers. This lack of metaphysical relevance is one reason why conditional analyses are not so helpful in understanding powers from the inside and are more conducive to networking accounts (see Section 0.7). By contrast, my purpose has been to give an informative account (not an analysis) of the metaphysics of powers.

Although conditional analyses of powers are problematic, conditionals are important to understanding powers. Therefore, I will show how my account of powers, in particular IT, can accommodate some central concerns of conditional analyses.

First, a little background on analyzing powers through conditionals. Conditional analyses use counterfactual statements to capture necessary and sufficient conditions for being a power. The basic idea is that an object, $x$, possesses a power to manifest if and only if, if $x$ were subject to the appropriate stimulus, then such-and-such manifestation would occur. One problem with this kind of analysis is its vulnerability to finks (Martin 1994). A fink prevents the manifestation of a power by taking the power away before it manifests. The stimulus causes $x$ to lose its power and a "finkish" power is one subject to such an event. For example, the electro-fink causes a live wire to become dead by detecting when the wire contacts a conductor, thus removing the power. Additional problems for the conditional analysis include masks (Johnston 1992) and antidotes (Bird 1998), cases where the power is triggered, the power remains intact (unlike with finks), yet the manifestation does not occur. The underlying problem in all these cases is that something prevents the power from realizing its manifestation – despite its being triggered in the case of masks and antidotes, or because of its being triggered in the case of finks. Therefore, conditional analyses of powers generally face the problem of prevention: Powers can (rather easily) be prevented from manifesting.

Lewis (1997) revises the conditional analysis, specifying that the causal basis of the power must remain intact for a sufficient length of time during and after the stimulation, thus ensuring that the manifestation occurs. This keeps finks out, but masks and antidotes could still prevent the manifestation. Bird (2007a: 37) accounts for preventers by including a *ceteris paribus* clause in the analysans, such that no condition obtains that would prevent the manifestation from occurring.[18] This is problematic because the *ceteris paribus* clause effectively says that the entire triggering and manifestation process must not be interfered with by any number of preventing conditions, arguably trivializing the conditional analysis. Nonetheless, Bird's modification does in fact rule out the common problems of finks, masks, and antidotes.[19]

Given that powers are subject to possible preventers, I argue that the conditional analysis of powers is subject to a dilemma. Either the conditional analysis does not specify possible preventers, or it does so by incorporating a prevention clause. On one hand, if the conditional analysis does not specify possible preventers, then the analysis will not work because the triggering of the power will not always suffice for its manifestation. On the other hand, if the conditional analysis does specify possible preventers (like on Bird's proposal), thus ruling them out, then the analysis will be implausible. It is implausible because it is both ad hoc and cumbersome. It is cumbersome since it requires a profligate *ceteris paribus* clause. In effect, it eliminates the problem of prevention simply by stipulating that no preventers occur. The "no preventers" clause must implicitly contain a lengthy list of possible prevention conditions.

This dilemma has force under the assumption that powers are subject to prevention. If this assumption is false, then powers are "perfect" in the sense that their manifestation will always occur given the appropriate trigger because they cannot be prevented. However, this is problematic, because only some powers, if *any*, are perfect. We can imagine some

---

[18] Steinberg (2010) also proposes a subjunctive analysis of powers qualified with a *ceteris paribus* clause.

[19] For a comprehensive survey of analyses of powers, see Choi and Fara (2018).

powers being immune to prevention. For example, an all-powerful being might have some perfect powers, even ones that, when triggered, the being itself cannot prevent. Or, in a simple universe with only two electrons, they will always repel each other. But most powers are imperfect.[20] The conditional analysis of powers is certainly not hopeless (see Choi 2006, 2008) and deserves continued evaluation and development.[21] But the prevention dilemma at least motivates the exploration of other options.

I have not analyzed powers in terms of information or intentionality. Rather, IT and PIT are attempts to characterize the nature of powers from the inside. Specifically, my information-theoretic account of powers can be tied to counterfactual conditionals and thus account for some of the motivation behind conditional analyses. That is, it can subsume the counterfactual content that conditional analyses posit without committing to a reductive analysis. It can do so because the information contained in each power's $\beta$ can plausibly support counterfactual claims (Williams 2019: 92). In effect, the information in each power can be interpreted as counterfactual information, a point I will further address in Section 6.6.

## *The Power/Quality Distinction*

The distinction between powers and qualities (dispositions and categorical properties) is central to contemporary metaphysics of science. It is relevant to understanding laws of nature, fundamental ontology, and issues in philosophy of mind. I have assumed a distinction between the two thus far (although, in Chapter 1, I argued that what are posited as qualities on nonpowers models of modality are in fact powers). What does IT imply about the power/quality distinction?

According to PIT, powers are essentially directed whereas qualities are not essentially directed. As argued in Chapter 2, to be a power is to be a directed property: Power = Directedness. Whereas powers satisfy the essential marks of intentionality, qualities do not satisfy these marks. If qualities *seem* to exhibit these marks, it is due to the laws of nature that they contingently obtain directedness and become powers-like. Laws confer powers upon qualities.

---

[20] Moreover, "perfect" powers might be impossible if powers always carry a unique dispositional modality (Anjum and Mumford 2018; Mumford and Anjum 2011: 193–194). Although I disagree with the dispositional modality, as argued above, I do admit it as an open question that deserves further attention.

[21] Corry (2019: 43–63), for instance, gives a new defense of the simple conditional analysis (with modifications) that fits within his account of powers in terms of causal influence.

But IT also implies an important and intriguing difference between powers and qualities. Powers inherently carry information for their various manifestations and are interconnected because their blueprints overlap. Owing to their informational content, powers carry their lawfulness, so to speak, inside their very being, whereas qualities do not. By "lawfulness" could be meant either something law-like or genuine laws of nature. I assume that laws of nature are irreal (Mumford 2004), therefore the lawfulness implied by the information carried inside powers is only law-like or serves a similar function to laws of nature. But what if, as a powers theorist, one is fully committed to laws being real? Then the "lawfulness" inside powers would have to be genuine laws. One might maintain that laws of nature supervene on powers (Bird 2007a) and claim that the supervening laws somehow remain inside the very being of powers. However, on this view, laws do not really do anything (since the power does all the work, the law is redundant) unlike the active role that laws play on the Universals Model. But a possible powers-based view on which laws are essential to the course of the universe, not just added on via supervenience, is nomic dispositionalism (Dumsday 2019). On this view, there are real powers and real laws. The laws, which play a governing role (2019: 9), are *ceteris paribus* clauses constituted by all the possible interferences that could block a power from manifesting (2019: 13). Laws and powers together underpin modal features of the world. My suggestion is that an advocate of this view could accept that the laws, as abstract entities (2019: 9), somehow reside inside the being of powers.

I will not resolve here whether powers theorists should accept laws of nature as real or whether laws play a governing role if they are real. Although I am strongly inclined toward the view that laws are irreal, my main point is that since powers inherently carry information that is essential to their modal force, it sets them apart from qualities.[22] Laws of nature represent modal information that determines what pure qualities are disposed to do in various circumstances. Qualities themselves do not carry information for their potential activities; they need laws. Qualities, absent laws, are perfectly uniform: They are raw, causally undifferentiated properties. According to the Universals Model and the Neo-Humean Model,

---

[22] There seem to be two questions about laws: what is their content and what is the status of their being (Esfeld and Deckert 2018: 1)? On the latter question, I disavow that laws have reality. Modality resides in causal powers, which serve the role of laws while having the benefit of being properties borne directly by the objects whose behavior needs explaining. The former question, about content, remains. The content of powers is their informational blueprint.

the laws of nature determine what powers these qualities will confer upon the objects bearing them. The laws of nature give qualities informational content that they would not otherwise have, thereby conferring them with powers. That is, on pure qualities views, the qualities that become "empowered" by laws are undifferentiated prior (in an ontological sense of "prior") to nomological conditions at a world determining the causal roles of qualities. So, qualities have a "just-there-ness" (Armstrong 2004: 141) feel to them – and if I am right, they are *just there* awaiting informational content and thus empowerment.

In Chapter 1, I argued that qualities-based views of modality are in fact committed to powers, and nothing in this chapter changes that argument. But if I am wrong that qualities on the Neo-Humean and Universals Models of modality collapse into powers, and there is a real distinction between qualities and powers, then IT provides a way to make the distinction: Powers are inherently informed whereas pure qualities become informed by the laws of nature.

## 6.6   Revisiting the 3d Account of Powers

I have pursued a theory of the internal nature of powers that centers on the Physical Intentionality Thesis (PIT) and the Informational Thesis (IT). In this section, with the Pure Powers Model defended (Chapters 1–2) and discussions of PIT (Chapters 3–5) and IT (Sections 6.1–6.5) complete, I will further explore the relationship between powers, information, and intentionality.

PIT and IT together undergird the **3d** account: that powers (**d**ispositions) possess physical intentionality (**d**irectedness) and carry information (**d**ata) for various manifestations. The 3d account is a nodal account of powers that opens a window into the "black box" that causal powers appear to be from the perspective of networking accounts.[23] According to the 3d account, a property is a directed power (i.e., a directedness) that carries or embodies information. A power's informational structure, captured by its blueprint, β, orients its directedness toward various collaborating powers (powerful partners) and specific manifestations. PIT concerns the fact of physical intentionality: *that* the power is directed. IT concerns

---

[23] Powers since Aristotle are commonly thought to exist behind a *"veil of manifestation"* (Marmodoro 2021: 20): they are known entirely through their manifestations. Therefore, their internal nature beyond their manifestations and their relations to other powers remains hidden. This is another way of saying that powers remain a black box and thus a nodal account is welcome.

the content of physical intentionality: *what* the power is for or directed toward. Similarly, there is the fact of a mental state being directed and the content of that mental state: what it is about. Although a power carries informational content (which is representational yet nonpropositional) it is not identical to that content. Compare a thought: a thought is directed toward the object of the thought but the directedness is not identical to its content.

Counterfactuals are intimately tied to our understanding of powers and physical modality in general. Can IT accommodate this fact? Yes. The information that defines each power's potentiality is real and supports counterfactual claims. It supports counterfactual claims in that the information blueprinted into each power is specifiable counterfactually: "If P were stimulated in such-and-such circumstances, then it would M" – where P is a power, M is a manifestation, and the stimulus is typically another power in the system of which P is one member. So, the information is primarily for P's manifestation, yet this entails the presence of information for P's manifestation partner (powerful partner) given that two (or more) powers are necessary for M to occur. This "counterfactual information" reflects the potentiality of each inherently modal power.

When I say "counterfactual information" I only mean that the information, the raw differences embodied in each directed property, is specifiable counterfactually. The information that defines what a power is directed toward is the metaphysical grounds for explaining why the counterfactuals are true, thus reflecting the notion of "why-grounding" as opposed to "how-grounding" (Richardson 2020). Why-grounding involves why-explanations, that is, answers to why-questions: in this case, why is such-and-such counterfactual true? Because this power is directed toward manifestations of the type specified by its informational content.

Even though counterfactual analyses of powers are unsatisfactory due to prominent counterexamples (see Section 6.5), they do provide insight into the nature of powers and powers are strongly associated with counterfactuals. That is, although powers are not reducible to counterfactual statements and although counterfactuals cannot provide a fool-proof conceptual analysis of powers, they provide a way of specifying the instructional information – the information *for* reality – that powers carry. IT stands in contrast to hypotheticalism about modality, the view that counterfactuals or subjunctives are the fundamental modal elements of reality,[24]

---

[24] For discussion of hypotheticalism, see Koons and Pickavance (2017: 84–86).

yet does recognize the importance of counterfactuals by specifying that powers' inside information can be interpreted counterfactually.

Although I maintain that the 3d account provides a coherent package of theses that illuminate powers, I am more confident in the second "d" (i.e., directedness or physical intentionality) than in the third "d" (data or information). But there must be some explanation concerning how powers "know" what to do. IT, at least, provides that. In sum, PIT and IT together provide a better, more complete explanation of the internality of powers than either alone (see Figure 6.2). Furthermore, the two theses conjointly have the benefit of more convincingly distinguishing powers from qualities. Qualities do not possess physical intentionality; they are not inherently directed toward manifestations. Rather, qualities are fully "manifest" or revealed as the properties they are at all times. And qualities do not contain information about manifestation partners or their potential to enter reciprocating relationships, for they have neither manifestations nor manifestation partners. They need no information for fitting into a network.

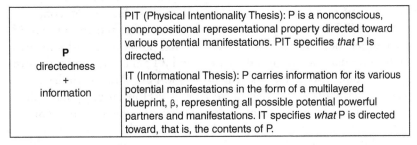

| **P**<br>directedness<br>+<br>information | PIT (Physical Intentionality Thesis): P is a nonconscious, nonpropositional representational property directed toward various potential manifestations. PIT specifies *that* P is directed. |
| --- | --- |
| | IT (Informational Thesis): P carries information for its various potential manifestations in the form of a multilayered blueprint, β, representing all possible potential powerful partners and manifestations. IT specifies *what* P is directed toward, that is, the contents of P. |

Figure 6.2   A power, P, from the inside

One might object that the 3d account is no better off from an ontological point of view than the Identity View (i.e., power = quality), since both views are committed to identity claims in elucidating powers (given that on the 3d account, power = directedness, where information *for* determines what the power is directed toward). However, the identification of power and quality presents more problems than the identification of power and directedness. For unlike "quality," "directedness" is already a modal notion. Directedness essentially involves that which is directed (i.e., the power) and that which the directed thing is directed toward (i.e., the manifestation). So, the notion essentially involves possibility since the directed thing (the power) might not achieve its aim.

Is it problematic that there are several interrelated concepts on the 3d account, none of which are completely unambiguous nor reducible to any of the other concepts? I think this worry is mitigated to the extent that the central concepts on my account – directedness and information – illuminate the modal nature of powers. And they do illuminate powers, in part because all these concepts have overlapping features. Powers are directed toward manifestations because they carry information for those manifestations. Yet this information itself is arguably intentional, since it is for or about something that might or might not occur. A degree of circularity is unavoidable since we are dealing with a family of related concepts. Yet, as I have argued, each element serves a specific role in illuminating powers and their inherent modality.

How does the 3d account relate to the Point Theory proposed in Chapter 2? According to Point Theory, excluding any powers that are extrinsically grounded, pure powers are self-grounded properties existing at spacetime points. On this view, pure powers are causal profiles at spacetime points. But these causal profiles are an epistemic stand-in for the real information that each power carries. Causal profiles are specified counterfactually, which is epistemically useful, but the underlying reality is the fundamental information (data or differences) that gives powers their directedness content.

IT and PIT mutually give us a better picture of powers from the inside than either thesis alone. They are claims that powerful qualities theorists *could* potentially accept into their view, and if I am right, powers theorists *should* accept. But questions remain. If the Pure Powers Model is correct, can we *really* know what powers are like? How far can philosophical investigation take us concerning these questions, which are relevant to a fully informed scientific understanding of the world yet inherently reach beyond the methods of science? This kind of investigation always retains a strong speculative element. But we are in no worse of a position here than if we accepted the Neo-Humean or Universals Models of modality.

A big implication of the 3d account is that, to the extent that causal powers pervade nature, an aspect of mind, that is, intentionality, pervades nature and is not just found in conscious beings. Nature's intentionality runs all the way from the smallest particles up through complex organisms with conscious minds. But fundamental intentionality, found in the causal powers of the smallest particles, is not conscious intentionality. This is not panpsychism, but a kind of panintentionality, where everything with causal powers possesses an important precursor to full, conscious mind. I will fully address this implication in Chapter 8. Before that, I turn to systems of powers and the appearance of qualities.

# CHAPTER 7

# Powers from the Outside
## Systems of Powers and the Appearance of Qualities

## 7.1 Systems of Powers

Type 1 objections to powers concern the nature of single instances of powers. Are pure powers grounded? What is their ontological status when not manifesting? The focus of type 1 objections concerns powers "from the inside," as Chapters 3 through 6 discussed. Type 2 objections to powers concern systems of powers, including the following issues. How can we distinguish two or more pure powers of the same type (Hawthorne 2001)? If a system of pure powers is entirely relational, what are the anchors of the relations (Heil 2003: 97–107; Jacobs 2011: 85)? Type 2 objections are more about powers "from the outside," so to speak. The Type 2 worry that concerns me here is: How might qualities, especially those possessed by macro objects, come to be instantiated from within a system of pure powers? At a minimum, how can we account for the *appearance* of qualities arising from a system of powers?

Given how powers interact in a system, we need to account for either the appearance that qualities emerge – because it at least *appears* that some properties in the world are qualitative – or the actual emergence of qualities.

A system of powers consists of two or more instances of powers in a dynamic relation. By "dynamic relation" I mean that no power in the system is entirely isolated from others. Every power in the system has at least one manifestation partner with which it can interact. If there are only two powers in the system, then they are mutual manifestation partners.

A system of powers contains no qualities. So, the powers must work together to produce higher-level properties, such as those found in the macro world or the world of everyday experience. The Pure Powers Model must explain how a system of powers is sufficient for all of the nonfundamental properties of the world to exist. The problem seems more pressing if the higher-level properties, underpinned by powers, are qualities. But a fundamental ontology of powers must also be capable of explaining how such a system can account for higher-level powers as well, for it is not obvious that lower-level powers can combine to form all the higher-level powers that we find in reality (Mumford and Anjum 2011: 101–105).

In this chapter, I explore the metaphysics of systems of powers. In Section 7.2, I delineate different kinds of multilevel systems of properties, specifying how powers and qualities might be related across different systems. In Section 7.3, in characterizing what it means for powers to form a unified "system," I build on the idea of powers holism introduced in Chapter 6. In Section 7.4, I proceed to discuss the possibility of ontologically emergent properties (particularly qualities) appearing out of a system of powers. Contrary to views that hold that powers reduce to qualities (Lewis 1986a), must have qualitative bases (Prior et al. 1982), or are identical to qualities (Heil 2003, 2012; Martin 2008), I hold that powers come first, qualities second – *if* there are qualities at all, for I argue that what appear to be genuine qualities might be quasi-qualities.

## 7.2   Powers and Multilevel Property Systems

A system of powers, S, existing at a single level of reality, contains two or more powers and no qualitative properties. If the powers were powerful qualities, then S would be capable of all the same actions, yet each power would be identical to a quality; in that case, many though not all of the questions explored below would be irrelevant. When I state "power" I mean pure power.

In using the phrase "levels of reality" I do not mean distinct ontological levels. Rather, I assume that there are organizational levels of properties, where properties at a "higher" or increased level of complexity come to exist as a result of the action of properties at a "lower" level of complexity. Carbon atoms in the appropriate relation will realize the hardness of a diamond (Gillett 2002). The hardness, I contend, does not exist at an ontologically higher level. Levels are metaphors and the reality of levels has more to do with the complexity of a system and the arrangement of its elements (properties, parts, ideas, etc.). The patterns and actions of the "lower-level" properties are sufficient to bring about (generate, realize, produce, etc.) the "higher-level" properties. What is built up is due to the patterns or actions of the building entities.[1]

---

[1] Bennett (2011) argues for a general building relation that subsumes cases of lower-level entities *generating, realizing, grounding*, and so on, higher-level entities. That is all I mean by the terms "realize" or "generate" – a general building relation – until the point later at which it is explicitly asked whether *emergence* (a specific building relation) is needed.

Two conditions define S. First, all the properties within S are pure powers; no qualities or powerful qualities allowed. Second, powers within S have no causal dependence on any properties external to S. So, properties outside of S are neither causally relevant to the manifestation of powers within S, nor causally necessary for the instantiation of powers within S.

I am concerned with the possibility of a multilevel system in which S generates a higher-level system of properties, $S^H$. What kinds of properties can piggyback on S at a higher level of organization? They could, in the simplest case, be higher-level (more complex) powers. That might be sufficient as an ontological basis for the world as we find it. But could the properties in $S^H$ be qualities? Could they be a mix of qualities and powers? Could they be powerful qualities? These more extravagant options might be required to explain the world of appearances – but, in turn, might require some form of emergence.

Figure 7.1 displays possible combinations of two organizational levels of properties. There are three kinds of property systems, consisting of either qualities only, powers only, or a mix of the two. Further, a mixed system comes in two varieties: with distinct powers and qualities, or powerful qualities. If there are only two levels – assumed for the sake of simplicity – then there are nine possible combinations of property systems yielding various types of multilevel property systems.

| Types of multilevel systems of properties | Lower-level system | Higher-level system |
|---|---|---|
| Type 1 | Powers | Powers |
| Type 2 | Powers | Qualities |
| Type 3 | Powers | Mixed |
| Type 4 | Qualities | Powers |
| Type 5 | Qualities | Qualities |
| Type 6 | Qualities | Mixed |
| Type 7 | Mixed | Powers |
| Type 8 | Mixed | Qualities |
| Type 9 | Mixed | Mixed |

Figure 7.1    Multilevel property systems

My concern is with multilevel systems type 1, 2, and 3. I am especially concerned whether S, a system of powers, can generate or realize higher-level nonpowers (i.e., qualities). In other words, are multilevel systems of type 2 or 3 possible and, if so, how are the qualities at the higher level produced?

Before pursuing that question, however, I will dig further into the nature of a system of powers. What makes a powers system an organized, unified whole capable of producing anything at a higher level?[2]

## 7.3   Systematizing a Powers System

### *The Problem of Fit or Unity*

Investigating the problem of fit for systems of powers provides a window into understanding the nature of powers and their interrelationship. Given that powers must work together to produce manifestations (i.e., reciprocity holds), yet powers are not merely relations (i.e., intrinsicality holds), and they cannot change their roles to fit changing circumstances (i.e., essentialism holds), there is a problem inherent in a powers theory of reality (Williams 2010, 2019: 85–95): how is that all the powers and their activity are so well arranged to issue a coherent, unified world?[3] The problem is that powers are in some sense ontologically isolated from each other – having essential, intrinsic features – yet their nature is to interact to produce manifestations. So how do they form a unified system that gets things done? Powers *do* work together; they do *fit* as parts of a whole network. The problem is explaining why that is so.

The problem of fit is similar to the combination problem in philosophy of mind (Brüntrup and Jaskolla 2016; Chalmers 2016; James 1950: 160)[4] and any general unity problem concerned with how a set of elements combines into a coherent whole. How do various elements (parts, properties)

---

[2]  My only concern here is with systems of properties. But one might also wonder about the systematization and interconnectedness of laws of nature within various property systems (categorical or dispositional), especially on necessitarian accounts of laws that some powers theorists maintain. For discussion of "nomic networks," and an argument that all possible laws are actual laws, see Bostock (2003).

[3]  The essentialist thesis is universally agreed upon by powers theorists. Reciprocity, the claim that powers must work together to manifest (e.g., salt's power to dissolve in water needs the dissolving power of water), is widely accepted (Heil 2003; Martin 2008; Mumford and Anjum 2011). Intrinsicality, the claim that powers are not relations, faces challenges from arguments that some powers are extrinsic (McKitrick 2003a), including even some sparse powers (Bauer 2011). However, even if some sparse powers such as mass are extrinsic, the problem of fit is still generated because their being extrinsic (or extrinsically grounded) does not necessarily mean that they are relational properties. Relational does not equal extrinsic (nonintrinsic). Even if that were so, then although the problem of fit could be avoided for some subsets of powers, for other subsets (excluding extrinsic powers but including intrinsic powers) the problem would be unavoidable.

[4]  The combination problem concerns how "smaller" mental states (e.g., nano-intentional states) combine to form fully-fledged consciousness or "bigger" mental states with higher-level intentionality.

fit together or combine to form a unified, systematic whole? The problem can be approached from the perspective of the elements (how are they structured or designed to work together?) or from the perspective of the whole (how is it composed or unified?). But the problem concerns one central question: the integration of various discrete elements – powers, gears, puzzle pieces, words – into one unified system.⁵ Given this understanding of the problem, I will treat "fit" and "unity" as perspectives on the same question. So, when I talk of a system of powers being unified, I mean that they fit together into a whole structure.

The main idea of unity I have in mind is that a system's entities (the components of a system) are interdependent in such a way that a change in the identity of any one entity affects the identity of at least some other entities in the system. It is a kind of causal or functional unity. In particular, I propose what I call "directed unity," which is engendered by the intentionality of powers, such that each power is directed at its manifestation partners and the manifestations which they are collectively for. This thesis, however, is built on top of powers holism.

### Powers Holism

Williams (2010, 2019: 85–95) develops powers holism to solve the problem of fit. Powers holism effectively shows that a system of powers is indeed a single, unified system. However, when supplemented by PIT, the unity of a powers system becomes even stronger, as I will argue.

According to powers holism, the identity conditions of any given power arise from the other powers in the system. Even if we assume powers are intrinsic properties (as William does) of their bearers, their causal roles (their identities) are codependent – they come packaged as a system, not as discrete entities. It takes (at least) two to tango. As such, powers must be "engineered" to have proper fit, therefore Williams (2010: 95) holds that each power must carry instructions or a blueprint of all possible interactions throughout the universe. This information ensures that any given power will be for a certain set of manifestations, typically requiring interactions with another power or powers. In a sense, the powers will "know" each other. For example, only because two electrons separately possess negative charge and "recognize" this in each other, will they repel each other.

---

⁵ Such a problem does not arise in a single-entity universe, such as a lone "atom" with no proper parts, or a lone property.

Each power having information in the form of a blueprint strongly suggests physical intentionality, although Williams does not explicitly endorse that idea in addressing the problem of fit. Before getting into those details, however, let us look closely at powers holism.

According to powers holism, the identity (but not necessarily the ontological ground) of any given power is determined by its relation to all the other powers in a system of powers (Mumford 2004: 182; Williams 2010: 96). These partnerships determine all the possible manifestations of any given power. On powers holism, "the constituents [the powers] of the whole determine their natures collaboratively" (Williams 2010: 96). As Mumford (2004: 182) puts it, "a property cannot stand alone, unaffected by and unconnected with anything else. A world comes with a whole, connected system of properties." I need to qualify this by emphasizing that while a power's *identity* cannot stand alone – its identity necessarily references other properties which might or might not be instantiated – there could be a one-power universe where the lonely power has unrealized connections (and information for) other powers (as discussed in Section 0.7, Section 2.5, and Section 6.3). Sans other powers, this lone power will not actually do anything, but it *could* if other powers were instantiated in the system. So, it must have a blueprint, β, relating it to other powers. When all the powers of a system are actually present, they form an interconnected web, meaning that no property is causally isolated from the others. Powers produce effects when triggered by other properties, and these effects are further properties capable of interacting with further powers for further effects, and so on.

Suppose that I am incorrect and powers holism does concern the ontological grounding of pure powers, not just their identity conditions, thus all powers in the network are, by implication, extrinsically grounded. In that case, the need for self-grounding and the claim that some pure powers are self-grounded (Chapter 2) might yet remain in force. This is because the powers of the network as a whole (as embodied by the universe) would have powers – powers to evolve, powers to gain or lose powers, and so on – and these would need to be self-grounded. That is, arguably, powers of the whole system would be self-grounded.

The causal interdependence of properties that powers holism requires bears strong resemblance to semantic holism (Williams 2010: 96). On semantic holism (Esfeld 1998: 374), the meanings of terms are interdefined, so a language (or a set of propositional attitudes) forms a coherent system. If the meaning of one term changes, the meanings of other terms in the semantic system should also change (if a lake is a body of water, then if the meaning of "water" changes, the meaning of "lake" will too). A change in one belief affects others in the same belief system. Likewise, powers form a coherent system in virtue of their interdependency. If one power in the system is changed (e.g., the range of its manifestation types is altered), the others necessarily change (Mumford 2004: 182).[6] This suggests unity to the system of powers – *one* system – for only in a unified system is there such metaphysical sensitivity. Throw a rock into a pond, there is a ripple effect; likewise, when a power's nature is changed.[7]

There are also interesting parallels between powers holism and Searle's framework for intentionality. Searle (2015: 36) holds that intentional states come packaged in what he calls a "Network." Similarly, powers come in a network in which they determine each other's triggering conditions and circumstances of manifestation. Intentional states do not function atomistically or independently (2015: 44) – they function holistically. If you believe one thing, by implication there are other things you will believe. If you believe the apple is red, you believe that people will tend to use "red" when describing it, that animals will respond to it in certain ways, and so on. This is analogous to powers holism. If a power is for one type of manifestation, it will also be for related types of manifestations. If a glass is disposed to break, it will be disposed to break in a variety of ways and places – it is connected to many powerful partners.

To the Network of intentional states, Searle (2015: 44) adds "a Background of pre-intentional capacities" required for the intentional states to function (however, he does not think there is a principled way to distinguish the Network and Background). For example, intending to A requires ability to perform A. This is questionable. Why can I not intend to do something for which I am not equipped at this point? Nevertheless, this aspect of Searle's view is not directly relevant to powers holism, for powers on my view *are* intentional and they *are* capacities. Capacities are not in the background: There is no distinction between capacities and the network of intentional states in systems of powers, because the capacities (powers) are intentional states, per PIT.

---

[6] A reviewer asked if this claim is consistent with essentialism. I think part of Mumford's point is that if one power were changed, the result would be *a different system of powers*. So, it is not metaphysically possible (though it might be logically possible) for just one power to change without changes in the whole system. (However, it might not be that *every* other property that makes up the entire system must change if one is changed; there could be powers on the periphery of the system, distant from the one power that hypothetically changes, which are not affected at all.) This observation shows both the sensitivity and connection between powers, that is, their systematicity and unity.

[7] If one rejects holism, Mumford (2004: 183) claims that one must then accept a theory of discrete properties (discreta) with quiddities. Perhaps, but I will not evaluate that claim here.

How do any two powers match up, as pieces of a jigsaw puzzle do, to causally cooperate for a manifestation? A system of powers must be built according to a plan specifying how each power interacts with its reciprocal powers. Signaling an information-theoretic approach, Williams (2010: 95) argues that each power effectively embodies a set of information or instructions (as introduced in Chapter 6) specifying and enabling these possible interactions. This explains the fit between powers and hence the unity of a powers system. Each individual power carries or embodies information that guides its action and ensures a system-wide coherency.

However, in order to "instruct" a single power, thereby blueprinting or informing it, all other powers that it could interact with also need blueprints (Williams 2010: 97). Thereby, each power's plan (set of possible interactions) is made consistent with other powers' plans. But how is this started, unless all the plans are determined at once? The powers' plans cannot be individually determined but must be done so collectively or holistically. If a power's nature were determined individually, it is not clear how it could be an effective part of a system of powers, capable of collaborating with other powers that thus mutually produce manifestations. It would be like the role of an individual gene in a genome being determined without accounting for how it interacts with other genes in the genome to produce phenotypic expressions.[8] Since the identity of each power depends on all the others, they are all "for" each other and so fit together naturally in a whole system.

Given these considerations, as foreshadowed in Section 6.3, I contend that each power's blueprint, $\beta_{P_1}$, $\beta_{P_2}$, and so on must be multidimensional or multilayered, each layer a slight variation of adjacent layers, thus mapping the full array of possible combinations of background conditions, power interactions, and outcomes specific to powers $P_1$, $P_2$, and so on (see Figure 6.1).

If this view of a system of powers is correct, then the identity of each power in a system is defined in terms of other powers as represented by their blueprints. No power's line of possible effects is an isolated series of manifestations toward some isolated end, disconnected from other powers. All powers (and manifestations of powers, which are further powers)

---

[8] At least, if powers' natures were determined individually (without reference to other powers), it would be metaphysically more complicated in contrast to the more organic simplicity of powers holism. This is because it would require an external metaphysical force or external instruction (e.g., a governing law) to regulate the potential interactions of powers in the "system." The systematicity would come from outside the system.

are part of a whole. So, there is no regress toward some infinite end, but a web-like series of powerful actions.[9]

### Directed Unity

Given powers holism, we have a plausible sense of how powers are unified in a coherent, self-contained system. In sum, two or more powers, P1, P2, P3, and so on are unified if the identity of P1 (its role in a system) ontologically depends on the identity of P2, P3, and so on. On this view of identity, the functions of all the powers in a system are ontologically interdependent. As such, the powers that make up the system are capable of affecting each other: when one undergoes a change, the system is appropriately affected. Thus, powers holism shows how a collection of powers can fit together into a unified system. However, powers holism derives further explanatory power from physical intentionality. While powers holists need not accept physical intentionality, doing so strengthens the unity provided by powers holism.

Although powers holism and physical intentionality are logically independent theses, physical intentionality provides a metaphysical framework to explain how and why powers are fitted for each other. Imagine two types of unity. There is *undirected unity* in which each power of a system is simply defined (i.e., given identity conditions, as represented by each power's blueprint) in terms of its role alongside other powers of the system. Then there is *directed unity* in which the powers of a system are not only interdefined but "reach out" to each other. They reach out, or are directed, in the way that psychological states reach out to the objects they are about (these objects could be other psychological states, as when a belief is about another belief). More specifically, each power carries fundamental informational content that represents both its possible manifestations and the other powers that are necessary for those manifestations. Reciprocal powers partners must represent, or have intentional states concerning, each

---

[9] Armstrong (1997: 80) argues that if all properties of particulars are powers, as in powers holism, then these "particulars would seem to be always re-packing their bags as they change their properties, yet never taking a journey from potency to act." Each act is just a new power or potency; as such, particulars would be "always packing, never traveling" as the argument is frequently summarized. This argument has received much attention. For a detailed analysis of the argument, see McKitrick (2009). For a detailed evaluation, see Molnar (2003: 173–180), who concludes that all attempts to show the regress as vicious face difficulties and none "uncovers an actual contradiction in pandispositionalism" (2003: 180) or any system of pure powers for that matter. For further discussion and defense of the powers regress, see Inghthorsson (2015).

other in order to achieve their manifestations. If powers come in a holistic set and PIT is true, then the intention – directedness – of $P_1$ is fixed by that of $P_2$, $P_3$, and so on. Directedness figures into an explanation of identity conditions. Each power is related to other powers in a system by directedness and informational content, per the 3d account, and this system holistically determines identity conditions.

I see powers holism as providing merely undirected unity to the universe's powers. Mumford (1999) explicitly denies PIT.[10] Although Williams (2010) emphasizes the for-ness of powers, and metaphorically attributes a kind of information-bearing blueprint to each power, this runs short of accepting PIT, and thus what I call directed unity. The blueprint might be metaphor, but the information and intentionality are not.

Williams (2010: 90) claims that "nothing about the intrinsicality or necessity of the powers prepares the properties to fit together" and thus causally interact. However, powers are directed toward their manifestations – and, importantly, toward each other to interact to produce manifestations – thus making them naturally engineered to cooperate or interact with other powers necessary for those manifestations. Why do such basic powers integrate and unify? My answer is: the directedness of powers. As such, the unity produced in this kind of system should be called directed unity. Assuming that IT is correct, then the interlocking feature of powers' directedness is further explained by their informational overlap (sharing of blueprints).

What I have in mind with directed unity is that two (or more) powers, $P_1$ and $P_2$, collaborate with each other, not just because they are interdefined per powers holism, but because they are mutually directed toward manifestations. Each is directed in two mutually dependent ways: toward each other – toward interacting with each other – and toward a manifestation. The mutual directedness toward a manifestation requires them to collaborate and respond to each other. As with $P_1$ and $P_2$, the same holds for $P_2$ and $P_3$, and $P_1$ and $P_3$, and so on as further powers are added to the system.

$$[P1*P2] \rightarrow \text{Manifestation 1}$$
$$[P2*P3] \rightarrow \text{Manifestation 2}$$
$$[P1*P3] \rightarrow \text{Manifestation 3}$$

Figure 7.2    Unity through directedness in a three-power system (* = collaboration between powers, → = mutual directedness toward a manifestation, M) (Originally printed in Bauer 2019. Reprinted by permission.)

[10] See also Mumford and Anjum (2011: 186–189).

Figure 7.2 represents a simple, three-power system: each power partners up with every other possible power and no more than two powers
partner up in any instance, toward one manifestation. As a system of powers becomes more complex (as in the actual world), some powers will of
course not have primary connections to each other, for it is not the case
that every set of two powers is directed toward a mutual manifestation.
But they will all make connections to each other through secondary, ter-
tiary, and further partnerships.

The directedness of powers creates a network of interdependence represented by each power's blueprint. For two powers, P1 and P2 – each
necessary for realizing a family of possible manifestations – P1 is directed
toward P2, and vice versa. The different but related possible manifestations
are captured in each power's multilayered blueprint, β. If the two states
are about (directed toward) each other then they are unified owing to their
being *for* a set of possible manifestations; that is, they jointly possess a singular purpose or directedness. But P1 and P2 are also separately partnered
with P3 for different manifestations. Since each power is partnered with
each other power, and each is directed toward the other to interact toward
a manifestation, there is a kind of intentional symmetry. Consequently,
they are unified in "intention" or directedness toward outcomes.[11]

How do the powers communicate? That is, how do they stay functionally integrated and thus unified? Just as intentional states reach out to the
world, representing objects and possibilities, powers reach out to partner
powers such that each power represents each other's contribution to their
potential joint manifestations. There are various ways to imagine these
connections. Imagine a kind of information-bearing signaling transmitted
instantaneously as what seems to occur between two or more subatomic
particles in a quantum entangled system. Changes in one particle seem to
affect an entangled partner instantaneously. We can imagine fundamental
power-bearing particles participating in a kind of superluminal information transmission. Though admittedly highly speculative, that would allow
them to "coordinate" their behavior on a continual basis. Alternatively, the
coordination between powers might be supported by a broader metaphysical feature.

Williams (2010: 98) thinks that for powers holism to take hold, it needs a
broader metaphysic – something to create conditions for the proper fitting

---

[11]   The unifying power of directed unity is somewhat like the phenomenal bonding relation advanced
by Goff (2016) to solve the combination problem. Directed unity creates a kind of *intentional* bonding relation.

(and thus systematization) of powers. Imagine a body of water in which billions of water molecules fit together in an otherwise empty space. Now imagine that same space filled with billions of distinct membranous pores (one for each water molecule), such that each molecule is surrounded by a membrane. In this situation, the molecules will not form a body of water because they need relatively empty space to interact and bond with each other. Similarly, we need a broader metaphysics that allows the powers to "communicate" and be "available" to each other (2010: 98), thus obtaining the interdependency required for fitting (and unification).

Here are three options (Williams 2010: 98–101). First, one could opt for brute force, holding that powers are necessarily holistically intertwined, and *that's it* – no further metaphysic needed. However, that view too easily dismisses the problem or stops the problem-solving too short. Second, one could adopt Platonism, claiming that powers enjoy a nonspatiotemporal existence in which they are timelessly and perfectly available to communicate, thereby obtaining the appropriate fit and unity. Third, one could take up a naturalistic form of monism – particularly, Priority Monism (Schaffer 2010b) – holding that powers are entirely spatiotemporal entities (thus denying Platonism) networked as part of a fundamental whole, the cosmos itself. Williams argues for the third view, urging to repudiate brute force solutions if others are available, and to avoid the supernaturalism associated with Platonism.[12]

I suggest that we do not need a further metaphysical framework to undergird powers holism, yet that does not mean we accept the brute force option. The intentionality built into each power can do the unifying work more parsimoniously than adding a further ontological posit. Physical intentionality internally governs the behavior of powers and guides their collaboration. This approach is not a brute force solution, but a particular interpretation of the nature of powers as defended in Chapters 3–5.

However, in Section 5.3, I gave some reasons to support Priority Monism in the context of defending the claim that powers satisfy Extrinsic-G. I stand by that limited defense of Priority Monism – if the Argument from Particle Physics, also discussed in Section 5.3, proves insufficient to show that powers satisfy Extrinsic-G. So, although I do not maintain that we need a broader metaphysic to support powers holism, since directed unity

---

[12] Another possibility is that the network was intelligently designed. But given my (tentative) suggestion that God = Nature (see Chapter 8), there would be no design or designer independent of the network of powers. (Thanks for a reviewer for suggesting this as a fourth solution to Williams' query.)

can do the job, if we do add a broader metaphysic then Priority Monism remains, to my mind, the most plausible.

Moreover, to say that some parts are parts of a larger, single whole is just for those parts to form a holistic system from the get-go (compare the claim that the cells in a body collaborate because they are generated by and embedded within that one body). According to monism, there is one fundamental thing manifesting fine-grained particularity in all the derivative parts. The powers of these parts fit together and form a whole owing to their derivation from the whole. Holism and monism seem to be similar, though not identical, theories of the same basic structural reality. So, we do not need both if one will provide the necessary metaphysical apparatus. I agree that Priority Monism *can* underpin powers holism, and that it is the best option of the three sketched by Williams. But it is not necessary, given the overall view of powers holism plus directed unity as outlined above.

Even if the Platonic or monistic framework is emplaced to underpin powers holism, directed unity still adds some explanatory force by specifying the nature of the connections between individual power tokens.

In sum, bolstered by their physical intentionality and informational nature, powers are networked in a system of powers. It is powers' networked nature that readies them for action with other powers with which they collaborate.[13] That completes a picture of what a system of powers is like. An important question remains: What can be ontologically derived from such a system? Can such a system generate qualities or at least explain the quality-like features of the world?

## 7.4   The Appearance of Qualities

### *Two Senses of "Appearance"*

Just as the advocates of Neo-Humeanism and the Universals Model should try to account for the appearance of powers out of a system of qualities, advocates of the Powers Model (especially the Pure Power Model) should try to account for the appearance of qualities out of a system of powers.

So, I am concerned to explain the appearance of qualities out of a system of powers, as represented in multilevel property systems 2 or 3 (see

---

[13] This bears some analogy to the proposal, known as Wild Systems Theory, that living systems are embodied in contexts that they are in turn *about* (Jordan 2018).

Figure 7.1). The "appearance of qualities," as I use the term, has two senses. In a weak sense, there is the mere appearance of qualities: they are quasi-qualities, not genuine qualities but outwardly appearing to be qualities (manifested, stable properties) due to the interactive work of powers. In a strong sense, they are genuine qualities, which "appear out of" or ontologically emerge from a system of powers. It also seems possible for a system of powers to produce emergent powers (Mumford and Anjum 2011: 101–105), but I am concerned here with emergent qualities.

One might wonder, when powers manifest, does this necessarily introduce qualities into the system? Is a manifestation necessarily a quality? No. A manifestation is the result of a process that a power undergoes when it is triggered. But this result is itself a further property and it is a power. It is capable of further contributions to the system – interactions with other properties in the system. If the manifestations of powers did nothing – if they were powerless – then "properties would not form a causal net, but rather several singular causal relations, and the causal work would soon come to an end" (Gozzano 2020: 1050). In other words, it would not be a system of powers and there would be no need for powers holism. So, powers manifesting within S simply produce further powers within S. From a powers point of view, the natural view is that manifestations are further powers, a thesis widely accepted thesis amongst powers theorists.

### The Argument from Composition and the Possibility of Emergent Qualities

The argument from composition holds that qualities cannot arise from, or be composed out of, a system of powers (Heil 2003: 114–115). Heil frames the argument in terms of the properties of a whole arising from the properties of the whole's parts, but I will focus on "higher-level" properties arising from "lower-level" systems of properties. This argument is one reason why Heil and others favor the Powerful Qualities Model over the Pure Powers Model. If a theory of reality requires genuine qualities – something more than quasi-qualities – then the argument from composition tries to show that qualities cannot be produced by a pure powers system.

The key idea behind the argument from composition is that an object cannot acquire an entirely new type of property out of a system consisting entirely of another type or property. So, a kind of property reductionism is assumed: token properties of a given property type must reduce to tokens of the same type. So, the *qualities* of an object must reduce to *qualities*, not powers, of the parts of the object. Therefore, assuming that objects do have qualities, they must have some fundamental qualities: It cannot be all powers at the bottom. Therefore, it is not possible for a powers system to realize higher-level qualities.[14]

The argument from composition challenges the idea that a powers system can compose qualities. However, it also shows that if qualities cannot be merely composed out of pure powers, then emergence is necessary for qualities to be produced.

I contend that just because a system has qualities at the system level – specifically when the system is kind of complex whole or object as Heil has in mind – does not necessarily mean that the system must contain qualities. This is because, in contrast to the reductionist principle behind the argument from composition, qualities could emerge from a system of powers (or the powers of the parts of a system if that system is a complex object). For example, a ball might be purple (suppose purple is a quality, not a power) but the quarks and electrons that make up the ball have no qualities whatsoever (including purple) but are propertied entirely by powers. If emergence is real, powers must work somehow to form qualities. This would be a form of ontological emergence, in which a new kind of property comes to be from another type of property operating at a more basic level.

In addition to ontological emergence, there is an epistemic conception of emergence. It is important to distinguish these because a proponent of the principle of composition could accept epistemic emergence while denying ontological emergence. This distinction reflects, in all ways relevant for my purposes, the difference between strong and weak emergence (Chalmers 2006). A phenomenon X is strongly emergent means that X is determined by lower-level facts but X is not deducible from them (or reducible to them); for strongly emergent phenomena we need new fundamental laws (or modal principles of some sort). This is the ontological sense of emergence. A phenomenon X is weakly emergent means that although X's arising from the lower level of reality is unexpected by the observer, no new law is needed. This is an observer-dependent, epistemic sense of emergence.

An epistemically emergent property might be surprising to an observer, despite complete knowledge of the pre-emergent properties in the system. However, the new property is ultimately explainable in terms of

---

[14] Heil (2003: 31–39) does not accept ontological levels of reality. However, this does not preclude organizational levels, or increasing complexity, of the kind identified in Section 7.2.

and reducible to the pre-emergent properties. By contrast, an ontologically emergent property is genuinely irreducible to and not explainable in terms of the pre-emergent properties. They just appear at some point from the system of pre-emergent properties. Therefore, although ontologically emergent properties might be surprising like their epistemically emergent cousins, this is not constitutive of their emergent status.

We can now distinguish two forms of ontological emergence (Searle 1994: 112).[15] Searle calls these emergent1 (the weaker variety) and emergent2 (the stronger variety). To be emergent1, a property or phenomenon X must be caused by the interaction of elements of a system, not just their arrangement (mere arrangement does not underpin any kind of emergence relation).[16] Consciousness seems like this, contends Searle, but not the shape and weight of a stone, for instance, for the properties of the stone can be explained just be citing the composition and arrangement of the parts. However, I think that this distinction (between the mere composition of the parts and the interaction of the parts) is illusory; all parts of a particular thing and all things in a system, so far as physics tells us, are continually interacting. The particles of a stone are in dynamic interaction; the quantum world is buzzing with activity. But I grant that there might be special kinds of interaction that are behind emergent1 phenomena, such as consciousness. Emergent1 can be epistemically surprising, as with Chalmers' weak emergence, and it is an ontological emergence; but it falls short of strong emergence.

Emergent2, however, is "a much more adventurous conception" than emergent1 (Searle 1994: 112). To be emergent2, a phenomenon X must possess causal powers inexplicable in terms of the interactions of the elements of the system out of which X arises. Emergent2 properties are not deducible from lower-level activity. If consciousness were emergent2, it would get "squirted out" of the behavior of neurons and then take on "a life of its own" (1994: 112). This is suggestive of the idea that the emergent phenomena require new laws of nature, for having "a life of its own" means not having a life explainable entirely in terms of lower-level action. If real qualities are generated by systems of powers, it seems that they would be emergent2 phenomena and fundamentally different from powers. If only

---

[15] Specifically, for Searle, these are kinds of causal emergence. But they have a clear ontological flavor.

[16] Similarly, Heil (2012: 30) contends that emergence is a causal notion: when two particles collide and produce a new kind of particle that possesses properties that the original two particles did not possess, the novel properties are genuinely emergent. The two original particles have caused a new particle with new properties to emerge.

emergent1 phenomena were in play, then any "qualities" that emerged, I suggest, would just be quasi-qualities.

There could be either emergent2 powers or qualities, or both. But the question of emergent2 qualities is the more intriguing problem and my concern here.

The idea of "qualities-emerging-from-powers" appears a bit unusual. It runs counter to the typical concern to explain the emergence of higher-order causal powers; accounts of emergence often refer to the emergence of higher-order, unique powers (see O'Connor 2020: Section 2). However, if we take the fundamental properties to be powers (i.e., we accept dispositional monism), yet hold that some nonfundamental properties are qualities, the latter needs to be accounted for in our ontology (unless we accept that there are entirely separate realms of powers and qualities having nothing to do with each other). So, the possibly of emergent qualities should be considered.[17]

### Qualities and Emergence

If qualities emerge2 out of S, they constitute a new type of property. An emergent2 quality is not just a continually manifesting power or set of powers, appearing to be qualitative; rather, it is a stable, irreducible quality. On the emergence account I propose, two or more powers interacting produce a quality. The quality, Q, irreducibly appears out of the interactions of powers within S (see Figure 7.3).[18] It could be a conscious quale (e.g., redness), some kind of structural property (e.g., rectangularity), or something else (e.g., a chemical property as simple as wetness).

---

[17] It must be pointed out that according to Wilson (2021), for whom strong emergence is both viable (2021: 16) and involves new powers coming to be instantiated at a higher level in a way incompatible with physicalism (2021: 17), what she labels the "*New Power Condition*" (2021: 51) is explicitly metaphysically neutral with regards to the reality of powers and causes (2021: 32–33). Emergent "powers" could very well be purely qualitative properties that are only metaphysically contingently involved in modal relations. So, one could be a strong emergentist in Wilson's sense without claiming that the emergent "powers" are *real causal powers*. If pure qualities are to emerge from real causal powers, as I contend is possible, and if one wants to give them any kind of powers interpretation, then these qualities must not be interpreted as anything other than "weak powers" or "moderate powers," as opposed to "robust powers" (Azzano 2019) (see footnote 32 in Chapter 1 for further discussion of Azzano's distinction).

[18] The issue lurking here is a sort of special composition question (SCQ) for powers to qualities. Assuming that qualities emerge2 out of powers, *when and how do qualities emerge out of the interactions of powers?* This is analogous to the SCQ for higher-order powers, concerning when powers compose higher-order, more complex powers (Bird 2020: 166), which in turn is modelled on the SCQ originally raised for objects (Van Inwagen 1990: 20): What are the conditions under which two or more objects compose one object?

$$S^H \qquad \{Q\}$$
$$S \qquad [P1*P2] \rightarrow M1$$
$$[P2*P3] \rightarrow M2$$
$$[P1*P3] \rightarrow M3$$

Figure 7.3   The emergence of a quality, Q, out of a powers system, S (the curly brackets around Q represent that Q is emergent2)

The core idea is that powers $P_1 \dots P_n$ (a relevant subset of powers within S or all of the powers within S) can activate each other in such a way to yield Q, whose metaphysical nature and causal-nomological role goes beyond those of $P_1 \dots P_n$. The generation of Q is a causal process: the powers' activity generates Q, but it is inexplicable beyond the fact that such-and-such powers interacting will generate such-and-such a quality. Imagine fragility and hardness, under some special conditions, together producing green, not brokenness. Once the relevant powers interact, they generate Q. More specifically, the powers are directed toward their mani-festation partners and distinctive manifestations $M_1$, $M_2$, $M_3$, and so on, as represented in Figure 7.3, but not directed toward producing Q. Rather, Q arises emergently out of some unspecified interaction of powers. Q is nomologically independent from S and irreducible to powers within S.

As a pure quality, the emerged Q does not play an inherent causal role within $S^H$. It is not intrinsically directed toward outcomes, but only contin-gently as specified by relevant laws of nature per the standard understand-ings of the Neo-Humean and Universals Models of physical modality. Q would qualify as a weak power, gaining dispositional capacities in response to its nomological environment. The metaphysical mechanism by which Q emerges from S is not explanatorily reducible to the interaction of pow-ers in S, despite the fact that it is the activity of powers in S that somehow produces Q; the powers in S are sufficient, but perhaps not necessary, to produce Q.

If Q were only emergent1, then Q would collapse into what I call a quasi-quality, a property that appears to be a quality but is really just the continual manifesting of powers in S so as to appear qualitative. So, on my view, genuine qualities *cannot* be emergent1, only emergent2. If the life of a supposedly emergent property is explanatorily reducible to the interac-tion of powers in S, then the powers would do all the explanatory work and the emergent property cannot be a new kind of property (a quality). Therefore, there would be no need to posit a new ontological reality. In that case, we would only be justified in positing quasi-qualities, not genu-ine qualities.

## Quasi-Qualities and the Interaction of Powers

Although the emergence of qualities from systems of powers is possible, I do not think we are justified in accepting emergent2 qualities. Given considerations of simplicity and explanatory power, I argue that the appearance of emergent2 qualities is illusory. What appear to be real qualities are only quasi-qualities: quality-like, stable manifestations generated by the continual interaction of multiple powers (two or more) within S. Quasi-qualities are not real qualities (not quiddities; not categorical); they appear as qualities, but they have no independent status since they are reducible to the work of powers stably interacting for prolonged periods of time. What is created by powers' interaction is a new power that appears to be a quality but is not genuine.

In this sense, the appearance of qualities out of powers (as I theorize) mirrors the appearance of powers out of qualities (as advocates of pure qualities theorize). Azzano (2019: 340–342) calls the powers that qualities appear to have "weak powers." For example, when we disquote the claim "birds can fly" we get the truth that birds can fly, and presumably we want to ascribe the power to fly to birds; but Neo-Humean and Universals Model theorists will reduce this "power" to qualities. Similarly, we can disquote the claim "the ball is round" to obtain the truth that the ball is round; this appears to be a quality, but by the light of the Pure Powers Model is just the appearance of a quality – a quasi-quality – as the power to fly is the appearance of a power. It is not a quality that makes it true that "the ball is round," rather a relevant set of powers interacting and manifesting. So, the "quality" is reduced to powers.

These quasi-quality producing powers are directed toward manifestations of structures, shapes, colors, and all the other qualitative appearances. This view does not deny the appearance of such properties, it only denies that their appearance is due to either a pure quality or a powerful quality. Some of these powers capable of producing quasi-qualities will be continually, long-manifesting powers, accounting for the stability of the qualitative appearance of the world. These properties, in some cases, reach the minds of perceivers; here too we can deny qualities, but account for the phenomena in terms of powers. The qualia within conscious experience are quasi-qualities, the complex work of interacting powers manifesting within consciousness. But that is a claim needing detailed, separate examination.[19]

---

[19] Gozzano (2020), for example, defends a dispositional theory of phenomenal states.

In sum, fundamental reality – the level with the least organizational complexity – consists of powers in a unified system. It appears that qualities arise out of such systems, because there appear to be qualities in our ordinary experience. But what appear to be qualities are actually quasi-qualities produced by the continual interaction of complexes of powers ultimately bottoming out in the pure powers of S. In short, powers undergird an arrangement of quasi-qualities.

However, I do leave open the possibility of genuine qualities emerging from a system of powers. There might be some special cases of genuine ontological emergence where real qualities are produced somehow by lower-level powers. This is a more ontologically heavyweight claim, but it cannot be ruled out. In this case, a special law connecting the powers system to the emergent, higher-level qualities would be necessary, as well as special laws for the role of qualities at the higher level.

## 7.5   Beyond Fundamental Powers and Quasi-Qualities

Applying the principle of parsimony, I argued above that we should favor a one-type-of-property worldview. Powers fit the bill and can plausibly account for quasi-qualities. In the concluding chapter, I turn from fundamental physical powers to powers of the biological and social domains, as well as to some of the larger implications of the Pure Powers Model. In particular, I will argue that there is a continuum of intentionality from the most fundamental elements of the world up through minds and societies.

CHAPTER 8

# Nature's Intentionality Continuum

## 8.1 Varieties of Intentionality and the Intentionality Continuum Thesis

Intentionality is instantiated in many ways across many types of systems. In earlier chapters, I defended PIT (the Physical Intentionality Thesis) and discussed a classification scheme for intentionality. To recap, there is conscious and unconscious intentionality, and representational and nonrepresentational intentionality. This feature-based way of organizing categories of intentionality is not the only way. We can also categorize types of intentionality by association with different levels of complexity found throughout the world. There is some overlap in feature-based and complexity-based ways of categorizing intentionality because conscious intentionality seems to occur only at relatively higher levels of complexity.

I will argue that intentionality pervades the world. The warrant for this claim is that the world is inhabited through-and-through by powers possessing physical intentionality, as PIT maintains. Building on previous chapters' conclusions, I will sketch various organizational levels of intentionality and speculate as to how they interconnect through physical processes and biological evolutionary developments. In sum, I argue that there is an intentionality continuum as represented by the following thesis.

> **The Intentionality Continuum Thesis**: Physical reality is structured by an intentionality continuum. Intentionality is not a local phenomenon, present only in creatures with minds, but a global phenomenon present in fundamental physical phenomena, biological cells, plants, animals and humans, and human societies.

The theoretical attractiveness of the Intentionality Continuum Thesis lies in the fact that it presents a unified picture of nature: It shows us reality – mind and matter – unified by the thread of intentionality. From the smallest constituents of reality to large, complex nonliving systems built out of powers as well as living systems, there is an essential thread of intentionality. Thus, the Intentionality Continuum Thesis supports the Argument from the Unity of Nature, introduced in Section 3.1. This is the second supporting argument for PIT (the first being the Argument from the Marks of Intentionality).[1]

I hypothesize that there exists a continuum of intentionality in nature, from the physical intentionality of fundamental powers to the complex, higher-level psychological properties of organisms as well as social groups. Through these instances of intentionality there is a reasonable case for a continuity of increasing grades of intentionality. Nonetheless, all intentionality is ultimately physical because it is grounded in the intentionality-laden powers of fundamental physical particles. There is, as discussed in Chapter 3, potentially a fundamental division between representational and nonrepresentational intentionality. But if the nonrepresentational is only found in limited cases of mental states such as bodily sensations, then representationality is largely present throughout the entire continuum.

Subatomic and atomic particles, molecules, relatively simple organisms, more complex organisms, psychological systems (minds), and societies all, to some extent, exhibit intentionality. In short, intentionality occurs all the way up and down the levels of physical complexity. It is not surprising to find that this is the case, given the 3d account, for powers and informational structures are present throughout nature – thus, along with them, intentionality.

A continuum is a continuous set of elements (properties, objects, events, etc.) that are only slightly different from each other; although the end points can be very different from each other, they retain fundamental similarities. The natural continuum of intentionality consists of intentionality that is essentially the same throughout in its basic form (as PIT maintains). However, in its particular instances, intentionality occurs in varying and increasingly complex objects and systems (particles, molecules, organisms, societies) with a mix of differentiating properties, and for that reason presents itself differently. For example, when intentionality is mixed with

---

[1] If taken in isolation from other considerations, the Argument from the Unity of Nature is an abductive argument that runs as follows: If intentionality occurs throughout nature (i.e., PIT is correct), then nature is more unified than otherwise; without such metaphysical unity, there would be two metaphysical realms, one saturated with intentionality and one free of intentionality; the theoretical desirability of metaphysical unity thus positions us to abductively infer the reality of physical intentionality. However, if the Argument from the Marks of Intentionality is sound, as I contend, then we can avoid the abductive inference and simply deductively infer the unity of nature provided by intentionality: since intentionality runs throughout nature, nature is more unified than otherwise. The fact that the argument is defensible on either deductive or abductive grounds enhances its overall plausibility.

consciousness, it takes on a qualitative feel but the essential nature of the intentionality remains the same; that is, the core marks of directedness, intentional inexistence, and intentional indeterminacy remain the same.

To conclude this chapter's introduction, the Intentionality Continuum Thesis reasonably implies a mild form of panpsychism and potentially even pantheism, as I will argue later in the chapter. To ease the minds of those who might balk at panpsychism or pantheism, a few preliminary remarks about these views are warranted. Panpsychism has a long history of support in the West, from some pre-Socratic thinkers through Spinoza, Leibniz, Schopenhauer, William James, and Whitehead, amongst many others.[2] Although it fell out of favor during the twentieth century, it is making a strong comeback and receiving significant attention.[3] That does not imply that panpsychism is true, but simply that it is worthy of serious investigation. Similar comments apply to pantheism: It is receiving fresh attention from analytic metaphysicians and philosophers of religion and is also worthy of serious investigation.[4]

Before diving further into panpsychism, pantheism, and their connection (Sections 8.4 and 8.5), I will discuss the possibility of emergent powers (Section 8.2) and explore the thread of intentionality running through increasing levels of complexity in the world (Section 8.3).

## 8.2 Emergence and the Special Composition Question for Powers

As systems within nature become more complex – from basic physical systems, to biological organisms and systems, to social systems – we find increasingly complex systems of powers. Along the way, new features like perception and consciousness crop up and complement intentionality. These new features, some of which are quasi-qualities (see Chapter 7) and some of which are more complex powers, arise from the more fundamental powers of these systems. So, if we want to explain how varieties of intentionality arise, we need to explain the increasing complexity of powers. Unlike with the appearance of qualities out of powers, we do not need to concern ourselves with how intentionality appears out of powers because intentionality is there from the beginning. If we are to trace the

---

[2] For surveys, see Goff et al. (2020) and Skrbina (2005).
[3] To explore further, see Brüntrup and Jaskolla (2016), Goff (2017, 2019), Goff et al. (2020), Griffin (1998), Meixner (2016), and Strawson et al. (2006).
[4] To explore further, see Buckareff and Nagasawa (2016) and Mander (2020).

powers backbone all the way through the intentionality continuum, what we need is some view of how higher-level, complex powers come to be out of basic powers. Lurking in these observations about the building up of powers is a sort of special composition question (SCQ) for higher-level powers, concerning when powers compose higher-level, more complex powers (Bird 2020: 166).[5]

The discussion in this section complements themes from Chapter 7. Whereas the focus there was on the appearance of qualities out of a system of powers, the focus of this section is on the generation of higher-level powers out of a system of powers.

In some cases of higher-level powers, there is no mystery how the higher-level power is realized. These are cases where we can easily "identify a whole with a function" (i.e., a power of the whole) generated by more basic powers (Bird 2020: 166).[6] For example, the cardiovascular system (a whole) has the power to transfer oxygen from breathed air to organs, but this power requires the powers of the heart to pump blood and the powers of the lungs to absorb oxygen. The more complex, higher-level cardiovascular power is composed of simpler component powers.

Although he claims that there is no simple answer to the SCQ for higher-level powers, Bird (2020: 166) offers some clues. He maintains that although there is some vagueness concerning when simple powers form higher-level powers, this should not force us into unrestricted composition (that powers always form more complex powers) or nihilism (that powers do not ever form more complex powers). For these reasons, I adopt a moderate view: restricted composition of powers into higher-level powers. Sometimes more fundamental powers do genuinely compose higher-level powers but other times they do not.

Furthermore, genuine higher-level powers – those constituted by assemblages of more basic powers – are those that form new mechanisms (Bird 2020: 166). These mechanisms are not found amongst the composing powers alone (as the cardiovascular example demonstrates). Building on Bird's idea, I layer a further condition on the metaphysics of powers composition, which is that the relevant powers involved in the instantiation of a higher-level power must carry appropriate informational content in order to serve their function.

---

[5] Compare the special composition question for objects (Van Inwagen 1990: 20).
[6] I use the term "powers," not "dispositions" as Bird does. Although Bird (2013) distinguishes between powers and dispositions, I do not think this affects his main points about the compositionality of one or the other. Even if the distinction did change how we think about compositionality in the two cases, we could simply ask two questions: the SCQ for powers and the SCQ for dispositions.

If IT is correct, then besides physical intentionality, relevant informational content must be involved in the metaphysical operation of realizing a higher-level power. The information that distinct powers carry is relevant to the information carried by the higher-level power created by the compositional operation. Specifically, the higher-level power must have new information, which determines its causal profile and thus how it is directed toward the kind of mechanistic functions it serves. This new information, the content of the higher-level power, is distinct from the information found in each of the composing powers. In order to account for the higher-level power's new directedness (i.e., its new function, a function of the whole that possesses the new power), the higher-level power needs to carry not only distinct, but perhaps more complex, information compared to the information carried by the more basic powers.

Could these higher-level powers be emergent? Mumford and Anjum (2011: 101–105) suggest that it is quite possible that emergent powers exist, perhaps powers attending to some social phenomena such as language. Still, some argue that even with higher-level phenomenon and the increasing complexity of powers in nature, the hope of reductive explanation to a base of causal powers remains strong (Corry 2019).

Some higher-level powers, instantiating complex mechanisms, might be weakly emergent (i.e., surprising) while others might be strongly emergent (i.e., neither deducible from nor reducible to lower-level powers). Weak emergence needs no new metaphysical account, but if strong emergence holds then we will have to commit to new metaphysical principles, perhaps for both the emergent powers themselves and the emergent information they would need to contain; henceforth, when I use "emergent" I mean strongly emergent or emergent2, as discussed in Chapter 7.[7] I think it remains a genuinely open question whether there are emergent powers. However, if emergent powers are needed, I would like to sketch a model for how they might come to be. I am not arguing for this theory of emergence; rather, it is a sketch toward showing the possibility of emergent powers if such entities are required by the world. Also, note that emergent properties are typically properties of complex wholes. But this does not imply that the whole itself is an emergent object; the whole, qua object, might reduce to its parts, while the powers of the whole might not reduce to powers of the parts.

---

[7] Chalmers (2006) makes the distinction between strong and weak emergence whereas Searle (1994: 111–126) makes the distinction between emergent1 and emergent2.

My proposal is inspired by the fusion theory of emergent properties (Humphreys 1997). I contend that the reciprocal manifestations of two or more pure powers, $P_1$ and $P_2$, if they are of the relevant type and operating in the relevant circumstances, can yield an ontologically distinct, emergent power, $P_e$. Their reciprocal activity generates and sustains $P_e$, but $P_e$'s instantiation is not metaphysically explainable in terms of the information carried by $P_1$ and $P_2$ alone. Something not only unpredictable but reductively unexplainable occurs; the best we can do is, postfusion, discern that when $P_1$ and $P_2$ interact and "fuse" together in appropriate conditions, $P_e$ is generated.

$P_1$ and $P_2$ are not destroyed during this fusion process but work interactively to generate a higher-level, emergent property. This process is dissimilar to the process, for example, of fragility and hardness producing breaking. Although the hardness might remain, the fragility is often destroyed – meaning that the fragile thing will no longer be fragile, because it will have exhausted its capacity to break or crack, or simply no longer exist as a whole object. By contrast, consider water. The powers of two hydrogen atoms and one oxygen atom collaborate in forming a water molecule. They interact and mutually manifest but do not go away. The powers fuse to form new powers that the complex whole, the $H_2O$ molecule, possesses but the component parts do not. It is something of a marvel that these atoms form water molecules and that water molecules form bodies of water. The workings of the component atoms, attributable to their causal powers, create new properties not found amongst the component parts. This phenomenon exemplifies a standard conception of ontological emergence, according to which components "generates properties that none of the individual micro-level components possess, and these higher-level properties in turn can have causal efficacy" (Mitchell 2009: 36).[8] The causal powers of water, I suggest, are strong candidates of examples that require the fusion theory of powers.

There is a case to be made that the powers of a water molecule are emergent, in particular its "anomalous properties" including surface tension, hydrophobic effect, and power to act as a solvent; these powers are owed to water's hydrogen bonds, which are in turn owed to the molecular structure of the water molecule (Stump 2013: 55). Hydrogen and oxygen atoms alone do not possess these powers. But relevant powers of hydrogen and oxygen must be present and active for the molecular structure to obtain and instantiate higher-level powers. Stump (2013) makes a case, from an

---

[8] Mitchell (2009: 36), however, argues that new scientific conceptions of emergence go beyond the standard conception, positing dynamic "forward and reverse feedback loops" that ground self-organization.

Aristotelian metaphysical viewpoint, that these higher-level powers are emergent. However, I maintain only that such emergence is possible and might be needed to account for the increasing complexity of powers as nature moves toward larger wholes and more complex, macro processes.[9]

If there are emergent powers, they too will have physical intentionality as PIT implies. But how does IT relate to emergent powers and to the intentionality continuum? In a system of powers, the information carried by the powers becomes more complex as we move into increasingly complex systems of intentionality. As we move from fundamental to abundant powers, and from fundamental physical systems to biological and psychological systems, the complexity of information will increase. If the information carried by emergent powers is also emergent, it will not be just surprising but irreducible to the pre-emergent information. One way the informational content of higher-order powers could be irreducible and thus emergent in the relevant sense (i.e., emergent2) is if the information of the lower-order powers is integrated such that it concerns potential manifestations that the lower-level powers alone could not be sufficient to produce.[10] That is, the higher-order information, arising from lower-order informational content of the more fundamental powers, would be for new types of outcomes. Correspondingly, these intentional systems should become more sophisticated as new features of these systems are instantiated: basic physical systems lead to organic systems, organic systems lead to life, life leads to consciousness. This kind of view is not unprecedented. For example, Dretske (1981) theorized levels of intentionality tied to informational structures. However, the backbone of my view remains powers.

---

[9] Are the emergent powers on the proposed ontology really strongly emergent? Yes, quite possibly. If these emergent powers were only weakly emergent (or nonemergent altogether), then their informational content would be derivable from the informational content of the more basic powers. However, that is arguably not the case: The informational content of the emergent powers is not derivable. It is genuinely new. There is precedent for this kind of informational uniqueness in the Integrated Information Theory proposed by Tononi (2008). According to Tononi's theory, consciousness arises where information integrates, that is, where there arises informational content "above and beyond" the informational content found in the parts of a system (2008: 216). (I further discuss Integrated Information Theory in Section 8.5.) Integrated information is arguably strongly emergent. It is not derivable from the component parts (information) but it does require them. I am not asserting that this theory is true (it is way too early in the philosophy and science of consciousness to assert that any theory of consciousness is correct). Rather, I am claiming that it is logically possible and shows, by analogy, that the informational content of an emergent power can be "above and beyond" that generated by the powers that underpin the emergent power in question.

[10] This reflects something comparable to the integrated information that make consciousness possible, according to Integrated Information Theory (Tononi 2008), as mentioned in the previous footnote and which I will address more in Section 8.5.

## 8.3   Intentionality beyond Fundamental Powers

I turn now to the corresponding intentionality of higher-level powers as found in increasing degrees of complexity in nature. I will argue for the existence of an intentionality continuum. I will explain how the intentionality of fundamental powers relates to higher orders of intentionality; the general idea is that the intentionality of fundamental powers compositionally feeds into higher-level forms of intentionality. Along the way, I will compare my view to other views that also assign intentionality widely. I focus primarily on the biological realm, including cells and whole organisms, but will also address the psychological and social realms.

### Biological Intentionality

Biological entities – not only brains and nervous systems but cells, organs, systems (e.g., the respiratory system), organisms, and perhaps even populations – exhibit intentionality. Chemical and biological processes link more fundamental powers – including atomic and molecular powers – to more complex biological entities such as cells, organs, and organisms. Some organisms display psychological states and consciousness, mental phenomena which are quite plausibly underpinned by chemical and biological processes.

Cells and organs are built out of elements exhibiting physical intentionality, and this intentionality carries over to organisms. As elements of these more fundamental biological entities interact and form complex relationships with their environments (much like fundamental powers form holistic systems), their intentionality becomes even more apparent. For example, organs are directed toward various processes and outcomes, although these outcomes might not occur and are ontologically indeterminate (following the essential marks of intentionality).

The physical intentionality of fundamental properties is necessary but insufficient for more advanced, complex, forms of intentionality, such as conscious intentionality. The latter arises from the interactions of more fundamental entities – neuronal, molecular, atomic, subatomic – possessing intentionality-laden powers. In general, higher-level intentionality requires lower-level intentionality, plus relevant physical, chemical, and biological processes that determine the natures of complex wholes.

To explore these initial observations further, consider Dennett's view on the beginnings of agency. Dennett (1995: 202) suggests that molecular biology allows us "to witness the birth of agency, in the first macromolecules that have enough complexity to 'do things'." This does not involve representation of reasons or conscious decision making, but it underpins the development of genuine intentional action. The molecular actions necessary for life Dennett (1995: 202) calls "quasi-agency" – "quasi" because "there's nobody home" – there is no representation of reason, no consciousness, no reflection. On this view, quasi-agency does not strictly involve intentionality, "but it is the only possible ground form which the seeds of intentional action could grow" (1995: 202).

So, Dennett finds the origins of agency and intentionality in the biological realm. However, according to PIT, nonconscious intentional action occurs in the fundamental, prebiological properties of reality. To the extent that intentional action is agential action – that entities exhibiting intentionality have the most basic kind of agency – agency is born in the roots of being, not the biological level as Dennett argues. But fundamental intentionality only makes for a simple form of agency not involving any cognitive capacities. I will return to the agency-intentionality connection later.

Fitch (2008) goes a step beyond Dennett by ascribing genuine intentionality to eukaryotic cells to account for cells' self-organizing capabilities. He does so in attempting to find a way between Dennett's dilemma between derived intentionality (where something has intentionality simply because of its intended function), including words and artificial objects such as thermometers, and supposedly intrinsic or original intentionality (the intentionality present in conscious minds) (Dennett 1987: 287–321).[11] Fitch argues that there is a basic kind of intrinsic intentionality, "nano-intentionality," found at levels of complexity well short of human consciousness. Nano-intentionality lacks representationality but serves as a building block to the more complicated kind of macro-intentionality found in mammals (2008: 165). Contra Bird (2007a: 117), intentionality on Fitch's account (as on my own) is compositional because intentionality in more basic systems can spill over into more complex systems. Therefore, despite not involving representationality according to Fitch, nano-intentionality strengthens the argument for an intentionality continuum. (Of course, if nano-intentional states are representational, this would not prove problematic for my 3d account.)

Let us take a closer look at Fitch's nano-intentionality and how it supports the intentionality continuum. Fitch (2008: 158) defines nano-intentionality as "a microscopic form of aboutness, inherent in individual eukaryotic cells,

---

[11] Dennett (1987: 299–300) argues that all intentionality is ultimately derived from evolutionary processes; intrinsic or original intentionality is illusory.

that includes a goal-directed capacity to respond adaptively to novel circumstances." He specifically frames this capacity in terms of causal power. Eukaryotic cells, including everything from amoebas to neurons, possess a causal power to arrange their constituent molecules and change their physical structure in a manner sufficient to living and functioning appropriately in their immediate environments (Fitch 2008: 158–159).[12]

Nano-intentionality is necessary, I suggest, to account for a variety of cellular phenomena, including especially the "interactome." This is the whole set of molecular interactions occurring in cells and essentially "maps the positions of proteins with unknown functions within a cellular network" (Landry 2011: 533). Scientists have developed such protein interaction maps for various fungi, bacteria, animals, and plants. Where does nano-intentionality fit in to our understanding of the interactome? The main point is that all the molecular interactions within cells must be directed toward particular outcomes for the cell to function. This strongly suggest that intentionality is needed. On one hand, if PIT is correct as I have argued, then the molecular interactions will depend on more fundamental, intention-laden causal powers, and nano-intentionality is just a natural extension of the underlying intentionality of physical powers. On the other hand, if one rejects PIT, then the facts of interactive cellular mechanics as indicated by interactomes could drive one to posit nano-intentionality as the first layer of intentionality in the world.

I agree with the existence of nano-intentionality. But I claim that, to the extent it involves real causal powers possessing representational directedness (see Chapter 4), then nonconscious *representational* intentionality is present in eukaryotic cells.[13] Furthermore, in order for cells to exhibit nano-intentionality, for example to rearrange themselves in adjusting to changing environmental circumstances, they also require information for various arrangements and directedness toward these arrangements. Thus, IT is consistent with and supports the positing of nano-intentionality.

How does nano-intentionality fit into the intentionality continuum? Nano-intentionality is a bridge between the physical and chemical worlds and the biological world. Given PIT, fundamental powers of elementary particles and fields possess physical intentionality. It would not be surprising for this intentionality to carry over to atoms and basic molecular

---

[12] Nano-intentionality "is related to, but much more specific than, Aristotelian 'telos' or Schopenhauerian 'will'," according to Fitch (2008: 159).

[13] Nonetheless, we can also allow for some instances of nonconscious, nonrepresentational intentionality, given a pluralist understanding of intentionality and directedness as presented in Chapter 4.

structures such as water. On the other end of the spectrum, we know that human consciousness is imbued with intentionality and the same probably goes for other mammals as well as most, if not all, animals. What about eukaryotic cells? That is where Fitch's thesis fits in. Eukaryotic cells display nano-intentionality when they adjust to new situations and new information by rearranging their internal components to meet rapidly changing demands. Fitch recognizes that this is simpler than macro-intentionality as found in humans and other animals. But nano-intentionality – a form of original, intrinsic intentionality (not derived intentionality, to use Dennett's distinction) – is an important ingredient in the building up to more complex forms of intentionality. Therefore, nano-intentionality supports the Intentionality Continuum Thesis. However, plants as well as societal phenomena remain lacunas to be addressed.

There is growing support for the claim that plants have a form of mind, display intelligent behavior, and communicate with each other. For instance, Maher (2017) argues for an "enactivist" theory of mind. According to this view, "to have a mind is to 'enact' or disclose a value-laden world, an environment or niche, an array of things that matter in various ways" (2017: 115). This view implies that all living things have minds, including plants, because they are autopoietic ("self-producing," i.e., the ability to reproduce and self-maintain, or persist as a living thing) and adaptive ("adjusting effectively in response to conditions that affect viability"). Possession of these two features positions a living thing to disclose "a value-laden world" or "field of things that have significance, opportunities, and threats [...]" for it (2017: 115).

Since plants typically exhibit both autopoiesis and adaptivity (Maher 2017: 120), they have minds. But plant minds are not equivalent to conscious, reasoning minds. Rather, being cautious, they are "proto-minds or minimal minds" (2017: 115). Even if they are minimal minds, plant minds are on the continuum of things that have minds. Although Maher does not make intentionality an explicit part of his thesis, plant minds as he describes them – goal-oriented, self-organized, and so on – clearly possess intentionality. Plants' activities, driven by their causal powers, are directed toward outcomes essential to their flourishing.[14]

---

[14] Maher maintains that having a mind does not require representational states. As compared to the computational theory of mind, which requires representations, Maher's enactivist theory of mind avoids that commitment. Yet if my interpretation of directedness in terms of representationality is correct, then representationality should carry through, vis-à-vis physical powers, to plants. With or without representationality, plant intentionality supports the claim that there is an intentionality continuum.

It is instructive to consider another view in comparison to the Intentionality Continuum Thesis. John Searle develops a comprehensive view concerning the place of intentionality and teleology in nature. He assigns intentionality somewhat generously, though still more restrictively than I do.

There is "nothing intrinsically mysterious about intentionality" (Searle 2015: 43) and intentional phenomena comes in a variety of ontological forms, to include "events, processes, and dispositions" (2015: 33). Although this does not imply identity between physical and psychological intentionality, as PIT entails, it does suggest a motivational consistency between PIT and Searle's view. Furthermore, on his account of intentionality, teleological phenomena are natural and thus teleological explanations serve as a subclass of scientific explanations (Searle 1984: 98). This follows as a logical consequence of ascribing goals, aims, purposes, and intentions to biological organisms (1984: 98). On Searle's view, intentionality seems to have ontological priority over teleology, with teleological phenomena arising as a result of intentionality. These teleological states are "future-directed Intentional states" with a world-to-mind direction of fit, capable of causally bringing about their "conditions of satisfaction" (1984: 98).[15]

Intentionality is a natural, biological phenomena according to Searle (2015: 34), not a fundamental physical phenomena as PIT maintains. So, my view is more permissive than Searle's. However, I suggest that to the extent that biological entities possess powers, as Searle appears to hold, and more complex powers arise from more fundamental ones, it is plausible to hold that the fundamental powers also possess intentionality. Thus, short of committing to an emergent2 type of process where biological intentionality emerges out of nonintentional prebiological properties, we can instead infer PIT from Searle's premise that intentionality is a biological phenomenon. PIT helps explain how intentionality enters the biological world: It is already there before biological phenomena. If intentionality exists at the most basic level of physical phenomena, as I maintain, there is nothing mysterious about biological (and, ultimately, psychological) intentionality. Accepting PIT diminishes that mystery in the way the mass of complex objects (atoms and up) is explained by the mass of simple objects (i.e., fundamental particles). What about consciousness? Searle (2015: 51) thinks that consciousness is necessarily a biological phenomenon, that is,

---

[15] Compare powers: The world can satisfy the power when the power brings about the manifestation it is directed toward, and the power plays a causal role in doing so. See Section 5.5 for further discussion of direction of fit.

it must occur "in some system composed of cells." These biological systems are composed of lower-level properties (2015: 51) that do *not* have consciousness. I tend to agree with that claim, but if PIT is correct then basic physical (nonbiological) states have an essential ingredient for consciousness: intentionality.[16]

### *Interlude: A Challenge to the Intentionality Continuum Thesis*

One might challenge the Intentionality Continuum Thesis by arguing that we have no reason to believe that physical intentionality explains mental intentionality (Bird 2007a: 115–118). This implies that even if PIT is correct it could not form a continuum with mental intentionality: There is a disconnect between physical and mental intentionality. As I have argued, the differences found in the continuum are not due to intentionality itself being fundamentally different in physical and mental systems. For according to PIT, physical intentionality = mental intentionality. Still, for mental intentionality to arise, elements bearing physical intentionality need to compose into more complex mind-inducing structures with the intentionality coming along for the ride. But Bird (2007a: 117) claims intentionality is noncompositional: "It is clear that the intentionality of the mind or of its modules is not built up out of the intentionality of the smaller parts of its physical realizer."[17] For example, "the causal relation that is supposed to explain" the intentionality of the thought of Napoleon is "between Napoleon and at least some structure of neurons, not between Napoleon (or anything else) and individual neurons" (2007a: 117).

However, neuroscientific evidence suggests that individual neurons might indeed be one of the relata in some instances of intentionality (Quiroga et al. 2005). The idea is that a single neuron might be activated in response to an image or string of letters, suggesting that individual neurons are strongly associated with intentional states. This is bolstered by Fitch's argument for nano-intentionality, as discussed above. Nano-intentionality is a general claim about eukaryotic cells that subsumes neurons, therefore individual neurons would have intentionality too. Fitch's thesis directly challenges Bird's claim about the noncompositionality of intentionality. Therefore, if PIT is true and bolstered by scientific findings about neurons

---

[16] Similarly, Djedovic (2020: 1) argues for a spectrum view in the building up from life to mind and that it is no surprise that mind develops out of life since natural agency is already there.

[17] In total, Bird gives three accounts of intentionality and explains how none of them entail that intentionality is compositional.

as well as the nano-intentionality thesis, the possibility of compositional-ity becomes more attractive. Why is the mind intentional? Because the parts – with their corresponding causal powers – that make up the mind are intentional. So, there is intentionality all the way down. Therefore, there is an intentionality continuum.

### From Psychological to Collective Intentionality

Nonpropositional, representational physical powers play a role in the gen-eration of entities at all levels of reality. At some point, sufficient complex-ity must be achieved to generate the forms of intentionality we find in our species: mental intentionality with propositionality and thus semantic representationality, along with consciousness and other distinctively men-tal features. These more complex forms of intentionality are only found, so far as we know, in organisms with sophisticated mental powers such as humans. The claims of physical intentionality and biological intentional-ity, discussed earlier, are modeled on mental intentionality. If accurate, they provide support for the thesis that intentionality runs through all of nature, not just minds.

There is a building up from physical intentionality to biological and men-tal intentionality. But how do we get from mental intentionality to col-lective, or social, intentionality? Through social interaction, minds create forms of collective intentionality. What I call "social intentionality" is the collective intentionality of groups of humans. It might be a unique feature of humans that we create vast social networks, economic structures, and politi-cal institutions through the convergence of our individual imaginations and wills upon collaborative plans of living. So, in a sense, there are broad inten-tional states that we can assign to groups. There are countless examples of a culture or society, as a whole, believing that $p$ is the case: Americans believe in the value of the dollar, football fans believe in the rules of the game, and so on. These collective intentional states, which help construct new realities, do not perish when one or a few individuals of the relevant group stop believing that $p$. So, to some degree, collective intention (and its outcome) has some independence from the individuals that underly the intention.[18]

As background, we should look at differences in the causal powers of basic physical agents (such as fundamental particles) and social agents. Ellis (2013) provides a fascinating analysis of the nature of agency based on

---

[18] In humans especially, forms of group and collective intentionality have become highly complex and are crucial to our distinctive social worlds (Tomasello 2014).

causal powers. Although he does not explicitly accept physical intentionality, his characterization of powers in terms of agency is not only consistent with, but strongly suggests, that PIT or something close to it is correct.[19] Furthermore, agency and intentionality go hand in hand. Agency requires intentionality because agency requires acting *for* something (directedness) that might not be achieved (intentional inexistence). Since intentionality is an inherent component of agency, Ellis' discussion of agential powers, from basic physical agents all the way up through simple organisms and rational agents, provides support for the existence of an intentionality continuum. A closer look is in order.

Ellis (2013: 190) posits that "an agent is something that is disposed to act or react in some way to cause something to happen." The primary agents in nature are (a) things like protons and electrons with "intrinsic causal powers" and (b) radioactive substances and excited atoms with powers (propensities) "to decay or radiate energy" (2013: 191). Although these primary physical entities are agents, their agency is "fixed [by nature] and very limited" (2013: 191). They either necessarily or probabilistically do what they do. There is no decisioning process by these entities. While the identity conditions (i.e., the causal profiles) of particles cannot be changed, the identity conditions for more complex and sophisticated systems composed of these particles can change (2013: 192). That is, the powers of these more complex and typically larger entities can be modified (in some cases, self-modified) without the entities in question losing their identities. For instance, a tree remains a tree and a bee remains a bee – and numerically the same tree and bee – even if their powers are modified. Supposing the water-absorbing power of the tree's roots are decreased, or the bee's power to navigate is weakened, the tree and the bee remain the same individual entities. These nonfundamental, complex entities have what Ellis (2013: 192) calls "variable agencies." Thus, their power profiles are contingent. This is necessary for living things – to their various particular degrees dependent on their abilities to anticipate and evaluate their environments as well as modify goals – to be self-directed agents (Christensen and Hooker 2001).

Ellis (2013: 192) contends that "Everything that is modifiable, evolves, grows, or learns from experience has variable agency, because its causal powers must vary as it is modified, evolves, grows, or learns." This principle constitutes what I identify as a biological link connecting the physical intentionality of basic physical systems to more complex systems in which biological evolutionary principles reign and biological intentionality is realized. Intentionality

---

[19] Armstrong (2002) suggests that Ellis should accept PIT.

is retained through these evolutionary and growth processes; it is essential to entities at "intermediate" levels of complexity in order to maintain their existence and reproduce (recall the discussion of Fitch's nano-intentionality thesis). Many nonhuman animals (maybe not amoebas, but almost certainly bees and birds), as with humans, have variable agencies. Although Ellis (2013: 192) holds that changes can take place in the "causal power profiles" of nonhuman animals, they do not typically acquire new capacities or new causal powers. However, their powers can be improved or weakened.

Causal powers play a role in fundamental physical systems up through human beings and social systems (Ellis 2002, 2013). Human agency is a power – specifically a meta-causal power to modify our causal powers and action profiles (2013: 186). But this meta-power, I suggest, feeds into creating and sustaining collective acts of intentionality; individuals can modify their action profiles so that their behavior sustains, rather than harms, various institutions created by acts of collective intentionality.

My interest here is that if powers run up to the highest levels of social organization, then so does intentionality – recognizing that society as we know it is largely ontologically dependent on human action, thought, and decision-making (agency) and therefore on human intentionality.[20] Collective intentionality is ultimately a product of complex interactions of more fundamental powers and the intentionality that they exhibit, running down through biological and fundamental physical levels. This holds, I contend, provided that powers and intentionality necessarily undergird agency – that agency is a power or complex of powers.

In response to the claim that there are higher-level social powers (and that this is part of the explanation of the intentionality continuum at the upper end of the continuum), one might argue that the causal powers often posited by social ontologists in explaining social powers (e.g., abilities to exercise sociopolitical powers, create social realities, and so on) are not real causal powers, that is, they are not intrinsic powers of the objects (people, institutions) that bear them. This is the line of reasoning taken by Wahlberg (2020). Therefore, since intentionality does not track perfectly with real powers all the way up, the intentionality continuum cannot be accounted for in terms of powers when we reach the more complex, upper end of the continuum.

Wahlberg (2020) argues that social powers tend to be extrinsic and grounded in more fundamental constituents. Although they are

---

[20] For example, see Harari (2015: 112–118) and Searle (2010). See Elder-Vass (2010) for detailed defense of the causal powers of social entities.

characterizable by conditional statements and meet other marks of powers, this does not imply they are intrinsic and therefore real causal powers. They can make a causal difference (just as distance between particles exercising powers can) but this does not imply that they are powers (just as distance is not a power). However, Wahlberg's argument can be questioned on several grounds. First, extrinsic powers – such as weight, visibility, and vulnerability (McKitrick 2003a) are not only difference makers but seem to be genuinely causally relevant and therefore real. Second, some sparse powers, such as mass, are arguably extrinsic yet definitely causally relevant and real (Bauer 2011). Third, distance and spatiotemporal relations in general might well be causal powers (see Mumford 2004: 188; Bird 2007a: 161–168, 2017). Therefore, I will continue to assume that there are real social powers; whether they are extrinsic or not is irrelevant.

Our individual social powers provide the backbone for collective intentionality – our "intersubjective order" or "shared imagination" (Harari 2015: 117) – which is responsible for many of our most cherished institutions (law, money, religion, etc.). But it is not, perhaps, just the individuals within a society that create social realities. If groups (above and beyond their individual members) have collective purposes, intentions, and agency (Mulgan 2018: 100), we can again extend the intentionality continuum further under the domain of powers, to the extent that group powers are responsible for group intentionality. Figure 8.1 shows the thread of intentionality running throughout nature.

| **Entities exhibiting intentionality** | Subatomic particles<br><br>Atomic particles<br><br>Molecules | Biological cells, organelles, organs<br><br>Biological systems, organisms, colonies | Psychological systems, or thinking systems, with conscious and unconscious domains, containing beliefs, desires, other mental states | Social groups exhibiting collective intentionality (e.g., populations of social animals) |
|---|---|---|---|---|
| | Physical intentionality [= →] Biological intentionality [= →] Psychological intentionality (physics, chemistry) (biochemistry, genetics, biology) (psychology, sociology) | | | |

Figure 8.1   The building up of intentionality through a powers-based ontology ("=" means that the intentionality per se is the same, while "→" indicates that intentionality is both instantiated and involved in building toward greater levels of complexity; relevant sciences are in parentheses)

A few qualifications concerning Figure 8.1 are necessary. First, physical intentionality = psychological intentionality. So, the first two columns should not be conceived as just forms of "physical intentionality" (associated with nonminds) and the second two as just forms of "psychological intentionality" (associated with minds). If PIT is correct, then instances of intentionality at each organizational level are fundamentally the same. Second, a single intentional state itself does not increase in amount or degree of intentionality or complexity; for any given intentional state, it cannot be more, or less, intentional. However, as the objects that bear intentional states become more complex, the number of intentional states that they can exhibit increases; and as other features mental features are added, the objects can accrue increasingly complex forms of intentionality (e.g., conscious intentionality). Third, related to the second point, I add "biological intentionality" to the diagram to indicate the presence of intentionality in the biological domain (same for "psychological intentionality"). But, again, the differences in intentionality at each level are due to the arrangements of physical structures that arise as nature builds up in complexity, not the intentionality itself. There are no strict boundaries between these intentionality categories.

## 8.4 Panintentionality: Toward a Unification of Mind and Matter

The common thread of intentionality running throughout nature helps unify mind and matter. If the idea of an intentionality continuum is correct, it does not solve the so-called mind–body problem but it does appear less problematic. For the continuum implies that there is no bright line between mind and matter, thus raising the possibility of panpsychism. PIT and the Intentionality Continuum Thesis underpin a theory of reality that is a precursor to panpsychism, namely panintentionality (Pfeifer 2016). Given that intentionality is found in all powers and powers are found in all aspects of reality from fundamental particles through social organizations, there is a necessary element of mind permeating reality.

Panpsychism, as traditionally conceived, claims that mind resides in every element or aspect of the universe. It comes in two basic types. One basic type of panpsychism is panexperientialism (conscious experience exists at a fundamental level throughout the world) and the other basic type is pancognitivism (thought exists at a fundamental level throughout the world), although panexperientialism is the most commonly proposed type (Goff et al. 2020). As noted in Section 8.1, this ancient view is making a strong comeback in contemporary philosophy of mind, exemplified by Strawson et al. (2006) and Goff (2017, 2019). Although I disagree with full-blown panpsychism, panintentionality has a natural kinship with this view. For, if intentionality is spread throughout reality, then something essentially related to and necessary for mind pervades everything.

Furthermore, fundamentally intentional properties (i.e., causal powers) ultimately generate cognition and consciousness at higher levels of organization (as suggested in Section 8.3). So, panintentionality is quite plausibly a form of pan*proto*psychism (following the terminology of Chalmers 2016). Other versions of panprotopsychism might posit panX, where X is not intentionality but some other ingredient of mind (e.g., teleological states, some mental ingredient that is not itself consciousness, or anything that is a first step to a preferred form of panpsychism).

Panpsychism implies the full unification of mind (consciousness) and material reality. By contrast, panintentionality implies a partial unification, because an essential ingredient of mind (intentionality) is unified with matter, while consciousness and other mental phenomena such as perception and metacognition remain exclusive to sophisticated minds.[21] Therefore, panintentionality helps bridge the gap between mind and matter.

Does the Intentionality Continuum Thesis water down the concept of mind? No. Recognizing similarities across nature, such as the presence of intentionality in all things, does not prevent recognition of important differences. Conscious minds have perception, cognition, and emotion, which are features almost certainly not found in fundamental physical particles, yet both conscious minds and fundamental physical particles possess intentionality. Likewise, bacteria – presumably nonconscious – can metabolize and reproduce just as animals can, yet animals but not bacteria can perceive and feel emotions. We can recognize that all living things are intelligent without ignoring the important features that differentiate them (Maher 2017: 123); similarly, we can recognize that all entities have intentionality without ignoring the important features that differentiate them.

## 8.5  From Panintentionality to Pantheism

There is a case to make that panintentionality supports pantheism. Prior to making that argument, pantheism needs conceptualizing. Pantheism

---

[21] Maybe plants have minds, as suggested above, but they are not conscious and so not as sophisticated as mammal and other animal minds.

minimally "means that the Cosmos has a divine quality, that all material objects (including humans) are part of that divinity" (Skrbina 2005: 20). At a minimum, everything would have this divine quality derivatively from the divine quality in the fundamental constituents and properties of the Cosmos. On this view, God is not a person, is not transcendent but immanent, and did not create the world (2005: 21). The simplest understanding of pantheism is that God = Nature. This is "classical pantheism" (2005: 88) roughly as developed in Spinoza's (2006) *Ethics*.

It is useful to contrast pantheism (God *is* Nature) and pan*en*theism (God is *in* all parts of Nature). These views are much more similar to each other than classical theism, whose god is transcendent, outside of time, perfect in all ways, and utterly distinct from Nature. Yet pantheism is distinct from panentheism. The latter typically means that God is in all the parts of the universe (yet, perhaps, remains something beyond as well, contrary to pantheism). The motto of panentheism is "God in all, and all in God" (Johnston 2009: 119). But that does not mean "God *is* all, and all *is* God." Against such identification of nature and God, the panentheist will opine that "God is partly constituted by the natural realm, in the sense that his activity is manifest in and through natural processes *alone*. But his reality goes beyond what is captured by the purely scientific description of all the events that make up the natural realm" (2009: 119). God is neither separable from Nature nor one and the same with it. What the "beyond" is could be natural or not, depending on whether one accepts that the scientific description of the world identifies the limits of naturalism.[22] By contrast, if the particular brand of pantheism assumed here is true, it does not go beyond the natural. It has metaphysical components (physical intentionality); however, these are supposed to be naturalistic (if not exactly *materialistic*) and could perhaps be part of a revised science that incorporates claims about the inner nature of matter being intentional.

In conceptualizing pantheism, I do not hypothesize that a strictly material universe, with no kind of mind-like feature whatsoever, is identical to God. That is one understanding, but it proves hard to see what the motivation for identifying nature with God would be if there was nothing of mind in the mix. For, if God has any features, it seems they must include some kind of mental features. Accordingly, on this kind of view what we have is a universe that physics describes (which standardly does not posit

[22] Baker (2009) worries about the coherence of the divine "reality" that supposedly goes beyond the scientific picture on Johnston's view.

mind in fundamental matter), but necessarily with some additional intrinsic mental or mind-like feature. If this feature is *physical* intentionality, it is in principle consistent with physical science.

As discussed in the previous section, panpsychism maintains that mind or consciousness pervades the cosmos (is in all things). It is not a specific theory of mind (of what mind *is*), rather it is a "meta-theory of mind" (Skrbina 2005: 2); whatever mind is, its reach is cosmic. I suggest two dimensions along which panpsychism, and thus pantheism to the extent that the former suggests the latter, can vary: (i) the sophistication level of mind, and (ii) the activation of mind within that level.

First, regarding sophistication levels, one can imagine a scale from a minimum amount of mentality to a maximal amount of mentality. At the minimal end, I imagine preconscious or proto-conscious states, something like nano-intentionality, which is necessary for macro-intentionality, as discussed previously. Or take PIT, which could serve as a basis for proto-consciousness. At a more sophisticated level of mind, the universe (or its parts) would be imbued with full sentience or consciousness. At a maximal level of mentality, the universe would have something like the mind associated with full personhood, including self-consciousness and rationality. Provided omniscience, this would include awareness of all possible states of the universe. Finer-grained possibilities, and variations within all these levels, are possible.[23]

Turning to the second dimension, the activation of mind within a level of sophistication refers to whether any given mental state is in an unmanifested or a manifested (occurrent) state. It is widely recognized that thoughts such as beliefs, desires, and so on can be plausibly conceived as dispositional or powerful properties.[24] If it is nonactivated, then it is latent, for instance being *disposed* to believe one is intelligent. That is a real but nonoccurrent belief. If it is activated, then it is occurrent, for instance consciously believing one is intelligent. The brand of panpsychism under consideration here involves (i) minimal sophistication of mind, though it is compatible with greater sophistication, and (ii) dispositional states that can be (and perhaps often are) activated.

---

[23] Meixner (2016) provides a list of four types of panpsychism, explicitly including idealism: dualistic atomistic panpsychism; dualistic holistic panpsychism; idealistic atomistic panpsychism; idealistic holistic panpsychism. Provided a less sophisticated kind of mind in nature, we could reasonably envision these as four types of panprotopsychism. Meixner's list excludes purely physicalist options: "physical atomistic" and "physical holistic" panpsychism. But I think Pfeifer's (2016) view, which is essentially the view I support, is intended as a kind of physical atomistic view, on which physical properties have intentionality naturally built into them.

[24] For example, see Ryle (1949), Clark and Chalmers (1998), and Schwitzgebel (2001, 2002).

Given the above background understandings of both pantheism and panpsychism, based on Pfeifer (2016), I will argue that panpsychism as well as panprotopsychism – to include the panintentionality that is essential to my 3d account – can serve as a metaphysical foundation for pantheism. Before examining the relevant details in the rest of this section, a summary of Pfeifer's argument should prove helpful. He argues in two basic steps. First, PIT implies panintentionality, which qualifies as panprotopsychism because intentionality is a significant and essential ingredient for conscious experience. Second, since panpsychism and panprotopsychism suggest pantheism, panintentionality also suggests pantheism. The second step involves conceiving of "God" as spread throughout the universe in all its powerful-intentional properties.

First, building on the discussion in Section 8.4, I turn to how PIT implies a form of panprotopsychism. Since powerful cum intentional states exist throughout the universe – that is, panintentionality obtains – mind is ubiquitous (Pfeifer 2016: 44). Matter alone is not conscious but neither is it empty of mentation. This type of panprotopsychism entails a loose sense of the term "mental" – it does not attribute any type of thinking or souls to atoms and rocks and trees – yet it does hold "that even the basic physical constituents of the universe have mental states" (2016: 44). Thus, panintentionality counts as a minimal sense of mentality, but one packed with potential for a pantheistic view.[25]

Physical intentionality is a type of panprotopsychism because intentionality is a necessary condition for consciousness per se, and it has long been recognized as a central feature, if not *the* central feature, of mind. Moreover, physical intentionality is preferable to other panprotopsychic or panpsychic views. First, it is consistent with physicalism (important if all powers are physical properties possessed by physical particles and objects). Second, PIT does not require positing an entirely new kind of particle – as with the micro-experience carrying "mentons" posited by Brogaard (2016) – but merely reconceives the properties of particles already accepted in a scientific ontology. Third, although powers are categorized as intentional states, this is not a property dualistic ontology. All in all, physical intentionality is an ontologically leaner view than many other panprotopsychic or panpsychic views.

---

[25] In other words, PIT implies that there is a fundamental thread of mind-likeness running through all of existence. This will be taken as a reductio ad absurdum by some thinkers with very strict criteria for attributing mental properties. But, as discussed in Section 8.1, panpsychism and related views are becoming more popular and seen as viable metaphysical views of mind and its place in nature. I count myself as a strong supporter of panintentionality but not panpsychism.

Turning to the second basic step, how can physical intentionality be interpreted as a mild form of pantheism? Pfeifer (2016: 43) conceptualizes God as spread throughout the universe via all the powers. This is accomplished by categorizing "God" as a mass term (versus a count term). A mass term is a noun that refers to noncountable stuff ("gas," "water") whereas count terms refer to countable things ("cup," "chair"). Pfeifer hypothesizes a substance called G. Similar to how fields can exist spread throughout the universe, G is everything and G is in all the parts; no part of G is not itself G (2016: 43). It is something like a basic "metaphysical substratum" (2016: 44). Thus, G is like the pantheistic conception of God, but what actually fills this role if anything is to be determined, though Pfeifer (2016: 44) speculates that fields of force might fill this role.[26] Also, since no part of G is not G itself this conception is pantheistic, not panentheistic.

In sum, we obtain a panpsychic turned near-pantheist view based on the ontology of powers. But to complete the pantheist picture, we need a sufficiently complex structure of powers (which are necessarily intentional properties) to form higher-level (more complex and sophisticated) intentional states worthy of divine attribution. On Pfeifer's conception, clusters of powers laden with information serve as neural-like structures. Crucially, these powers compose higher-level properties, thus forming the basis for a divine cosmic brain. Let us look at this claim in more detail.

Pfeifer (2016: 46) cautions not to attribute higher-level intentionality to fundamental physical powers such as mass and charge. The intentionality found there is different than the intentionality associated with thoughts or perceptual powers, for example. Somehow, we need to get from basic physical intentionality to full-fledged mental intentionality. To this end, Pfeifer invokes a distinction between various orders of intentionality based on the work of Dretske (1981: 171–173). Dretske's theory allows for a natural building up of higher-level intentionality out of lower-level intentionality. While lower-level intentionality is found in purely physical, nonsemantic informational structures, higher-level intentionality is found in cognitive systems and includes states such as beliefs. I hasten to add that, as I am

---

[26] Pfeifer (2016: 44) contends that "G must be of such a nature as to underlie and underwrite the diversity or lack of solid sameness manifest throughout our universe." On this view, objects, persons, and properties are distortions of fields (or G). This could be interpreted as a form of supersubstantivalism, according to which spacetime is the one and only substance, with objects and their properties reduced to points or events within this substance. For example, Sider (2011: 296) holds that material objects are identical to "sets of occupied points" and Heil (2012: 146–147) holds that material objects amount to "thickenings" of space. Priority monism (Schaffer 2010b) could be brought into play here as a background or framing metaphysic (see footnote 29 of this chapter for further discussion).

conceiving of higher-level level intentionality it is no different than basic physical intentionality. As I have argued, physical intentionality and mental intentionality, qua intentional states, are the same. Higher-level intentionality as we find in organismal minds is "higher" because of additional features that increasingly complex systems acquire through biological evolution: consciousness, perception, thinking, and the like.

On Dretske's information-theoretic approach to intentionality, Pfeifer (2016: 49) observes that "physical information is intentional in the same sense that dispositional properties are." Dretske (1981: 75–77) notes parallels between the intentionality of mental states and the intentionality carried by physical information-bearing states.[27] If this is correct, then Dretske's idea of orders of intentionality piggybacking on informational structures can reasonably accommodate powers too. Dretske (1981: 27–28) allows an overlap (but not an identity) between information flow and causality, and causality is consistent with and possibly supported by a powers-based ontology (Mumford and Anjum 2011). Thus, we can analogize Dretske's ideas and envision orders of power-intentionality, running from fundamental, physical powers up to biological and psychological powers.[28]

Following this framework, Pfeifer (2016: 46) proposes "that the high-grade intentionality of ordinary mental states" results from the integration of lower-grade powerful-intentional states. Suppose that powerful-intentional states saturate the brain and nervous system. These integrate in complex ways in the brain, creating more sophisticated "informational structures" – the fully fledged intentionality of the organism itself (2016: 47), what Pfeifer calls capital-I intentionality. Analogously, pantheism can coherently be viewed as follows: Powerful-intentional properties pervade the universe, from fundamental to more complex, resembling the vast informational structures of the central nervous system (2016: 48). So, the universe is a complex system of powerful-intentional states involving massive amounts of informational

---

[27] The presence of intentionality in information transmission is found in the lawful dependencies or regularities on which information transmission depends (Dretske (1981: 76). Law-like regularities are the source because they ensure one state X is about another state Y, that there is appropriate correspondence and thus "aboutness" as required for intentionality. Given the powers ontology we are working with here, these regularities must be grounded in or realized by powers (Pfeifer 2016: 49).

[28] It is important to note (thanks to a reviewer for pressing this clarification) that Dretske does not reference "powers" or "dispositions" in the context of grounding intentionality in nomic dependencies. Indeed, Dretske favors a universals-based account of laws of nature (Dretske 1977) similar to Tooley (1977) and Armstrong (1978, 1983). Although the argumentation here extends Dretske's framework beyond its intended boundaries, I (along with Pfeifer) think that talk of interconnections between dispositionality, information, and intentionality is logically consistent; consider that just as information is causal, so are powers.

flow across the system that integrates in locations where physical structures attain sufficient complexity, thereby creating higher-level intentional states. The "owner" of the integrated states is located at the sources (the fundamental powers) that give rise to those states, "namely *everywhere*" – at least everywhere there are physical elements with powerful properties (2016: 48). And "interfacing with every informational source might be regarded as tantamount to omniscience" (2016: 48). The main idea is therefore that this complex powerful-intentional activity generates something akin to God's (= Nature's) brain/mind.

Since this view is an instance of pan*proto*psychism, it is not panpsychicism and therefore neither a form of panexperientialism nor pancognitivism (Goff, et al. 2020). Indeed, I am not arguing that panprotopsychism leads to panpsychism: the view is only that fundamental reality consists of protopsychic properties (i.e., physical intentional states). I take no view about what kind of panpsychic states (experiential or cognitive) would come first when all the proto requirements are met. Moreover, because it is built on panprotopsychic states, the resulting pantheism does not involve a God (Nature) with occurrent thoughts or conscious experiences, but a God (Nature) with proto-thoughts or proto-consciousness. Thus, God on the pantheism I envision is unconscious and therefore not consciously thinking; rather, it exists in an unconscious or subconscious state of representational directedness toward outcomes. When Nature's powerful-intentional states are activated, they manifest but not necessarily as conscious, phenomenological states of any sort; instead, they manifest as natural activity.

Although the panprotopsychic and pantheistic view under examination here does not attribute consciousness to the cosmos, is it possible for complex powerful-intentional structures, underpinning informational flow, to generate consciousness and not just proto-consciousness? Perhaps. One contemporary theory of consciousness that fits naturally with the panpsychic theory just sketched – and which goes further to explain the importance of integrated information mentioned by Pfeifer (2016) – is the Integrated Information Theory proposed by Tononi (2008: 217) positing $\Phi$ as a measure of consciousness defined as "integrated information." Integrated information is "the amount of information generated by a complex of elements, above and beyond the information generated by its parts" (2008: 216). In the view under consideration here, the parts are the fundamental elements of reality. The powerful-intentional properties of these parts could presumably underpin information integration and flow. Paralleling Dretske's theory, as structures built of these elements complexify, there is greater capacity for integrated information and thus higher level, more complex forms of intentionality. Under assumption of Tononi's Integrated Information Theory, we could in principle measure $\Phi$ to determine the "amount" of integrated information – thus, the sophistication level of consciousness – contained by God (= Nature). Therefore, the Integrated Information Theory would, if accepted, complement panintentionalism and pantheism.

If we are to accept a theory of a divine reality, then pantheism is the most likely view because it presents a naturalistic, impersonal, immanent, and thus more scientific view of God. Neither Nature nor God has ontological priority, for they are the same thing. I have not directly and fully argued for pantheism. My point was only to show how a powers ontology combined with PIT, as well as ideas about informational structures similar to what IT implies, is compatible with a pantheistic view.[29]

## 8.6    Conclusion

Open questions remain. Which version of the Powers Model (Pure Powers or Powerful Qualities) is correct? Although I argued for the Pure Powers Model, I do not think that the debate is settled. Further analysis is required. Is PIT correct? I have conducted a robust but likely inconclusive investigation, for there will remain doubts about the marks of intentionality. I also argued for IT, implying that powers carry information, but the exact nature of information is a point of contention. How does physical intentionality fit in with consciousness and subjectivity? I have offered only an initial exploration of the building up of intentionality states and the intentionality continuum, and it is not clear how to get from intentionality to consciousness, although the former strongly seems to be required for the latter. Given that fundamental properties have some kind of purposiveness built into them – that is, powers are directed at outcomes – could this be

---

[29] Priority Monism (Schaffer 2010b) – which was assumed for the sake of the Argument from Priority Monism in Section 5.3 to argue that causal powers of subatomic particles can satisfy Extrinsic-G, thus representing a parallel to the extrinsicness of thoughts – could potentially bolster the case for pantheism here. Although not necessary to support pantheism, it would further support the metaphysical unity needed for the kind of panintentional cum pantheistic metaphysic being touted by Pfeifer (2016). If Priority Monism and Pfeifer's pantheism are packaged, then the cosmic mind = the World, so as one and the same thing they would "share" ontological priority (without Priority Monism, the cosmic mind will be built up out of fundamental constituents and their powers). However, directed unity, as I have argued in Section 7.3, also provides this unity and is my preferred metaphysical complement to powers holism (again, as argued in Section 7.3); still, directed unity does not rule out Priority Monism.

the source of "value" or "valuing" of certain ends? Perhaps. Purposiveness implies a valuing of that which is the goal (or manifestation or object) of intention, but if valuing requires subjectivity then fundamental powers do not fit the bill.

The most general question that this book answers is, "why does anything happen?" The short answer is: real causal powers. The longer answer involves a nuanced view of powers as intentional properties carrying information. While I am reasonably confident that the speculative claims in this book are coherent, plausible, and substantial, I certainly recognize that they could be wrong. I hope, at least, they are worthy of thoughtful criticism and encourage new thinking about powers and their place in contemporary metaphysics of science. The interpretation of the Powers Model that I have presented provides a framework on which other powers-based claims about the nature of reality can be built. It can also cause one to feel more connected – causally and intentionally – to the world we inhabit.

# Works Cited

Anandan, Jeeva and Brown, Harvey R. (1995) On the Reality of Spacetime Structure and the Wavefunction. *Foundations of Physics* 25(2): 349–360.

Anjum, Rani Lill, Lie, Svein Anders Noer, and Mumford, Stephen (2013) Dispositions and Ethics. In Ruth Groff and John Greco (Eds.), *Powers and Capacities in Philosophy: The New Aristotelianism*, pp. 231–247. New York: Routledge.

Anjum, Rani Lill and Mumford, Stephen (2018) *What Tends to Be: The Philosophy of Dispositional Modality*. New York: Routledge.

Anscombe, G. E. M. (1965) The Intentionality of Sensation: A Grammatical Feature. In Ronald J. Butler, (Ed.), *Analytical Philosophy: Second Series*, pp. 158–180. Oxford: Basil Blackwell.

Ariew, Roger (2014) *Descartes and the First Cartesians*. Oxford: Oxford University Press.

Aristotle (1941a) Metaphysics. In Richard McKeon (Ed.) and W. D. Ross (Trans.), *The Basic Works of Aristotle*, pp. 689-926. New York: Random House.

Aristotle (1941b) Physics. In Richard McKeon (Ed.) and W. D. Ross (Trans.), *The Basic Works of Aristotle*, pp. 218-394. New York: Random House.

Armstrong, D. M. (1978) *A Theory of Universals*. Cambridge: Cambridge University Press.

Armstrong, D. M. (1983) *What Is a Law of Nature?* Cambridge: Cambridge University Press.

Armstrong, D. M. (1989) *Universals: An Opinionated Introduction*. Boulder: Westview Press.

Armstrong, D. M. (1993) The Identification Problem and the Inference Problem. *Philosophy and Phenomenological Research* 53(2): 421–422.

Armstrong, D. M. (1997) *A World of States of Affairs*. Cambridge: Cambridge University Press.

Armstrong, D. M. (2002) Two Problems for Essentialism: Appendix in Brian Ellis, *The Philosophy of Nature: A Guide to the New Essentialism*, pp. 167–171. Montreal: McGill-Queen's University Press.

Armstrong, D. M. (2005) Four Disputes about Properties. *Synthese* 144(3): 309–320.

Armstrong, D. M. (2010) *Sketch for a Systematic Metaphysics*. Oxford: Oxford University Press.

Azzano, Lorenzo (2019) The Question of Realism for Powers. *Synthese* 196(1): 329–354.

Baez, John C. (2001) Higher-dimensional Algebra and Planck-scale Physics. In Craig Callender and Nick Huggett (Eds.), *Physics Meets Philosophy at the Planck-scale: Contemporary Theories in Quantum Gravity*, pp. 177–195. Cambridge: Cambridge University Press.

Baker, Lynn Rudder (2009) Review of Mark Johnston's *Saving God: Religion without Idolatry. Notre Dame Philosophical Reviews.* Notre Dame, IN: Department of Philosophy, University of Notre Dame. https://ndpr.nd.edu/reviews/saving-god-religion-after-idolatry/

Balashov, Yuri (2022) Dispositionalism, Causation, and the Interaction Gap. *Erkenntnis* 87(2): 677–692.

Baltimore, Joseph (2022) Dispositionalism, Causation, and the Interaction Gap. *Erkenntnis* 87(2): 677–692.

Barker, Stephen (2013) The Emperor's New Metaphysics of Powers. *Mind* 122(487): 605–653.

Bateson, Gregory (2000) *Steps to an Ecology of Mind.* Chicago: University of Chicago Press. (Originally published in 1972.)

Bauer, William A. (2011) An Argument for the Extrinsic Grounding of Mass. *Erkenntnis*, 74(1): 81–99.

Bauer, William A. (2012) Four Theories of Pure Dispositions. In Alexander Bird, Brian Ellis, and Howard Sankey (Eds.), *Properties, Powers and Structures: Issues in the Metaphysics of Realism*, pp. 139–162. New York: Routledge.

Bauer, William A. (2013) Dispositional Essentialism and the Nature of Powerful Properties. *Disputatio: International Journal of Philosophy*, 5(35): 1–19.

Bauer, William A. (2015) Why Science Needs Philosophy. *Life as a Human.* May 17, 2015. https://lifeasahuman.com/2015/mind-spirit/philosophy/why-science-needs-philosophy/

Bauer, William A. (2016) Physical Intentionality, Extrinsicness, and the Direction of Causation. *Acta Analytica* 31(4): 397–417.

Bauer, William A. (2019) Powers and the Pantheistic Problem of Unity. *Sophia* 58(4): 563–580.

Bennett, Karen (2011) Construction Area (No Hard Hat Required). *Philosophical Studies* 154(1): 79–104.

Bird, Alexander (1998) Dispositions and Antidotes. *The Philosophical Quarterly* 48(191): 227–34.

Bird, Alexander (2005) The Ultimate Argument against Armstrong's Contingent Necessitation View of Laws. *Analysis* 65(2): 147–155.

Bird, Alexander (2007a) *Nature's Metaphysics: Laws and Properties.* Oxford: Oxford University Press.

Bird, Alexander (2007b) The Regress of Pure Powers? *The Philosophical Quarterly* 57(229): 513–534.

Bird, Alexander (2013) Limitations of Power. In Ruth Groff and John Greco (Eds.), *Powers and Capacities in Philosophy: The New Aristotelianism*, pp. 15–47. New York: Routledge.

Bird, Alexander (2017) Manifesting Time and Space: Background-Free Physical Theories. In Jonathan D. Jacobs (Ed.), *Causal Powers*, pp. 127–138. Oxford: Oxford University Press.

Bird, Alexander (2020) A Dispositional Account of Causation, with Some Remarks on the Ontology of Dispositions. In Anne Sophie Meincke (Ed.), *Dispositionalism: Perspectives from Metaphysics and the Philosophy of Science*, Vol. 417 of Synthese Library, pp. 151–170. Cham, Switzerland: Springer Nature.

Bird, Alexander, Ellis, Brian, and Sankey, Howard (2012) *Properties, Powers and Structures: Issues in the Metaphysics of Realism*. New York: Routledge.

Blackburn, Simon (1990) Filling in Space. *Analysis* 50(2): 62–65.

Borghini, Andrea (2009) Dispositions and Their Intentions. In Gregor Damschen, Robert Schnepf, and Karsten Stüber (Eds.), *Debating Dispositions: Issues in Metaphysics, Epistemology and Philosophy of Mind*, pp. 204–219. Berlin: DeGruyter.

Borghini, Andrea and Williams, Neil E. (2008) A Dispositional Theory of Possibility. *Dialectica* 62(1): 21–41.

Bostock, Simon (2003) Are All Possible Laws Actual Laws? *Australasian Journal of Philosophy* 81(4): 517–533.

Bostock, Simon (2008) In Defence of Pan-Dispositionalism. *Metaphysica* 9(2): 139–157.

Bourget, David and Chalmers, David J. (2014) What Do Philosophers Believe? *Philosophical Studies* 170(3): 465–500.

Brentano, Franz (1911) Appendix to *The Classification of Mental Phenomena*. In Franz Brentano (2015) *Psychology from an Empirical Standpoint*, pp. 281–320. New York: Routledge.

Brentano, Franz (1966) *The True and the Evident*. Oskar Kraus (Ed.), Roderick M. Chisholm (Ed., English Edition), Roderick M. Chisholm, Ilse Politzer, and Kurt R. Fischer (Trans.). London: Routledge and Kegan Paul. (Translated from the German, *Wahreit und Evidenz*, 1930.)

Brentano, Franz (2015) *Psychology from an Empirical Standpoint*. New York: Routledge (Originally published in 1874.)

Broad, C. D. (1925) *The Mind and Its Place in Nature*. New York: Harcourt and Brace.

Brogaard, Berit (2016) In Search of Mentons: Panpsychism, Physicalism, and the Missing Link. In Godehard Brüntrup and Ludwig Jaskolla (Eds.), *Panpsychism: Contemporary Perspectives*, pp. 130-152. Oxford: Oxford University Press.

Brown, Harvey R. and Pooley, Oliver (2006) Minkowski Space-Time: A Glorious Non-entity. In Dennis Dieks (Ed.), *The Ontology of Spacetime*, pp. 67–89. Oxford: Elsevier.

Brüntrup, Godehard and Jaskolla, Ludwig (2016) Introduction. In Godehard Brüntrup and Ludwig Jaskolla (Eds.), *Panpsychism: Contemporary Perspectives*, pp. 1–16. Oxford: Oxford University Press.

Buckareff, Andrei and Nagasawa, Yujin (2016) Introduction: Alternative Conceptions of Divinity and Contemporary Analytic Philosophy of Religion. In Andrei Buckareff and Yujin Nagasawa (Eds.), *Alternative Concepts of God: Essays on the Metaphysics of the Divine*, pp. 1–18. Oxford: Oxford University Press.

Callender, Craig (2011) Philosophy of Science and Metaphysics. In Steven French and Juha Saatsi (Eds.), *Continuum Companion to the Philosophy of Science*, pp. 33–54. London: Continuum.

Camp, Elisabeth (2018) Why Maps Are Not Propositional. In Alex Grzankowski and Michelle Montague (Eds.), *Non-Propositional Intentionality*, pp. 19–45. Oxford: Oxford University Press.

Campbell, Keith (1981) The Metaphysics of Abstract Particulars. *Midwest Studies in Philosophy* 6(1): 477–488.

Campbell, Keith (1990) *Abstract Particulars*. Oxford: Basil Blackwell.

Carnap, Rudolf (1958) *Introduction to Symbolic Logic and Its Applications*. Mineola, New York: Dover.

Carroll, John (1994) *Laws of Nature*. Cambridge: Cambridge University Press.

Carroll, John (2008) Nailed to Hume's Cross? In Theodore Sider, John Hawthorne, and Dean W. Zimmerman (Eds.), *Contemporary Debates in Metaphysics*, pp. 67–81. Oxford: Basil Blackwell.

Cartwright, Nancy (2017) Causal Powers: Why Humeans Can't Even Be Instrumentalists. In Jonathan D. Jacobs (Ed.), *Causal Powers*, pp. 9–23. Oxford: Oxford University Press.

Cartwright, Nancy and Pemberton, John (2013) Aristotelian Powers: Without Them, What Would Modern Science Do? In Ruth Groff and John Greco (Eds.), *Powers and Capacities in Philosophy: The New Aristotelianism*, pp. 93–112. New York: Routledge.

Chalmers, David J. (1996) *The Conscious Mind: In Search of a Fundamental Theory*. Oxford: Oxford University Press.

Chalmers, David J. (2006) Strong and Weak Emergence. In Philip Clayton and Paul Davies (Eds.), *The Re-Emergence of Emergence: The Emergentist Hypothesis from Science to Religion*, pp. 244–254. Oxford: Oxford University Press.

Chalmers, David J. (2016) Panpsychism and Panprotopsychism. In Godehard Brüntrup and Ludwig Jaskolla (Eds.), *Panpsychism: Contemporary Perspectives*, pp. 19–47. Oxford: Oxford University Press.

Chisholm, Roderick (1957) *Perceiving: A Philosophical Study*. Ithaca, NY: Cornell University Press.

Choi, Sungho (2006) The Simple vs. Reformed Conditional Analysis of Dispositions. *Synthese* 148(2): 369–379.

Choi, Sungho (2008) Dispositional Properties and Counterfactual Conditionals. *Mind* 117(468): 795–841.

Choi, Sungho and Fara, Michael (2018) Dispositions. *The Stanford Encyclopedia of Philosophy* (Fall 2018 Edition), Edward N. Zalta (Ed.), Stanford, CA: The Metaphysics Research Lab, Philosophy Department, Stanford University. URL = https://plato.stanford.edu/archives/fall2018/entries/dispositions/.

Christensen, Wayne David and Hooker, Cliff A. (2001) Self-directed Agents. In Jillian Scott McIntosh (Ed.), *Canadian Journal of Philosophy Supplementary Volume 27: Naturalism, Evolution, and Intentionality*, pp. 19–52. Calgary: University of Calgary Press.

Clark, Andy and Chalmers, David J. (1998) The Extended Mind. *Analysis* 58(1): 7–19.

Coates, Ashley (2021) Making sense of powerful qualities. *Synthese.* 198(9): 8347–8363.

Collier, John (1990) Intrinsic Information. In Philip P. Hanson (Ed.), *Information, Language, and Cognition (Vancouver Studies in Cognitive Science, Volume 1),* pp. 390–409. Vancouver: University of British Columbia Press.

Collier, John (2008) Information in Biological Systems. In Pieter Adriaans and Johan van Benthem (Eds.), *Handbook of Philosophy of Science, Volume 8: Philosophy of Information,* pp. 763–787. Amsterdam: North-Holland.

Copeland, B. Jack (2020) The Church-Turing Thesis. *The Stanford Encyclopedia of Philosophy* (Summer 2020 Edition), E. N. Zalta (Ed.), Stanford, CA: The Metaphysics Research Lab, Philosophy Department, Stanford University. URL = https://plato.stanford.edu/archives/sum2020/entries/church-turing/

Corry, Richard (2019) *Power and Influence: The Metaphysics of Reductive Explanation.* Oxford: Oxford University Press.

Cross, Troy (2012) Goodbye, Humean Supervenience. In Karen Bennett and Dean. W. Zimmerman (Eds.), *Oxford Studies in Metaphysics, Volume 7,* pp. 129–153. Oxford: Oxford University Press.

Davidson, Donald (1987) Knowing One's Own Mind. *Proceedings and Addresses of the American Philosophical Association* 60(3): 441–58.

Davies, Paul (2010) Universe from Bit. In Paul Davies and Niels Henrik Gregersen (Eds.), *Information and the Nature of Reality: From Physics to Metaphysics,* pp. 83–117. Cambridge: Cambridge University Press.

Davies, Paul and Gregersen, Niels Henrik (2010) Introduction: Does Information Matter? In Paul Davies and Niels Henrik Gregersen (Eds.), *Information and the Nature of Reality: From Physics to Metaphysics,* pp. 1–12. Cambridge: Cambridge University Press.

Demarest, Heather (2012) Do Counterfactuals Ground the Laws of Nature? A Critique of Lange. *Philosophy of Science* 79(3): 333–344.

Dembski, William A. (2016) *Being as Communion: A Metaphysics of Information.* New York: Routledge.

Dennett, Daniel (1987) *The Intentional Stance.* Cambridge, MA: MIT Press.

Dennett, Daniel (1995) *Darwin's Dangerous Idea: Evolution and the Meanings of Life.* New York: Simon & Schuster.

Descartes, René (1985) *Principles of Philosophy.* In John Cottingham, Robert Stoothoff, and Dugald Murdoch (Trans.), *The Philosophical Writings of Descartes, Volume I,* pp. 177-292. Cambridge: Cambridge University Press. (Originally published in 1644.)

Dickens, Charles (1899) *A Tale of Two Cities.* New York: Charles Scribner's Sons.

Djedovic, Alex (2020) *From Life-Like to Mind-Like Explanation: Natural Agency and the Cognitive Sciences.* University of Toronto, PhD Dissertation. ProQuest. www.proquest.com/docview/2467622332

Dorato, Mauro (2005) *The Software of the Universe: An Introduction to the History and Philosophy of Laws of Nature.* Burlington, VT: Ashgate.

Dorato, Mauro (2007) Dispositions, Relational Properties and the Quantum World. In Max Kistler and Bruno Gnassounou (Eds.), *Dispositions and Causal Powers*, pp. 249–270. Burlington, VT: Ashgate.

Dorato, Mauro and Esfeld, Michael (2010) GRW as an Ontology of Dispositions. *Studies in History and Philosophy of Science Part B: Studies in History and Philosophy of Modern Physics* 41(1): 41–49.

Doyle, Tsarina (2018) *Nietzsche's Metaphysics of the Will to Power: The Possibility of Value.* Cambridge: Cambridge University Press.

Dretske, Fred I. (1977) Laws of Nature. *Philosophy of Science* 44(2): 248–268.

Dretske, Fred I. (1981) *Knowledge and the Flow of Information.* Cambridge: Cambridge University Press.

Dumsday, Travis (2019) *Dispositionalism and the Metaphysics of Science.* Cambridge: Cambridge University Press.

Ehrenfeucht, Andrzej, Harju, Tero, Petre, Ion, Prescott, David M., and Rozenberg, Grzegorz (2004) *Computation in Living Cells: Gene Assembly in Ciliates.* Berlin: Springer-Verlag.

Elder-Vass, Dave (2010) *The Causal Powers of Social Structures: Emergence, Structure and Agency.* Cambridge: Cambridge University Press.

Ellis, Brian (2001) *Scientific Essentialism.* Cambridge: Cambridge University Press.

Ellis, Brian (2002) *The Philosophy of Nature: A Guide to the New Essentialism.* Montreal: McGill-Queen's University Press.

Ellis, Brian (2010a) Causal Powers and Categorical Properties. In Anna Marmodoro (Ed.), *The Metaphysics of Powers: Their Grounding and Their Manifestations*, pp. 133–142. New York: Routledge.

Ellis, Brian (2010b) *The Metaphysics of Scientific Realism.* Montreal: McGill-Queen's University Press.

Ellis, Brian (2012) The Categorical Dimensions of the Causal Powers. In Alexander Bird, Brian Ellis, and Howard Sankey (Eds.), *Properties, Powers and Structures: Issues in the Metaphysics of Realism*, pp. 11–26. New York: Routledge.

Ellis, Brian (2013) The Power of Agency. In Ruth Groff and John Greco (Eds.), *Powers and Capacities in Philosophy: The New Aristotelianism*, pp. 186–206. New York: Routledge.

Ellis, Brian and Lierse, Caroline (1994) Dispositional Essentialism. *Australasian Journal of Philosophy* 72(1): 27–45.

Esfeld, Michael (1998) Holism and Analytic Philosophy. *Mind* 107(426): 365–380.

Esfeld, Michael and Deckert, Dirk-Andre (2018) *A Minimalist Ontology of the Natural World.* New York: Routledge.

Fara, Michael (2005) Dispositions and Habituals. *Noûs* 39(1): 43–82.

Fine, Kit (2005) *Modality and Tense: Philosophical Papers.* Oxford: Oxford University Press.

Fitch, W. Tecumseh (2008) Nano-Intentionality: A Defense of Intrinsic Intentionality. *Biology and Philosophy* 23(2): 157–177.

Floridi, Luciano (2009) Philosophical Conceptions of Information. In Giovanni Sommaruga (Ed.), *Formal Theories of Information, Lecture Notes in Computer Science*, pp. 13–53. Berlin: Springer-Verlag.

Floridi, Luciano (2010) *Information: A Very Short Introduction*. Oxford: Oxford University Press.

Floridi, Luciano (2011) *The Philosophy of Information*. Oxford: Oxford University Press.

Gamez, David (2018) *Human and Machine Consciousness*. Cambridge: Open Book Publishers. DOI: 10.11647/OBP.0107

Gozzano, Simone (2020) The Dispositional Nature of Phenomenal Properties. *Topoi* 39(5): 1045–1055.

Giannotti, Joaquim (2021) The Identity Theory of Powers Revised. *Erkenntnis* 86(3): 603–621.

Gillett, Carl (2002) The Dimensions of Realization: A Critique of the Standard View. *Analysis* 62(4): 316–323.

Goff, Philip (2016) The Phenomenal Bonding Solution to the Combination Problem. In Godehard Brüntrup and Ludwig Jaskolla (Eds.), *Panpsychism: Contemporary Perspectives*, pp. 283–302. Oxford: Oxford University Press.

Goff, Philip (2017) *Consciousness and Fundamental Reality*. Oxford: Oxford University Press.

Goff, Philip (2019) *Galileo's Error: Foundations for a New Science of Consciousness*. New York: Pantheon.

Goff, Philip, Seager, William, and Allen-Hermanson, Sean (2020) Panpsychism. *The Stanford Encyclopedia of Philosophy* (Summer 2020 Edition), Edward N. Zalta (Ed.), Stanford, CA: The Metaphysics Research Lab, Philosophy Department, Stanford University. URL = <https://plato.stanford.edu/archives/sum2020/entries/panpsychism/>.

Graziano, Michael (2013) *Consciousness and the Social Brain*. Oxford: Oxford University Press.

Gregersen, Niels Henrik (2010) God, Matter, and Information: Towards a Stoicizing Logos Christology. In Paul Davies and Niels Henrik Gregersen (Eds.), *Information and the Nature of Reality: From Physics to Metaphysics*, pp. 405–443. Cambridge: Cambridge University Press.

Grice, Paul (1989) *Studies in the Way of Words*. Cambridge, MA: Harvard University Press.

Griffin, David Ray (1998) *Unsnarling the World-Knot: Consciousness, Freedom, and the Mind-Body Problem*. Berkeley: University of California Press.

Groff, Ruth (2013) *Ontology Revisited: Metaphysics in Social and Political Philosophy*. New York: Routledge.

Groff, Ruth and Greco, John (2013) (Eds.), *Powers and Capacities in Philosophy: The New Aristotelianism*. New York: Routledge.

Gross, David J. (1996) The Role of Symmetry in Fundamental Physics. *Proceedings of the National Academy of Sciences* 93(25): 14256–14259.

Grzankowski, Alex and Montague, Michelle (2018) Non-Propositional Intentionality: An Introduction. In Alex Grzankowski and Michelle Montague (Eds.), *Non-Propositional Intentionality*, pp. 1–18. Oxford: Oxford University Press.

Handfield, Toby (2008) Unfinkable Dispositions. *Synthese* 160(2): 297–308.

Harari, Yuval Noah (2015) *Sapiens: A Brief History of Humankind*. New York: HarperCollins.

Harré, Rom and Madden, Edward H. (1975) *Causal Powers: A Theory of Natural Necessity*. Oxford: Basil Blackwell.

Hawthorne, John (2001) Causal Structuralism. *Philosophical Perspectives* 15(Metaphysics): 361–378.

Heil, John (2003) *From an Ontological Point of View*. Oxford: Oxford University Press.

Heil, John (2010) Powerful Qualities. In Anna Marmodoro (Ed.), *The Metaphysics of Powers: Their Grounding and Their Manifestations*, pp. 58–72. New York: Routledge.

Heil, John (2012) *The Universe as We Find It*. Oxford: Oxford University Press.

Holton, Richard (1999) Dispositions All the Way Round. *Analysis* 59(1): 9–14.

Horgan, Terence E. and Potrč, Matjaž (2008) *Austere Realism: Contextual Semantics Meets Minimal Ontology*. Cambridge, MA: MIT Press.

Hume, David (2002) *A Treatise of Human Nature*. Urbana, IL: Project Gutenberg. Retrieved July 7, 2022 from www.gutenberg.org/ebooks/4705. (Originally published in 1739.)

Hume, David (2003) *An Enquiry Concerning Human Understanding*. Urbana, IL: Project Gutenberg. Retrieved July 7, 2022 from www.gutenberg.org/ebooks/9662. (Originally published in 1748.)

Humphreys, Paul (1997) How Properties Emerge. *Philosophy of Science* 64(1): 1–17.

Hüttemann, Andreas (2009) Dispositions in Physics. In Gregor Damschen, Robert Schnepf, and Karsten Stüber (Eds.), *Debating Dispositions: Issues in Metaphysics, Epistemology and Philosophy of Mind*, pp. 223–237. Berlin: DeGruyter.

Ingthorsson, R. D. (2013) Properties: Powers, Qualities, or Both? *Dialectica* 67(1): 55–80.

Ingthorsson, R. D. (2015) The Regress of Pure Powers Revisited. *European Journal of Philosophy* 23(3): 529–541.

Isaacs, Alan (2000) *Oxford Dictionary of Physics*, fourth edition. Oxford: Oxford University Press.

Jacobs, Jonathan D. (2010) A Powers Theory of Modality: Or, How I Learned to Stop Worrying and Reject Possible Worlds. *Philosophical Studies* 151(2): 227–248.

Jacobs, Jonathan D. (2011) Powerful Qualities, Not Pure Powers. *The Monist* 94(1): 81–102.

James, William (1950) *The Principles of Psychology, Vol. I*. Mineola, New York: Dover. (Originally published in 1890.)

Jaworski, William (2016) *Structure and the Metaphysics of Mind: How Hylomorphism Solves the Mind-Body Problem*. Oxford: Oxford University Press.

Jenkins, C. S. and Nolan, Daniel (2012) Disposition Impossible. *Noûs* 46(4): 732–753.

Johnson, Monte Ransome (2005) *Aristotle on Teleology*. Oxford: Oxford University Press.

Johnston, Mark (1992) How to Speak of the Colors. *Philosophical Studies* 68(3): 221–263.

Johnston, Mark (2009) *Saving God: Religion after Idolatry*. Princeton: Princeton University Press.

Jordan, J. Scott (2018) It's Hard Work Being No One. *Frontiers in Psychology* 9(2632): 1–3.

Joy, Lynn S. (2013) The Ineliminability of Dispositions in Hume's Rejection of Causal Powers. In Ruth Groff and John Greco (Eds.), *Powers and Capacities in Philosophy: The New Aristotelianism*, pp. 69–89. New York: Routledge.

Koons, Robert C. and Pickavance, Timothy H. (2017) *The Atlas of Reality: A Comprehensive Guide to Metaphysics*. Malden, MA: Wiley Blackwell.

Kriegel, Uriah (2016) Brentano's Mature Theory of Intentionality. *Journal for the History of Analytical Philosophy* 4(2): 1–15.

Kriegel, Uriah (2018) Belief-That and Belief-In. In Alex Grzankowski and Michelle Montague (Eds.), *Non-Propositional Intentionality*, pp. 192–213. Oxford: Oxford University Press.

Kroll, Nick (2017) Teleological Dispositions. In Karen Bennett and Dean W. Zimmerman (Eds.), *Oxford Studies in Metaphysics: Volume 10*, pp. 3–37. Oxford: Oxford University Press.

Landry, Christian R. (2011) A Cellular Roadmap for the Plant Kingdom. *Science* 333(6042): 532–533.

Lange, Marc (2009) *Laws and Lawmakers: Science, Metaphysics, and the Laws of Nature*. Oxford: Oxford University Press.

Langton, Rae and Lewis, David (1998) Defining "Intrinsic." *Philosophy and Phenomenological Research* 58(2): 333–345.

Laplane, Lucie, Mantovani, Paolo, Adolphs, Ralph, Chang, Hasok, Mantovani, Alberto, McFall-Ngai, Margaret, Rovelli, Carlo, Sober, Elliott, and Pradeu, Thomas (2019) Why Science Needs Philosophy. *Proceedings of the National Academy of Sciences* 116(10): 3948–3952.

Leibniz, Gottfried Wilhelm (1991) *Monadology*. In Nicholas Rescher (Ed.), *G. W. Leibniz's Monadology: An Edition for Students*, pp. 17–30. Pittsburgh: University of Pittsburgh Press. (Originally published in 1714.)

Lewis, David (1986a) Introduction. *Philosophical Papers, Vol. II*. Oxford: Oxford University Press.

Lewis, David (1986b) *On the Plurality of Worlds*. Oxford: Basil Blackwell.

Lewis, David (1994) Humean Supervenience Debugged. *Mind* 103(412): 473–490.

Lewis, David (1997) Finkish Dispositions. *The Philosophical Quarterly* 47(187): 143–158.

Lewis, David (2008) Ramseyan Humility. In David Braddon-Mitchell and Robert Nola (Eds.), *Conceptual Analysis and Philosophical Naturalism*, pp. 203–222. Cambridge, MA: MIT Press.

Livanios, Vassilis (2017a) The Categorical-Dispositional Distinction, Locations and Symmetry Operations. *Acta Analytica* 32(2): 133–144.

Livanios, Vassilis (2017b) *Science in Metaphysics: Exploring the Metaphysics of Properties and Laws*. New York: Palgrave Macmillan.

Lloyd, Seth (2010) The Computational Universe. In Paul Davies and Niels Henrik Gregersen (Eds.), *Information and the Nature of Reality: From Physics to Metaphysics*, pp. 118–133. Cambridge: Cambridge University Press.

Locke, John (2004) *An Essay Concerning Human Understanding*. Urbana, IL: Project Gutenberg. Retrieved July 8, 2022 from www.gutenberg.org/ebooks/10615 (Originally published in 1689.)

Lowe, E. J. (1998) *The Possibility of Metaphysics: Substance, Identity, and Time*. Oxford: Oxford University Press.

Maher, Chauncey (2017) *Plant Minds: A Philosophical Defense*. New York: Routledge.

Mander, William (2020) Pantheism. *The Stanford Encyclopedia of Philosophy* (Spring 2020 Edition), Edward N. Zalta (Ed.), Stanford, CA: The Metaphysics Research Lab, Philosophy Department, Stanford University. URL = <https://plato.stanford.edu/archives/spr2020/entries/pantheism/>.

Manley, David and Wasserman, Ryan (2017) Dispositions without Teleology. In Karen Bennett and Dean W. Zimmerman (Eds.), *Oxford Studies in Metaphysics: Volume 10*, pp. 47–59. Oxford: Oxford University Press.

Marmodoro, Anna (2009) Do Powers Need Powers to Make Them Powerful? *History of Philosophy Quarterly* 26(4): 337–352.

Marmodoro, Anna (2014) *Aristotle on Perceiving Objects*. Oxford: Oxford University Press.

Marmodoro, Anna (2020) Review of Neil E. Williams' *The Powers Metaphysic*. *Notre Dame Philosophical Reviews*. Notre Dame, IN: Department of Philosophy, University of Notre Dame. https://ndpr.nd.edu/news/the-powers-metaphysic/

Marmodoro, Anna (2021) Causal Powers in Aristotle and his Predecessors. In Julia Jorati (Ed.), *Powers: A History*, pp. 10–27. Oxford: Oxford University Press.

Martin, C. B. (1993) Power for Realists. In John Bacon, Keith Campbell, and Lloyd Reinhardt (Eds.), *Ontology, Causality and Mind: Essays in Honour of D.M. Armstrong*, pp. 175–186. Cambridge: Cambridge University Press.

Martin, C. B. (1996) Properties and Dispositions. In Tim Crane (Ed.), *Dispositions: A Debate*, pp. 71–87. New York: Routledge.

Martin, C. B. (1997) On the Need for Properties: The Road to Pythagoreanism and Back. *Synthese* 112(2): 193–231.

Martin, C. B. (2008) *The Mind in Nature*. Oxford: Oxford University Press.

Martin, C. B. and Heil, John (1999) The Ontological Turn. *Midwest Studies in Philosophy* 23(1): 34–60.

Martin, C. B. and Pfeifer, Karl (1986) Intentionality and the Non-Psychological. *Philosophy and Phenomenological Research* 46(4): 531–554.

Maxwell, Nicholas (2020) Aim-Oriented Empiricism and the Metaphysics of Science. *Philosophia* 48(1): 347–364.

Maudlin, Tim (2007) *The Metaphysics within Physics*. Oxford: Oxford University Press.

McGinn, Colin (1989) Can We Solve the Mind-Body Problem? *Mind* 98(391): 349–366.

McKitrick, Jennifer (2003a) A Case for Extrinsic Dispositions. *Australasian Journal of Philosophy* 81(2): 155–174.

McKitrick, Jennifer (2003b) The Bare Metaphysical Possibility of Bare Dispositions. *Philosophy and Phenomenological Research* 66(2): 349–369.

McKitrick, Jennifer (2005) Are Dispositions Causally Relevant? *Synthese* 144(3): 357–371.

McKitrick, Jennifer (2009) Dispositional Pluralism. In Gregor Damschen, Robert Schnepf, and Karsten Stüber (Eds.), *Debating Dispositions: Issues in Metaphysics, Epistemology and Philosophy of Mind*, pp. 186–203. New York: Walter de Gruyter.

McKitrick, Jennifer (2017) Indirect Directedness. In Karen Bennett and Dean W. Zimmerman (Eds.), *Oxford Studies in Metaphysics: Volume 10*, pp. 38–46. Oxford: Oxford University Press.

McKitrick, Jennifer (2018) *Dispositional Pluralism*. Oxford: Oxford University Press.

McKitrick, Jennifer (2021) Powers in Contemporary Philosophy. In Julia Jorati (Ed.), *Powers: A History*, pp. 271–294. Oxford: Oxford University Press.

Meincke, Anne Sophie (2020) Dispositionalism: Between Metaphysics and the Philosophy of Science. In Anne Sophie Meincke (Ed.), *Dispositionalism: Perspectives from Metaphysics and the Philosophy of Science*, Vol. 417 of Synthese Library, pp. 1–12. Cham, Switzerland: Springer Nature.

Meixner, Uwe (2016) Idealism and Panpsychism. In Godehard Brüntrup and Ludwig Jaskolla (Eds.), *Panpsychism: Contemporary Perspectives*, pp. 387–406. Oxford: Oxford University Press.

Mendola, Joseph (2008) *Anti-Externalism*. Oxford: Oxford University Press.

Mitchell, Sandra (2009) *Unsimple Truths: Science, Complexity, and Policy*. Chicago: University of Chicago Press.

Molnar, George (2003) *Powers: A Study in Metaphysics*. Stephen Mumford (Ed.). Oxford: Oxford University Press.

Mulgan, Geoff (2018) *Big Mind: How Collective Intelligence Can Change Our World*. Princeton: Princeton University Press.

Müller, Thomas (2010) Formal Methods in the Philosophy of Natural Science. In Friedrich Stadler (Ed.), *The Present Situation in the Philosophy of Science*, pp. 111–124. New York: Springer.

Mumford, Stephen (1998) *Dispositions*. Oxford: Oxford University Press.

Mumford, Stephen (1999) Intentionality and the Physical: A New Theory of Disposition Ascription. *The Philosophical Quarterly* 49(195): 215–225.

Mumford, Stephen (2004) *Laws in Nature*. New York: Routledge.

Mumford, Stephen (2006) The Ungrounded Argument. *Synthese* 149(3): 471–489.

Mumford, Stephen and Anjum, Rani Lill (2011) *Getting Causes from Powers*. Oxford: Oxford University Press.

Mumford, Stephen and Anjum, Rani Lill (2015) Freedom and Control: On the Modality of Free Will. *American Philosophical Quarterly* 52(1): 1–11.

Mumford, Stephen and Tugby, Matthew (2013) Introduction: What Is the Metaphysics of Science? In Stephen Mumford and Matthew Tugby (Eds.), *Metaphysics and Science*, pp. 3–28. Oxford: Oxford University Press.

Nagel, Thomas (1974) What Is It Like to Be a Bat? *The Philosophical Review* 83(4): 435–450.

Nolan, Daniel (2014) *David Lewis*. New York: Routledge (First published in 2005 by Acumen.)

O'Connor, Timothy (2020) Emergent Properties. *The Stanford Encyclopedia of Philosophy* (Fall 2020 Edition), Edward N. Zalta (Ed.), Stanford, CA: The Metaphysics Research Lab, Philosophy Department, Stanford University. URL = <https://plato.stanford.edu/archives/fall2020/entries/properties-emergent/>.

Oddie, Graham (1982) Armstrong on the Eleatic Principle and Abstract Entities. *Philosophical Studies* 41(2): 285–295.

Oderberg, David S. (2017) Finality Revived: Powers and Intentionality. *Synthese* 194(7): 2387–2425.

Ott, Walter (2009) *Causation and Laws of Nature in Early Modern Philosophy.* Oxford: Oxford University Press.

Pfeifer, Karl (2016) Pantheism as Panpsychism. In Andrei Buckareff and Yujin Nagasawa (Eds.), *Alternative Concepts of God: Essays on the Metaphysics of the Divine*, pp. 41–49. Oxford: Oxford University Press.

Place, Ullin T. (1996) Intentionality as the Mark of the Dispositional. *Dialectica* 50(2): 91–120.

Plato (1997) *Sophist.* In John M. Cooper and D. S. Hutchinson (Eds.), Nicholas P. White (Trans.), *Plato: Complete Works*, pp. 235–293. Indianapolis: Hackett.

Powers, Thomas M. (2013) On the Moral Agency of Computers. *Topoi* 32(2): 227–236.

Price, Huw (1996) *Time's Arrow and Archimedes' Point: New Directions for the Physics of Time.* Oxford: Oxford University Press.

Priest, Graham (2005) *Towards Non-Being: The Logic and Metaphysics of Intentionality.* Oxford: Oxford University Press.

Prior, A. N. (1957) *Time and Modality.* Oxford: Oxford University Press.

Prior, Elizabeth (1985) *Dispositions.* Aberdeen: Aberdeen University Press.

Prior, Elizabeth W., Pargetter, Robert, and Jackson, Frank (1982) Three Theses about Dispositions. *American Philosophical Quarterly* 19(3): 251–257.

Psillos, Stathis (2006) What Do Powers Do when They Are Not Manifested? *Philosophy and Phenomenological Research* 72(1): 137–156.

Psillos, Stathis and Ioannidis, Stavros (2019) Review of R. L. Anjum and S. Mumford's *What Tends to Be: The Philosophy of Dispositional Modality. Notre Dame Philosophical Reviews.* Notre Dame, IN: Department of Philosophy, University of Notre Dame. https://ndpr.nd.edu/news/what-tends-to-be-the-philosophy-of-dispositional-modality/

Putnam, Hilary (1973) Meaning and Reference. *Journal of Philosophy* 70(19): 699–711.

Putnam, Hilary (1975) The Meaning of "Meaning." *Minnesota Studies in the Philosophy of Science* 7: Language, Mind, and Knowledge, pp. 131–193 Minneapolis: University of Minnesota Press.

Quine, Willard Van Orman (1980) Reference and Modality. In *From a Logical Point of View.* Second Edition, pp. 139–159. Cambridge, MA: Harvard University Press. (First edition published in 1953.)

Quiroga, R. Quian, Reddy, L., Kreiman, G., Koch, C., Fried, I. (2005) Invariant Visual Representation by Single Neurons in the Human Brain. *Nature* 435(7045): 1102–1107.

Randall, Lisa (2005) *Warped Passages: Unravelling the Mysteries of the Universe's Hidden Dimensions*. New York: HarperCollins.

Reichenbach, Hans (1951) *The Rise of Scientific Philosophy*. Berkeley: University of California Press.

Rescher, Nicholas (1991) *G.W. Leibniz's Monadology: An Edition for Students*. Pittsburgh: University of Pittsburgh Press.

Richardson, Kevin (2020) Grounding Pluralism: Why and How. *Erkenntnis* 85(6): 1399–1415.

Roberts, John T. (2008) *The Law-Governed Universe*. Oxford: Oxford University Press.

Rovelli, Carlo (1997) Halfway through the Woods: Contemporary Research on Space and Time. In John Earman and John D. Norton (Eds.), *The Cosmos of Science*, pp. 180–223. Pittsburgh: University of Pittsburgh Press.

Rovelli, Carlo (2017) *Reality Is Not What It Seems: The Journey to Quantum Gravity*. New York: Riverhead Books (Penguin).

Russell, Bertrand (1927) *An Outline of Philosophy*. London: George Allen & Unwin.

Ryle, Gilbert (1949) *The Concept of Mind*. Chicago: University of Chicago Press.

Schaffer, Jonathan (2001) The Individuation of Tropes. *Australasian Journal of Philosophy* 79(2): 247–257.

Schaffer, Jonathan (2003) The Problem of Free Mass: Must Properties Cluster? *Philosophy and Phenomenological Research* 66(1): 125–138.

Schaffer, Jonathan (2010a) The Internal Relatedness of All Things. *Mind* 119(474): 341–376.

Schaffer, Jonathan (2010b) Monism: The Priority of the Whole. *Philosophical Review* 119(1): 31–76.

Schaffer, Jonathan (2016) Grounding in the Image of Causation. *Philosophical Studies* 173(1): 49–100.

Schrenk, Markus (2017) *Metaphysics of Science: A Systematic and Historical Introduction*. New York: Routledge.

Schwitzgebel, Eric (2001) In-Between Believing. *The Philosophical Quarterly* 51(202): 76–82.

Schwitzgebel, Eric (2002) A Phenomenal, Dispositional Account of Belief. *Noûs* 36(2): 249–275.

Searle, John R. (1979) What Is an Intentional State? *Mind* 88(1): 74–92.

Searle, John R. (1983) *Intentionality: An Essay in the Philosophy of Mind*. Cambridge: Cambridge University Press.

Searle, John R. (1984) Intentionality and Its Place in Nature. *Dialectica* 38(2/3): 87–99.

Searle, John R. (1994) *The Rediscovery of the Mind*. Cambridge, MA: MIT Press.

Searle, John R. (2004) *Mind: A Brief Introduction*. Oxford: Oxford University Press.

Searle, John R. (2010) *Making the Social World: The Structure of Human Civilization*. Oxford: Oxford University Press.

Searle, John R. (2015) *Seeing Things as They Are*. Oxford: Oxford University Press.

Searle, John R. (2018) Are There Non-Propositional Intentional States? In Alex Grzankowski and Michelle Montague (Eds.), *Non-Propositional Intentionality*, pp. 259–271. Oxford: Oxford University Press.

Shannon, Claude E. and Weaver, Warren (1949) *The Mathematical Theory of Communication*. Urbana: University of Illinois Press.

Shoemaker, Sydney (1980) Causality and Properties. In Peter van Inwagen (Ed.), *Time and Cause: Essays Presented to Richard Taylor*, pp. 109–135. Dordrecht: Reidel.

Shoemaker, Sydney (1998) Causal and Metaphysical Necessity. *Pacific Philosophical Quarterly* 79(1): 59–77.

Sider, Theodore (2011) *Writing the Book of the World*. Oxford: Oxford University Press.

Skrbina, David (2005) *Panpsychism in the West*. Cambridge, MA: MIT Press.

Smolin, Lee (1991) Space and Time in the Quantum Universe. In Abhay Ashtekar and John Stachel (Eds.), *Conceptual Problems of Quantum Gravity*, pp. 228–291. Boston: Birkhäuser.

Spinoza, Benedictus de (2006) *Ethics*. In Michael L. Morgan (Ed.), Samuel Shirley (Trans.), *The Essential Spinoza: Ethics and Related Writings*, pp. 1–161. Indianapolis: Hackett (Originally published in 1677.)

Stapp, Henry (2010) Minds and values in the quantum universe. In Paul Davies and Niels Henrik Gregersen (Eds.), *Information and the Nature of Reality: From Physics to Metaphysics*, pp. 134–154. Cambridge: Cambridge University Press.

Steinberg, Jesse R. (2010) Dispositions and Subjunctives. *Philosophical Studies* 148(3): 323–341.

Strawson, Galen (2008) The Identity of the Categorical and the Dispositional. *Analysis* 68(4): 271–282.

Strawson, Galen, Carruthers, Peter, Coleman, Sam, et al. (2006) *Consciousness and Its Place in Nature: Does Physicalism Entail Panpsychism?* Anthony Freeman (Ed.). Exeter: Imprint Academic.

Stump, Eleonore (2013) Emergence, Causal Powers, and Aristotelianism in Metaphysics. In Ruth Groff and John Greco (Eds.), *Powers and Capacities in Philosophy: The New Aristotelianism*, pp. 48–68. New York: Routledge.

Swartzer, Steven (2013) Appetitive Besires and the Fuss about Fit. *Philosophical Studies* 165(3): 975–988.

Taylor, Henry (2018) Powerful Qualities and Pure Powers. *Philosophical Studies* 175(6): 1423–1440.

Tomasello, Michael (2014) *A Natural History of Human Thinking*. Cambridge, MA: Harvard University Press.

Tononi, Giulio (2008) Consciousness as Integrated Information: A Provisional Manifesto. *Biological Bulletin* 215(3): 216–242.

Tooley, Michael (1977) The Nature of Laws. *Canadian Journal of Philosophy* 7(4): 667–698.

Trigg, Roger (2015) *Beyond Matter: Why Science Needs Metaphysics*. West Conshohocken, PA: Templeton Press.

Tugby, Matthew (2013) Platonic Dispositionalism. *Mind* 122(486): 451–480.

Tugby, Matthew (2016) Universals, Laws, and Governance. *Philosophical Studies* 173(5): 1147–1163.

Van Fraassen, Bas C. (1989) *Laws and Symmetry*. Oxford: Oxford University Press.

Van Inwagen, Peter (1990) *Material Beings*. Ithaca: Cornell University Press.

Vetter, Barbara (2015) *Potentiality: From Dispositions to Modality*. Oxford: Oxford University Press.

Wahlberg, Tobias Hansson (2020) Causal Powers and Social Ontology. *Synthese* 197(3): 1357–1377.

Wang, Jennifer (2015) The Modal Limits of Dispositionalism. *Noûs* 49(3): 454–469.

Wheeler, John Archibald (1990) Information, Physics, Quantum: The Search for Links. In Wojciech H. Zurek (Ed.), *Complexity, Entropy, and the Physics of Information*, pp. 3–28. Redwood City, CA: Addison Wesley.

Williams, Donald C. (1953) On the Elements of Being: I. *The Review of Metaphysics* 7(1): 3–18.

Williams, Neil E. (2005) Static and Dynamic Dispositions. *Synthese* 146(3): 303–324.

Williams, Neil E. (2009) The Ungrounded Argument Is Unfounded: A Response to Mumford. *Synthese* 170(1): 7–19.

Williams, Neil E. (2010) Puzzling Powers: The Problem of Fit. In Anna Marmodoro (Ed.), *The Metaphysics of Powers: Their Grounding and Their Manifestations*, pp. 84–105. New York: Routledge.

Williams, Neil E. (2011) Dispositions and the Argument from Science. *Australasian Journal of Philosophy* 89(1): 71–90.

Williams, Neil E. (2017) Powerful Perdurance: Linking Parts with Powers. In Jonathan D. Jacobs (Ed.), *Causal Powers*, pp. 139–164. Oxford: Oxford University Press.

Williams, Neil E. (2019) *The Powers Metaphysic*. Oxford: Oxford University Press.

Wilson, Jessica (2010) What Is Hume's Dictum, and Why Believe It? *Philosophy and Phenomenological Research* 80(3): 595–637.

Wilson, Jessica M. (2021) *Metaphysical Emergence*. Oxford: Oxford University Press.

Wittgenstein, Ludwig (1922) *Tractatus Logico-Philosophicus*. New York: Harcourt, Brace & Company.

Yablo, Stephen (1999) Intrinsicness. *Philosophical Topics* 26(1/2): 479–505.

Yates, David (2015) Dispositionalism and the Modal Operators. *Philosophy and Phenomenological Research* 91(2): 411–424.

# Index